Practical Shader Development

Vertex and Fragment Shaders for Game Developers

Kyle Halladay

Apress®

Practical Shader Development: Vertex and Fragment Shaders for Game Developers

Kyle Halladay
Bristol, UK

ISBN-13 (pbk): 978-1-4842-4456-2   ISBN-13 (electronic): 978-1-4842-4457-9
https://doi.org/10.1007/978-1-4842-4457-9

Managing Director, Apress Media LLC: Welmoed Spahr
Acquisitions Editor: Jonathan Gennick
Development Editor: Laura Berendson
Coordinating Editor: Jill Balzano

Cover image designed by Freepik (www.freepik.com)

Distributed to the book trade worldwide by Springer Science+Business Media New York, 233 Spring Street, 6th Floor, New York, NY 10013. Phone 1-800-SPRINGER, fax (201) 348-4505, e-mail orders-ny@springer-sbm.com, or visit www.springeronline.com. Apress Media, LLC is a California LLC and the sole member (owner) is Springer Science + Business Media Finance Inc (SSBM Finance Inc). SSBM Finance Inc is a **Delaware** corporation.

For information on translations, please e-mail rights@apress.com, or visit www.apress.com/rights-permissions.

Apress titles may be purchased in bulk for academic, corporate, or promotional use. eBook versions and licenses are also available for most titles. For more information, reference our Print and eBook Bulk Sales web page at www.apress.com/bulk-sales.

Any source code or other supplementary material referenced by the author in this book is available to readers on GitHub via the book's product page, located at www.apress.com/9781484244562. For more detailed information, please visit www.apress.com/source-code.

Printed on acid-free paper

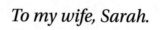

To my wife, Sarah.

Table of Contents

About the Author

Kyle Halladay is a professional game programmer living in Chicago. He has more than seven years' experience in writing shaders and building graphics technology for games and architectural visualizations.

About the Technical Reviewer

Ben Garney is the founder of The Engine Company, a technical consulting firm providing services ranging from implementation to product architecture and development to fractional CTO. Ben has had exits as key hire, cofounder, and founder. His work has powered hundreds of millions of user experiences, been shown on the TED Prime stage, and used in planetary robotics research. He cowrote a book, Video Game Optimization, and has done technical review for a number of others. His areas of expertise include internet video, AR/VR, game engines, and engineering team leadership. You can read his blog at http://bengarney.com/ or follow his Twitter account @bengarney.

Acknowledgments

I have to start by thanking my wife, Sarah, for all the support she's given me throughout writing this book. Not only did she read early chapter drafts and offer advice about how to make things clearer, but she also put up with me through all the weekends I spent hunched over my computer, and all the mornings when the first thing I wanted to talk about was the book. I truly appreciate all the love and support that you've shown me throughout this entire process.

My technical reviewer, Ben Garney, also deserves some special recognition. He took on this project despite barely knowing me, and not only delivered great feedback about my content, but also sage advice from his experiences with technical writing. It's safe to say that the book would not be nearly as complete (or accurate) without him.

Finally, I want to thank the team at Apress for giving me the chance to write an actual, physical, book! Thank you for all the time you spent guiding me through this process, providing feedback, and keeping me on schedule.

Introduction

Welcome to Practical Shader Development. This book is intended to be the gentlest introduction possible to the theory and practice of writing shaders for video games. Shader writing is a very large topic, and I can remember feeling very lost when I was starting out. My hope is that this book will help you avoid that same feeling and allow you to take your first steps into the vast world of shaders and game graphics quickly and confidently.

This book's guiding philosophy is: "a carpenter doesn't need to know how to make a wrench." Similarly, you don't have to know how to build a rendering engine to be able to use shaders to create beautiful visual effects, especially when you're just starting out. This book is all about empowering you to experiment, be creative, make cool things, and hopefully have some fun in the process. To that end, this book will not attempt to teach you how to be a graphics programmer or try to give you a systematic math education (although we'll cover a bit of math along the way). Instead, we're going to start at the very beginning and talk about how modern games put things on a screen, and then jump straight into writing shaders to make the things we put on screen look the way we want. There will be lots of example code, lots of pictures, and by the end of the book we'll have gone from the very basics of shader writing to writing shaders that use the same lighting found in some of the most popular games on the market.

If at the end of the book you decide that you'd like to dive deeper into graphics programming, and maybe even write your own rendering engine, or dive into more complicated shader techniques, this book will have provided you with a solid set of fundamentals to prepare you for tackling more complex subject matter.

Who Should Read This Book

This book is for anyone who wants to learn how to use shader code to create visual effects for games or real time applications. I'm going to assume that you already know how to write some simple C++, but that's all you need. I'll explain all the math that we're going to need (and you'll be surprised at how little of it there is), and break down every graphics technique we'll use, starting from what a 3D mesh is. If your C++ skills are a bit rusty, that's OK! Since the focus of the book is on shader development, we're not going to be writing much C++ at all, and what little we do write is going to be kept very simple.

How to Use This Book

The book is divided up into three main sections. Chapters 1-12 are concerned with teaching shader techniques and introducing new graphics concepts. If you're a complete beginner, I recommend starting at Chapter 1 and reading everything in order. Each chapter will build on the information contained in previous ones, so there's a chance you'll end up lost if you skip too far ahead.

If you already have some amount of shader development knowledge, you might have more fun skipping ahead to the first chapter that talks about something you haven't already learned before. If you hit a concept you don't understand, the index at the back of the book should be able to point you to when it was originally introduced, and you can skip back to there to get caught up.

Chapters 13 to 15 are concerned with debugging and optimizing shader code. If you're picking this book up because your project is running at 10 fps and you need to fix it, it might be worth jumping straight to there and dealing with your immediate problem before reading the first sections; otherwise you might be a bit frustrated by the relaxed pace of the early chapters.

Chapters 16 to 18 talk about how to implement the concepts taught in this book in three of the most popular engines being used today: Unity, Unreal Engine 4, and Godot. I recommend leaving those until the very end, when you're ready to apply the concepts taught in this book to your projects.

Finally, there is an Appendix at the end of the book that has a couple of important code snippets that are needed for some of the examples in the book. These snippets aren't shader code, and as such, aren't explained in depth by the chapter contents.

If you're reading this book without an Internet connection, you'll need to consult there to follow along with the chapter examples in the later chapters. The chapter text will tell you when to do this, so don't worry about it right off the bat, you won't need this code until the later chapters of Section 1.

Example Code Conventions

The book uses a lot of example code. To make it easier to talk about that code, these examples are annotated with numbered symbols, like the following:

```
int main(){
    return 0; ❶
}
```

Text referring to this example will refer to the return 0; line as "❶."

Software Requirements

Since we'll be using an open source coding framework called openFrameworks—which uses C++14 by default—your life will be easiest if you have a compiler capable of supporting C++14. We aren't going to be using any C++14 features, but the framework needs them under the hood. Your life will also be easier if you're using an IDE supported by openFrameworks. Luckily, there are a lot of them, and you'll be able to select which one you want when we get everything set up.

Finally, we'll be using OpenGL to run all our shaders. OpenGL is a "rendering API," which is a fancy term for a set of functions that we can use to communicate with our graphics card (GPU). There are a lot of different APIs to choose from, but OpenGL has the advantage of running on the widest range of hardware possible and being well integrated with openFrameworks. You should make sure that your GPU supports at least OpenGL version 4.1, which is what this book will assume you're using. As of OS X High Sierra, Apple has deprecated OpenGL for their desktop PCs, which means that the examples in the book may not work if you're following along on a Mac.

CHAPTER 1

Hello, Game Graphics

Before we can dive in to writing shaders, we first need to cover some background information about how games put things on screen, and some of the basic math that they use when doing so. In this chapter we're going to get a bird's-eye view of what rendering is, and how a game renders a frame of a video game. Next, we'll talk about what a shader is, and how it fits into the rendering process we just learned about. Finally, we'll end the chapter with a very brief introduction to what vectors are, which will give us all the information we need to start writing our own shaders in the subsequent chapters.

What Is Rendering?

In computer graphics, *rendering* is the process of creating an image from a set of 2D or 3D meshes, and information about the game scene like the position of lights or the orientation of the *game camera*. The image created by the rendering process is sometimes referred to as a *render* or a *frame*, and that image is what gets presented to the user on their computer screen many times a second. In fact, most games will render a new frame between 30 and 60 times per second.

A lot of rendering terminology is borrowed from film, because a lot of the general concepts are very similar between computer graphics and film-making. In our definition of rendering, I mentioned a "game camera," which is one of these borrowed terms. Just like in film, where the position and direction of the camera determines what's on screen, games use the concept of a game camera to mean essentially the same thing: a data structure that contains information about where the game scene should be viewed from. At its most basic, a game camera can be represented with just a position and a direction. This information is used to determine which objects in the game are currently visible and need to be rendered in the current frame.

© Kyle Halladay 2019
K. Halladay, *Practical Shader Development*, https://doi.org/10.1007/978-1-4842-4457-9_1

The part of video game code that's responsible for rendering frames is referred to as a *rendering engine*. If you've ever used a game engine like Unity, Unreal, or Godot before, you've worked with a rendering engine, even if you didn't know it at the time. The series of steps a rendering engine uses to turn mesh data into new frames is referred to as the *rendering pipeline* (or *graphics pipeline*). We'll talk about this pipeline in a moment, but first we should probably talk about what a mesh is, given that they're the things that the pipeline acts on.

What Is a Mesh?

Meshes are one of the methods we have for describing shapes in a way that will make sense to a computer. If you've ever played a video game or watched an animated movie before, chances are you've seen an awful lot of meshes. To define a shape, a mesh needs to store information about three things: *vertices*, *edges*, and *faces*.

Vertices are points in 3D space. If you only saw a mesh's vertices, it would look like the leftmost section of Figure 1-1. *Edges* are the lines that connect the vertices. These lines define how the vertices are connected to form a shape. You can see the edges of the mesh in the center section of Figure 1-1. Finally, *faces* are 2D shapes formed by three or more edges. You can think of faces as the space in between the edges of a mesh. In Figure 1-1, the sphere in the rightmost section looks solid, because all the faces of the mesh have been filled in. Mesh faces can be any 2D shape, but for speed and simplicity, many game engines require that the meshes they work with be triangulated (meaning that they contain only triangular faces).

Figure 1-1. *Examples of the different components of a mesh: from left to right we can see vertices, edges and faces*

One of the reasons that meshes are so popular in computer graphics is that they're very simple to define in code. Only a mesh's vertices are stored in memory, and the edges and faces of a mesh are defined implicitly by the order the vertices are in. Sometimes this vertex ordering is simply the order the vertices are stored in the mesh's shape data, and other times it's defined by a data structure called an *index buffer*, which we'll talk about in a later chapter.

The order of vertices is also important because it's used to define which side of a mesh face is considered the "front" of that face's 2D shape. For all the examples in this book, if when looking at a mesh face, the vertices are defined in a counter clockwise order around the center of that polygon, that side of the mesh face is the "front." Choosing counterclockwise here is an arbitrary choice, and other games or engines may choose to use the clockwise direction in this same calculation. Which direction you choose is referred to as a mesh's *winding order*.

To see an example of this, let's suppose that we want to define the triangle shown in Figure 1-2. We want the front of the triangle to be facing us, so we might define the vertices in the order (200,200), (400,100), and (400,300). We're going to work with meshes extensively throughout the book, so don't worry if this is all feeling a bit abstract. We're going to be creating our own meshes in the next chapter, so you'll get some hands-on experience very soon.

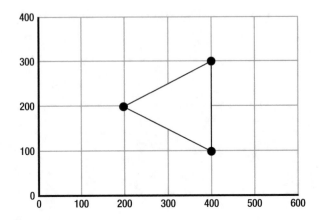

Figure 1-2. *A simple triangle mesh*

Which side of a face is the front is important because many games won't render the "back" side of mesh faces. This is an optimization known as *backface culling*, and is a common optimization used in games. There are lots of times when you may need to disable backface culling while working on a more complex scene, but it's much more common for games to have this enabled. To make things as simple as possible, the examples in this book won't have backface culling turned on, but it's important to know about it for your own projects.

One thing to note is that a mesh's vertices are defined using vectors, which are a very important bit of math to know about, since they're one of the fundamental data types used in shader code (so much so, that the programming languages that you write shaders in provide vector types by default). We're not going to get too deep into vector math right now, but it's important that we cover the basics before going much farther down the shader rabbit hole.

Vectors 101

Many people first learn about vectors in math class and get an explanation along the lines of "a vector is a quantity with both a direction and a magnitude," which is technically correct but not very intuitive. Instead, we can think about vectors like directions on a road trip. If we need to drive 3 miles north to get to the next gas station, we can think about that as a vector with a direction of "north" and a magnitude—or length—of 3 miles. Figure 1-3 shows two examples of what this vector might look like on a graph.

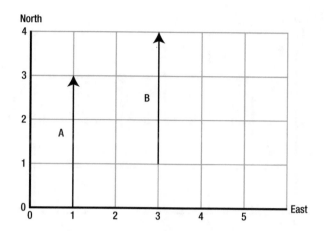

Figure 1-3. *Examples of the same vector at two positions*

One thing to notice is that both vectors have the same direction and magnitude despite being located at different positions. This is because vectors don't express any information about position, so they need a point of reference to make sense spatially. In the preceding diagram, depending on if our car was located at position (1,0) or position (3,1), our trip's vector would be A or B, respectively. This point of reference is called a vector's *initial point*, and the end point of a vector is called its *terminal point*. It's common to think about vectors as a movement from one point to another, and that's how they got their name: the name vector comes from the Latin word "vehere," which means "to carry," so feel free to think about a vector as carrying something from one point to another.

Despite vectors not expressing any information about position by themselves, it's very common to define a position with a vector. When a vector is used to refer to something's position, the initial point of that vector is assumed to be the zero point in whatever coordinate system our vector is used in. In 2D space, this is point (0,0), in 3D it's (0,0,0), etc. This "zero point" is known as the *origin*. So, when we say that an object is located at position (2,1), what we mean is that if you start at the origin, and move 2 units in the X axis, and 1 unit in the Y axis, you get to our position. Figure 1-4 shows a couple of examples of positions being plotted on a graph.

In Figure 1-4, the points on our graph are the terminal points of two different vectors, both of which start at the origin. If we added arrows to this diagram to show these vectors, the same diagram would look like Figure 1-5.

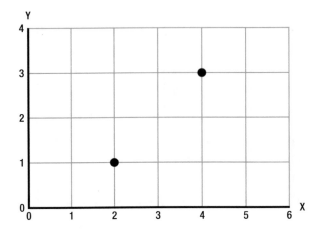

Figure 1-4. *Two positions in space. We usually represent positions like this as vectors.*

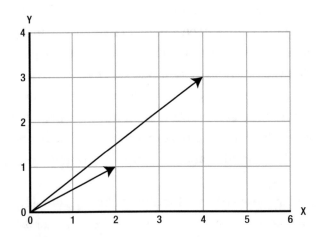

Figure 1-5. *Adding in vector lines to the positions in Figure 1-4*

As you may have noticed, vectors are often referred to as a series of numbers inside parentheses, like (1,2,3). These numbers are referred to as a vector's *components*, and the number of components a vector has determines how many dimensions we say that vector has. A 1-dimensional vector will contain a single value, while a 3-dimensional vector will have three of them. In practice, a vector can have any number of dimensions, but in graphics it's most common to work with vectors up to four dimensions.

For vectors up to three dimensions, it's common to see their values be named after the common names for the axes of a graph: X, Y, Z. When working with 4-dimensional vectors, it's common to refer to the last value as "W," so a 4D vector's components will most commonly be named X, Y, Z, and W. You'll often hear vectors being talked about in terms of the number of values they contain, rather than their dimensionality, so don't be thrown off if we start talking about a "4-component vector" rather than a "4-dimensional vector," they mean the same thing. As you'll see later, shader code also refers to vectors by their number of components, and we'll see lots of code that uses vec2, vec3, and vec4 variables, denoting 2-, 3-, and 4-component vectors, respectively.

While there are a lot of things you can do in vectors, there are only four operations that we need to know about to get started, and they should sound very familiar: addition, subtraction, multiplication, and division. We'll talk about addition and subtraction first, since they're the most intuitive to understand. To go back to our road trip metaphor: I said that a vector was like a single direction that we might follow as part of our trip (i.e., drive 3 miles north), but a road trip is never that simple and there's always a whole lot of different steps to follow to reach our destination. Adding vectors together is a bit like that—when you add vectors together, you get a vector that points in a straight line to the point that you'd reach if you followed each vector one after the other. Represented visually, it would look like Figure 1-6.

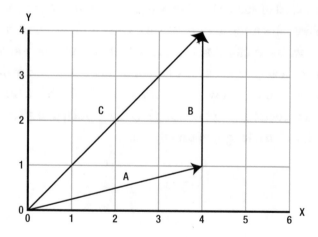

Figure 1-6. *The vectors A and B are being added together; the result is vector C*

You can see in Figure 1-6 that we have two vectors, A and B, which are being placed end to end. The third vector—labeled C—is the sum of these two vectors. You can see that whether you follow A and B in sequential order, or just follow C, you're going to get to the same position. That's how vector addition—and subtraction—work.

To add two vectors together, you consider each component of the vectors separately, so the X value of your resulting vector is the sum of the X components of both vectors being added, and the Y result is the sum of the Y components. Vector subtraction works the same way. This might be easier to understand if we look at it with some math notation:

$$(200, 200) + (200, 100) = (200 + 200, 200 + 100) = (400, 300)$$

$$(200, 200) - (200, 100) = (200 - 200, 200 - 100) = (0, 100)$$

Another important thing you can do with vectors is multiply them by a single number (called a scalar). If we multiplied our road trip vector by the number 5, it would be a bit like saying "drive 3 miles north, five times"—we would end up 15 miles north. In math notation, this works like this:

$$(1, 3) * 5 = (0 * 5, 3 * 5) = (0, 15)$$

One very special kind of vector is called a unit vector, which is a vector that has a magnitude of 1. These are important because if you multiply a unit vector by any number, you end up with a vector that has a length of the number you multiplied by, meaning that you can easily represent any length of movement in the direction of the vector. For example, Figure 1-7 shows two vectors, one of which is a unit vector and the second one is that unit vector being multiplied by 2.5. Notice that after multiplication, the product is a vector with a length of exactly 2.5.

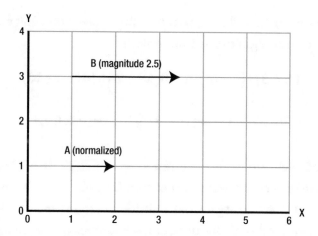

Figure 1-7. *Vector A is a normalized vector. If we multiply that vector by 2.5, we end up with vector B.*

Multiplying a vector by a scalar is a lot like addition and subtraction, because we're still just considering every component in isolation. Here's what the multiplication from the preceding diagram would look like if we wrote it down in math notation:

$$(1, 0) * 2.5 = (1*2.5, 0*2.5) = (2.5, 0)$$

The process of turning a nonunit vector into a unit vector is called *normalization* and is done by dividing each component of a vector by that vector's magnitude. For example, we know that vector B in Figure 1-7 has a magnitude of 2.5, because we created that vector by multiplying a unit vector by that value. If we wanted to renormalize vector B, which is (2.5, 0, 0), we would simply divide each component by 2.5, which would give us vector A (1, 0, 0). You don't have to remember this, as we're going to use a special shader function to normalize our vectors for us, but it's a handy thing to know regardless. What's important to remember right now is what a unit vector is, and why it makes sense to use unit vectors when we want to store direction (but not distance) information.

Dividing a vector by a scalar works the same way as multiplication—each component of the vector is divided in isolation:

$$(1, 2, 3) / (4, 5, 6) = (1/5, 2/5, 3/6) = (0.2, 0.4, 0.5)$$

The last bit of vector math we need to know before diving into shader code is how to multiply or divide a vector by another vector. Just like multiplying by a scalar value, these operations are done component-wise as well. These operations aren't commonly used on vectors that are storing spatial data, so rather than show you what they look like on a graph, I'm going to skip straight to the math notation:

$$(1, 2, 3) * (4, 5, 6) = (1*4, 2*5, 3*6) = (3, 10, 18)$$

$$(1, 2, 3) / (4, 5, 6) = (1/5, 2/5, 3/6) = (0.2, 0.4, 0.5)$$

If you've studied vectors outside of computer graphics, these two examples might confuse you because they're not really part of standard vector math. The reason for this is that although vectors have a very formal definition in math and physics, in code, a vector is just an ordered series of numbers, and sometimes the preceding operations will make sense—or just be convenient—for certain kinds of data. One example of when this is the case is when our vectors are storing colors instead of position and direction. Multiplying a color by another color in the way our example shows is extremely useful, but rather than explain why right now, we'll talk more about that in Chapter 3. For now, just know that multiplying and dividing a vector by another vector in graphics code works like the preceding example shows, even if those operations don't exist in the larger vector math world.

I just mentioned that we'll use vectors to store color information. Depending on the sorts of things you've programmed before, it might not be obvious how a vector would store color data, so let's take a moment to talk about how graphics code usually represents color.

Defining a Color in Computer Graphics

In all types of programming, it's common to see colors represented as a series of three values, one for how much red a color has, one for how much green, and one for how much blue. You sometimes hear these different values referred to as *color channels*. Sometimes these are represented as a series of integers (usually with a range of 0 meaning no color, up to 255), a series of floats, or a series of hexadecimal numbers. For example, Figure 1-8 shows a few different colors and different ways we can represent those colors numerically.

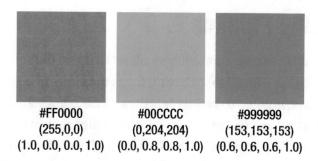

#FF0000 | #00CCCC | #999999
(255,0,0) | (0,204,204) | (153,153,153)
(1.0, 0.0, 0.0, 1.0) | (0.0, 0.8, 0.8, 1.0) | (0.6, 0.6, 0.6, 1.0)

Figure 1-8. *Examples of different ways programmers can represent colors*

In shaders, we almost always treat colors as a series of floats, but we also add one more number to the mix. This final value represents the amount of *alpha* a color has. Alpha is the computer graphics term for how opaque a color is. If you were looking at red box with an alpha of 1, you wouldn't be able to see what was inside. If you changed the color of that box to have an alpha of 0.8, you would be able to see inside, or through the box, as though it was made of colored glass. You can see what this looks like in Figure 1-9.

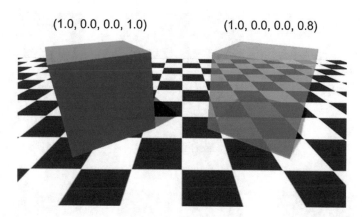

Figure 1-9. *The cube on the left has an alpha of 1.0, so it is solid; the right one has an alpha of 0.8*

In computer graphics, it's very common to use 4-component vectors (also called vec4s) to store color data, with the X,Y,Z components referring to the amount of red, green, and blue in that color, and the W component for the alpha. It's also common to see colors being represented as vec3s in cases where we know the alpha value of that color will always be 1. If you're using a vector to store color data, it's common to refer to the components of the vector as R,G,B,A instead of X,Y,Z,W; and as we'll see when we start writing our own shaders, you can use either of these naming conventions when writing code.

The Rendering Pipeline

We've already defined the term "rendering pipeline" to mean the series of steps that a graphics card (also called a *GPU*) takes to turn mesh data into an image on our screen. The rendering pipeline is going to be very important throughout this book, because shaders do their work as part of this pipeline. We're going to talk a lot more about what shaders are in a couple of pages, but for now, it's enough to know that shaders are small programs that execute during some steps of the rendering pipeline, to influence the output of these steps.

As such, it makes sense for us to have at least some knowledge of what the steps of the rendering pipeline are before we talk too much more about shaders. I'm not going to talk at length about every step (there are a lot, and we don't have to worry about most of them right now), but if we only consider the steps in the pipeline that we're going to think about in this book, the rendering pipeline looks like Figure 1-10.

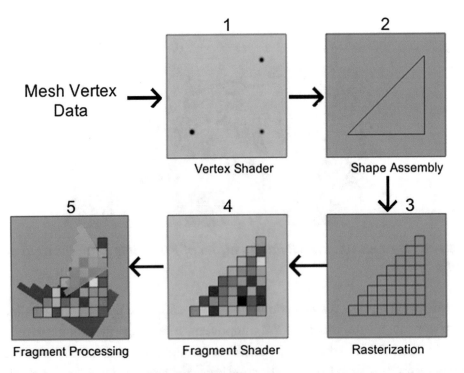

Figure 1-10. *A simplified view of the graphics pipeline. The order of the steps is shown both by the arrows and the numbers located over each box.*

This pipeline is run on every mesh that we tell our GPU it should consider for the frame it's currently rendering. Once every one of those meshes has been sent through the pipeline, we have our frame. These steps run exclusively on the GPU, and one of the reasons graphics cards are so important to games is that they're built to run the graphics pipeline as fast as possible.

You can see that vertex shaders are the first step in our simplified view of the pipeline. They are concerned with figuring out where on screen every vertex in the mesh currently being processed needs to be drawn. Remember earlier when we saw what a sphere mesh would look like if it was just vertices? A vertex shader would handle figuring out where to put each of those vertices on our screen. When an object moves in a video game, it's because that object's position is being sent to a vertex shader, which then combines that with other information, like data about our game camera's position and orientation, and uses all of that to decide where to place the vertices of that object's mesh on our screen.

After our vertex shader has finished processing all the vertices in a mesh, it sends all that data to the next step of the pipeline, which is called "shape assembly." This stage is responsible for connecting all those vertices that we just processed with lines. Essentially, this stage is responsible for putting our mesh's edges on screen.

The next stage in our simplified pipeline is rasterization. In this stage, the GPU figures out which pixels on screen our mesh might occupy, and for each one of these potential pixels, creates a *fragment,* which is a data structure that contains all the information needed to draw a single pixel on your screen. You can think of a fragment as a potential pixel, but not all fragments will end up as pixels on screen.

The rasterization step doesn't know anything about what the surface of our mesh looks like; it needs help from a fragment shader to fill in information about what color each of the fragments needs to be, so it sends all the fragments to the next step in the pipeline, where our code fills in that information for us. You can almost think about fragment shaders as coloring in the lines created by the shape assembly stage.

There's one more step before we get an image on our screen, which I've labeled in the diagram as "fragment processing." This stage of the pipeline has two major roles: fragment testing and blending operations. Fragment testing involves deciding what fragments to put on the screen, and which to throw away. Fragments are generated for meshes without any information about the rest of the scene, which means that the GPU usually creates many more fragments than your screen has pixels to fill. For example, if the player is looking at a brick wall that has a sports car behind it, the GPU will create fragments for all the pixels that the sports car would fill if the wall wasn't there, as well as fragments for all the pixels that the wall will cover. It isn't until the "fragment processing" stage of the pipeline that we figure out which fragments will appear on screen, and which will be discarded. Fragment blending is what allowed our alpha cube in Figure 1-9 to blend its color with the fragments behind it. Blending is very useful, but since we're going to devote a whole chapter to it later, I won't dwell on it too much here.

After the fragment processing step completes, our frame is ready to be displayed on screen. Remember that these are just the steps in the rendering pipeline that we need to think about to get started writing shaders, the real rendering pipeline has many more steps to it, but there's no reason to worry about them right now.

What Is a Shader?

We touched briefly on what a shader is in the last section, but now we have enough background knowledge to really define it. A shader is a program that gets executed on a graphics card. This is different from most programs that people write, which are usually executed by the CPU. This means that there are some things that shaders can do that regular programs can't. For our purposes, the most important thing they can do is to control parts of the rendering pipeline. A lot of the pipeline stays the same no matter what type of object is being rendered—GPUs will always generate shapes from vertices the same way, for example—but shaders allow us to control key parts of the pipeline to create games and applications that look exactly how we want them to.

Shaders that operate on different stages of the pipeline are given different names. As you may have guessed from Figure 1-10, we're going to be focusing on vertex shaders, and fragment shaders. These are the most commonly used shader types, since they're the minimum requirements to get something through the rendering pipeline and on the screen. Since each stage of the pipeline is different, shaders written for each stage are also different: you can't use a vertex shader to do fragment processing, or vice versa. Don't get too hung up on the fact that shaders are defined as "programs." While that is the correct term for what a shader is, I think that it's a bit confusing when you're first starting out. It's totally OK to simply think of them as bits of code that the GPU runs and not get too hung up on proper terminology.

Shaders are written in specialized programming languages called "shader languages." There are a lot of shader languages, but the reality is that they're all very similar. Once you're comfortable with one of them, it's not too difficult to learn the others. Since this book is using OpenGL for our graphics, we're going to be using GLSL, which stands for "OpenGL Shading Language." This language is going to look a lot like C, which means we can get up and running quickly without having to learn the basics of how its syntax works; if you know some C or C++, things will look very familiar.

We've gone over a lot of theory in this chapter, but it's all led up to now: we're finally ready to start writing our own application!

Summary

Here's a quick summary of what we covered in this chapter:

- Meshes are a collection of vertex positions, used to define a 3D shader in a 3D game or application.

- Vectors are a data structures consisting of two or more floats, which we will use to store position, direction, and color data.

- Colors are commonly represented as a 4-component vector, with the last component storing "alpha", which is the graphics term for opacity.

- We can add, subtract, multiply, and divide vectors from one another. All these operations are done in a component-wise fashion.

- GPUs follow a series of steps called the "rendering pipeline" to produce images on our screen. We went into detail about the steps in this process, which will be important for us throughout this book.

- Shaders are programs that execute during some steps of the rendering pipeline and are used to control the output of those steps.

CHAPTER 2

Your First Shaders

It's time to start building things! As I mentioned before, this book will not cover the code needed to write a rendering engine from scratch (since most of us have the luxury of using a game engine that provides one). However, this book is not about making shaders in a specific game shader. Rather than grab something like Unity, UE4, or Godot, we're going to use a creative coding framework called openFrameworks. openFrameworks has the advantage of being minimal enough that it will do "just enough" to let us focus on shaders, while not being as complicated as a full game engine. It's also completely open source, MIT licensed, and works on every major operating system. Hopefully, openFrameworks will work for you, no matter what platform you're on, or what your end goal is for shader development.

To get started, head to `http://openframeworks.cc/download/` and download it. This book was written with version 0.10.0, so for the best luck when following along, grab that version. openFrameworks ships as source only, and how you build the framework and create a project with it can change a lot depending on what operating system and IDE you're using. Since I expect that most readers will be working with Windows and Visual Studio, I'm going to walk through getting things set up for that use case. This will be one of the few times that the book will focus on a single platform, so don't worry if you're on a different platform. If you aren't using Windows, openFrameworks has setup guides for every platform they support. Head back to the download page, and you should find links for your operating system under the heading "Setup Guides." Then, instead of following along with the next section here, follow the steps in the setup guide for your use case. For the rest of us, let's see how to set things up for Windows and Visual Studio.

© Kyle Halladay 2019

K. Halladay, *Practical Shader Development*, https://doi.org/10.1007/978-1-4842-4457-9_2

Setting Things Up on Windows

The biggest difference between setting up a regular project in Visual Studio and using openFrameworks is the project generator application that comes with openFrameworks. This is a small utility that will handle creating a new Visual Studio project that links correctly against openFrameworks and has the minimum amount of code needed to create a window. This makes getting up and running with openFrameworks much easier than with most third-party code. All the steps we need to take are outlined in the following list:

1. Unzip the compressed archive you downloaded from openFrameworks to wherever you want the framework to live on your hard drive.

2. Navigate into the projectGenerator-vs folder and run projectGenerator.exe. You should be presented with a window that asks for some project setup details, like name and file path.

3. Enter a name for your project and specify where you'd like it to be put. Then click "Generate."

4. You should see a new screen show up that has a button labelled "Open in IDE"; click that. That will open a Visual Studio solution that contains two projects: one for the openFrameworks library and one for your project.

5. Build the solution for the project you just created (it will also automatically also build openFrameworks for you), and then run it. Your program will consist of a gray window. If that's what you see, you're good to go.

Setting Up Our Project

From here on out, I'm going to assume that you have an openFrameworks project created, and that you're following along with the examples in your own code. By default, a new openFrameworks project will have three source code files: main.cpp, ofApp.h, and ofApp.cpp. main.cpp has our program's main() function and is responsible for creating an object of type OfApp and then telling that object to take over from there. If we don't do anything to main(), it will create an OfApp object that's configured to use OpenGL version 2.0. OpenGL is a "rendering API," which is a fancy term for a set of functions that we can use to communicate with our GPU. There are a lot of different APIs to choose from, but OpenGL has the advantage of running on the widest range of hardware possible and being well integrated with openFrameworks. We're going to work with something a bit more modern than OpenGL 2.0 though, so we need to modify main() a little bit to specify what version of OpenGL we want to use. Your main() function should start off by looking like Listing 2-1.

Listing 2-1. Our Initial main() Function

```
#include "ofMain.h"
#include "ofApp.h"

int main( ){
        ofSetupOpenGL(1024,768,OF_WINDOW); ❶
        ofRunApp(new ofApp());
}
```

By default, we start off with two function calls inside main(). The first of these (at ❶) is what sets up OpenGL for us and creates the window that our app will display frames on. Next, we call ofRunApp() to hand control flow over to an ofApp object. Notice that functions provided by openFrameworks are all prefixed with "of," which makes them easy to distinguish from the code that we'll write for our examples.

Right now, main() is nice and minimal, but unfortunately, we need to make it a bit more verbose in order to configure our OpenGL version. To do that, we need to replace line ❶ with the code snippet in Listing 2-2.

Listing 2-2. Setting Up a Window to Use GL 4.1

```
ofGLWindowSettings glSettings;
glSettings.setSize(1024, 768);
glSettings.windowMode = OF_WINDOW;
glSettings.setGLVersion(4, 1);
ofCreateWindow(glSettings);
```

This should be all we need to do to main() to get things set up properly. We'll be spending a lot more time in the other two files that were generated for us, ofApp.h and ofApp.cpp, since these files are for the ofApp() object that our main function creates. The default ofApp files that get generated for us already contain overloads of several functions from our base class (ofBaseApp) that we can use to respond to openFrameworks events. By default, all these overloads are empty functions, but we'll fill them in as our examples get more complex.

To start with, we're going to look at the setup() function in ofApp.cpp. This is called when our ofApp object is constructed, and is a good spot to load resources or create objects that will be used to render the first frame of our application. We know shaders control stages of the rendering pipeline and that the rendering pipeline operates on meshes, so the first thing we're going to put into our setup() function is the code to create a mesh.

Creating Your First Triangle

The class for a mesh in openFrameworks is called ofMesh. Creating an ofMesh and adding vertices to it is very simple, all that's required is to create an ofMesh object using its default constructor, and provide vertex positions in the form of 3-component vectors to that object's addVertex() function. openFrameworks uses a math library called "GLM" to handle vector math, so our vec3 data type will come from the glm namespace. This looks like Listing 2-3.

Listing 2-3. Creating a Triangle Mesh

```
void ofApp::setup()
{
    ofMesh triangle;
    triangle.addVertex(glm::vec3(0.0, 0.0, 0.0));
    triangle.addVertex(glm::vec3(0.0, 768.0f, 0.0));
    triangle.addVertex(glm::vec3(1024.0, 768.0, 0.0));
}
```

This code is all that's needed for us to create our first mesh, but unfortunately not enough for us to see it on the screen. To do that, we need to modify our ofApp's draw() function. This function is called once per frame and is responsible for recording a series of commands that the GPU will then execute as part of the rendering pipeline.

Confusingly, the ofMesh class also has a function called draw(), and it's what we'll use to tell our GPU that we want it to draw our mesh this frame. The most convenient way to do this is to move the declaration of our triangle into our header and then call our mesh's draw() inside ofApp's draw(). This looks like Listing 2-4.

Listing 2-4. Drawing Our Triangle Mesh

```
void ofApp::draw()
{
        triangle.draw();
}
```

If we don't specify any shaders ourselves, openFrameworks gives our mesh a default vertex and fragment shader. These default shaders interpret our vertex coordinates as screen pixel coordinates and render our mesh as a solid white shape. If we run our app right now, we'll see a white triangle that covers half of our screen—which is otherwise gray. This looks like Figure 2-1.

Figure 2-1. *A white triangle covers half our window*

You might be surprised to see that the two vertices we created with a Y coordinate of 768 are located at the bottom of the screen. In OpenGL, pixel coordinates start at the top left of the screen, and the Y axis increases as you go down. This means that if we wanted to put a vertex at the top right corner of our screen, we could put it at coordinate (1024.0,0). This can be a bit confusing, so let's modify our program a bit to give us a practical way to experiment with screen pixel coordinates.

We're going to modify the keyPressed() function to let us move one of the vertices of our triangle in response to a key press. You can do this by adding the code in Listing 2-5 to your ofApp.cpp file.

Listing 2-5. Moving a Triangle in Response to a Key Press

```
void ofApp::keyPressed(int key)
{
    glm::vec3 curPos = triangle.getVertex(2);
    triangle.setVertex(2, curPos + glm::vec3(0, 20, 0));
}
```

The code in Listing 2-5 is going to cause the bottom right vertex of our triangle to move upward by 20 pixels every time we press a key on our keyboard. Once you have that working, try modifying the vector that we're using to move our vertex so that instead of moving upward, it moves to the left (toward the bottom left vertex) instead.

Shader writing involves a lot of different coordinate systems and we're going to get introduced to one more very soon, so it's important to take a moment right now and make sure that you have a good handle on how screen pixel coordinates match up to locations on your screen. Next, we're going to replace the default openFrameworks shaders with our own vertex and fragment shaders, so once you feel comfortable with the example we've built so far, it's time to write your very first shaders!

Your First Vertex Shader

Shader code is usually placed in files that are separate from C++ code. By convention, vertex shaders in GLSL are stored in files that end in ".vert" and are normally placed in the same location that you would store assets like images or meshes, rather than where your code files live. This is because shaders are loaded at runtime like any other type of asset. For our openFrameworks app, that asset directory is the "bin/data" folder. Create a new file there called "first_vertex.vert" and open it up.

I often feel like it's better to get introduced to new code syntax by walking through example code, so let's start by just looking at what the simplest vertex shader possible might look like, and then talking about each line. To kick things off, copy the code in Listing 2-6 into your vertex shader file.

Listing 2-6. Our First Vertex Shader

```
#version 410 ❶

in vec3 position; ❷

void main()
{
        gl_Position = vec4(position, 1.0); ❸
}
```

We're going to walk through each line, but it might help to have a high-level summary of what's going on here before we dig into minutia. A vertex shader tells the rest of the pipeline where on screen each vertex of a mesh should be positioned. Vertex shaders operate on a single vertex at a time and have no information about the other vertices of the mesh unless we manually give them that data. This vertex shader is simply taking the position of each vertex and passing it unchanged to the rest of the pipeline. With all that in mind, let's go line by line and see how this vertex shader works.

The #version Preprocessor Directive

We start by declaring what version of GLSL we're going to use (❶). For this book, we'll always use #version 410, which corresponds to our OpenGL version, 4.1. If in the future you were writing a shader that used a feature that was introduced in a newer version of GLSL, you would change this line to specify the version of GLSL that you wanted. For this book, the first line of every shader we write will be identical to the one we wrote here.

GLSL's *in* Keyword

Line ❷ is where we declare the mesh information that our vertex shader is going to use to do its job. Since our mesh only has position data, this is relatively simple for us. We can just specify that we are expecting a 3-component vector (which GLSL calls a vec3) of position data, since each vertex of our mesh is just a 3-component vector right now. If you've never seen shader code before, there are two things that likely stick out as a bit confusing in this line: the "in" keyword and the data type of our variable.

The "in" keyword is specific to GLSL. It's used to specify which data a shader expects to receive from the previous step in the rendering pipeline. For vertex shaders, the previous step in the rendering pipeline is when the GPU turns the mesh data it has been given by our program into a format that can be read by our vertex shader, and later stages of the pipeline. At ❷, what we're really saying is that we expect that our vertex shader is being used to process a vertex that is made up of a 3-component vector, and that we want to take that vec3 and put it in a variable called "position."

As you may have guessed, GLSL also has an "out" keyword, which is used to declare variables that we want to make available to the next stage in the pipeline. We'll talk about "out" variables more when we get to our fragment shader.

GLSL's vec Data Types

Let's talk a little bit more about the data type we're using to store our position data. Unlike our C++ code, we don't need to worry about using a math library like GLM to give us data types for vectors. Vectors are such an integral part of shader code that they are built-in data types in GLSL. Just like our GLM vec3 in C++ code, a vec3 in GLSL is just a collection of three floating point values, called x, y, and z, respectively. Also, GLSL gives us a vec2 data type, and a vec4 (which you can see used at ❸).

A lot of shader code involves manipulating vectors, and as such, there are a few conveniences that GLSL provides to make our life easier. One of these is the ability to use a smaller vector as part of the constructor of a larger one, like we just did (❸). In the example code, we're passing the position vec3 to the constructor for a vec4. This lets us use the x/y/z components of the vec3 and then manually specify our vec4's w component, which for position data will always be 1.0. There are a lot of math reasons why we need to convert our position vector to a vec4, but we don't need to dig into that. We have a lot of shader code to learn about already; there's no need for us to add a math lesson to the mix right now.

Writing to gl_Position

We know that GLSL uses the out keyword to define data that we want to pass from a shader to the next stage of the rendering pipeline, but that isn't the only way a shader can output information. GLSL also defines some special "built-in variables" that are used for different things. The gl_Position variable is one of these special variables and is used to store the position data that a vertex shader wants to send to the rest of the pipeline. Every vertex shader we write will involve writing a vec4 to gl_Position.

Normalized Device Coordinates

That covers all the code in our vertex shader, but if we were to run this vertex shader right now the results wouldn't be what we might expect. This is because the default openFrameworks shader was doing some extra work to make our vertex coordinates match up to screen pixel positions; vertex shaders don't naturally do that. Instead, positions that are output from a vertex shader are expected to be in *normalized device coordinates*.

Earlier in this chapter we talked about screen pixel coordinates, which put the position (0,0) at the top left corner of our window, and the position (1024,768) at the bottom right corner. One problem with using this coordinate system is that it's resolution dependent. If our window was 800 pixels wide and 400 pixels tall, then the bottom right corner of the window would be position (800,400) instead of (1024,768). This means that vertices with the same pixel coordinate would be displayed differently on different screen or window sizes. Normalized device coordinates solve this problem by mapping all screens to the same set of coordinates. If we wanted to put a grid on top of our screen that labelled our screen positions with normalized device coordinates, that grid would look like Figure 2-2. It's worth noting that Figure 2-2 shows how OpenGL handles normalized device coordinates. Other rendering APIs may handle them differently.

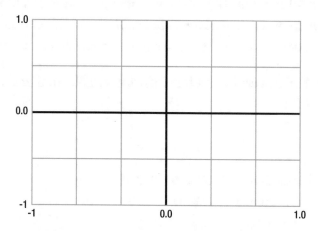

Figure 2-2. *What normalized device coordinates would look like if they were overlaid on our window*

Normalized device coordinates solve our earlier problem with screen pixel coordinates, because no matter what size your screen is, normalized device coordinates remain the same. For example, without knowing the size or shape of a screen, we can be certain that if we want a vertex to be in the center of the screen, it should be at coordinate (0,0). If we want our current vertex shader to output the same triangle as we saw before (with our three vertices lining up with three corners of our screen), we need to modify setup() to specify vertex positions in normalized coordinates. You can see this in Listing 2-7.

Listing 2-7. Specifying Vertex Positions in Normalized Device Coordinates

```
void ofApp::setup(){
        triangle.addVertex(glm::vec3(-1.0f, 1.0f, 0.0f));
        triangle.addVertex(glm::vec3(-1.0f, -1.0f, 0.0f));
        triangle.addVertex(glm::vec3(1.0f, -1.0f, 0.0));
}
```

Notice that we had to swap the signs on the Y components of all our vertices. This is because the direction of the Y axis is different between pixel coordinates and normalized device coordinates.

If we didn't want to modify the vertex positions of our mesh, we could instead change our vertex shader to perform the same math that the default openFrameworks shader was doing to convert our vertex positions from screen pixel coordinates to normalized device coordinates. This requires a bit of simple math (shown in Listing 2-8). To make things simple, Listing 2-8 hard codes the dimensions of our application's window (1024,768). If you wanted to use this approach in a larger application, you'd likely pass these dimensions to the shader from your C++ code so that you could support different resolutions.

Listing 2-8. How to Convert from Pixel Positions to Normalized Device Coordinates

```
void main()
{
        float x = (position.x / 1024.0) * 2.0 - 1.0;
        float y = (position.y / 768.0) * 2.0 - 1.0;
        gl_Position = vec4(x, y, 0.0, 1.0);
}
```

While Listing 2-8 will work, it's much more common to see a mesh use normalized device coordinates than it is to see one use pixel coordinates. So for now, our vertex positions will always be specified in normalized device coordinates, rather than having our shader code convert from screen pixel positions.

That covers our vertex shader, but that's not enough for us to see anything on screen. It's time to move on to our next shader.

26

Your First Fragment Shader

Just like vertex shaders, fragment shaders don't operate on all a mesh's fragments at once; instead they process one fragment at a time, and their main job is to decide what color each fragment should be. Remember that a "fragment" is the computer graphics term for the information needed to fill in one pixel on a computer screen.

To that end, our first fragment shader is going to set the color of every fragment generated by our triangle mesh to red. Just like before, I want to approach this by providing the entirety of the shader's code, and then talking about it afterward. Fragment shaders are typically stored in files that end in ".frag". If you're following along with the examples, create a new file in your project's bin/data directory called "first_fragment.frag" and copy the code in Listing 2-9 into it.

Listing 2-9. A Fragment Shader that Outputs Red

```
#version 410
out vec4 outColor;

void main(){
    outColor = vec4(1.0, 0.0, 0.0, 1.0);
}
```

After walking through our vertex shader, this probably looks a bit familiar. The biggest difference between this and our vertex shader is that we don't get a built-in variable to write our data to, so we need to declare our own. To do this, we need to declare a variable using the "out" keyword, which we mentioned briefly earlier but need to dive into now.

GLSL's *out* Keyword

We've already talked about the "in" keyword and how it's used to specify that a variable will be written to by an earlier stage in the rendering pipeline. The "out" keyword means the opposite. Variables declared with the "out" qualifier are written to by our current shader, and then passed to later stages of the pipeline. In Listing 2-9, we're using an "out" variable to pass the color of each fragment to the later stages of the pipeline so that those colors can make it to our screen.

It may seem odd that our vertex shader had a built-in variable to write to, while our fragment shader needs to define its own "out" variables. In older versions of OpenGL, fragment shaders also had a built-in variable to write to. As the API evolved, this was removed to give shader writers more flexibility with their fragment shaders. The fragment shaders we write in this book will always output a single color. However, many modern video games use fragment shaders that output multiple colors and sometimes ones that don't output a color at all.

Using Shaders in Our Project

Now that we've talked about using an "out" variable to output our color value, we've officially finished writing our first set of shaders! It's time to load them into our application and start using them. The class used by openFrameworks to store and work with shader code is called an ofShader, and we're going to declare a member variable of that type in ofApp.h. This means that our header file should have the two member variables from Listing 2-10 in it now, one for our mesh and one for our shader.

Listing 2-10. Member Variables to Hold a Mesh and a Shader

```
ofMesh triangle;
ofShader shader;
```

In ofApp.cpp, we need to tell this ofShader object to use the shaders we just wrote. This is very easy if you took my advice and placed the two shaders in the project's "bin/data" directory. It looks like Listing 2-11.

Listing 2-11. Loading Our Shader Files into an ofShader Object

```
void ofApp::setup(){
    triangle.addVertex(glm::vec3(-1.0f, -1.0f, 0.0f));
    triangle.addVertex(glm::vec3(-1.0f, 1.0f, 0.0f));
    triangle.addVertex(glm::vec3(1.0f, 1.0f, 0.0));
    shader.load("first_vertex.vert", "first_fragment.frag"); ❶
}
```

When we tell the GPU to render a mesh, we first need to specify which shaders we're going to use to render it with. Since we need to set all of these shaders up at once, it makes sense from an API standpoint to store them all in a single object so we can bind them with a single function call. To that end, ofShader objects can store both a vertex and fragment shader. You can see how to load our shader files into an ofShader variable at ❶. The paths given to ofShader's load() function are relative to the bin/data directory of our application, so if you've put your shader files there you can reference them with their filenames like the example is doing here.

Once our shaders are loaded, we need to tell our program to use them when rendering our triangle. This requires a slight modification to our draw function from earlier. Listing 2-12 shows the changes that need to be made.

Listing 2-12. Using a Shader in Our Draw Function

```
void ofApp::draw(){
        shader.begin(); ❶
        triangle.draw();
        shader.end(); ❷
}
```

Every time we call an ofMesh's draw() function, we're telling our GPU to render our mesh in the next frame, which means it will need to send that mesh's data through the rendering pipeline. In graphics terminology this is called "issuing a draw call," because we are telling our GPU to draw a specific thing.

In order to use a specific set of shaders to render a mesh, we need to signal what shaders we want to use before issuing the draw call for that mesh. This is referred to as "binding" a set of shaders. In openFrameworks this is done with the begin() function, which you can see at ❶. Once we've bound the shaders we want to use, we're free to issue draw() commands for every mesh that needs to use the set of shaders that we've bound. When it's time for us to finish drawing, or change what shader we're using, we need to tell the GPU to stop using our current shader, which is done with the end() function that we're using at ❷.

With those changes made, we should be able to run the program and see a handsome red triangle covering half of the window. If that's what you're seeing, it means that you've successfully written and used your first shaders! However, displaying a single color is only so exciting. Why don't we spruce our triangle up a little bit and have it display a whole bunch of colors instead? You can see what this will look like in Figure 2-3.

Figure 2-3. *Dapper, right?*

Adding Color with Vertex Attributes

We're going to create a triangle that displays a whole lot of different colors. We can do this by assigning a single color to each of the three vertices in our mesh: one will be pure red, one will be pure green, and one will be pure blue. Then in our fragment shader, we can blend between these three colors depending on how far away from each vertex that fragment is. Fragments closer to one vertex will get more of that vertex's color, which is how we'll end up with the triangle in Figure 2-3.

There are only a couple of ways to pass information to the rendering pipeline from C++ code, and the only way to have that data vary on a per-vertex basis is through our mesh's vertex data. The only data our mesh's vertices have right now is position data, but we aren't limited to that. We're free to store any numeric data that we want on our mesh's vertices as long as every vertex in our mesh has the same amount of that data. Storing colors is a very commonly seen example of this, and openFrameworks makes this very easy for us to do. In graphics terms this is called adding a "vertex attribute" to our mesh. To do this, we need to revisit setup() in ofApp.cpp and add a few more lines of code to our mesh creation logic. These are shown in Listing 2-13.

Listing 2-13. Adding Vertex Color to Our Mesh

```
void ofApp::setup(){

    triangle.addVertex(glm::vec3(-1.0f, -1.0f, 0.0f));
    triangle.addVertex(glm::vec3(-1.0f, 1.0f, 0.0f)); ❶
    triangle.addVertex(glm::vec3(1.0f, 1.0f, 0.0f));

    triangle.addColor(ofFloatColor(1.0f, 0.0f, 0.0f, 1.0f));
    triangle.addColor(ofFloatColor(0.0f, 1.0f, 0.0f, 1.0f)); ❷
    triangle.addColor(ofFloatColor(0.0f, 0.0f, 1.0f, 1.0f));

    shader.load("first_vertex.vert", "first_fragment.frag");
}
```

The function used to add colors to our mesh is called addColor(). The order that we call this function in must match the order that we defined our vertices in. If we want the second vertex we created (at ❶) to be our green vertex, we must make sure that green is the second color we add to the mesh (at ❷). The addColor() function makes this very simple but it also makes it seem like a vertex's colors are different from vertex position data, which is a bit misleading. As far as OpenGL is concerned, our mesh is simply a collection of numeric data. The GPU doesn't have any notion of position or color; it's up to us to write shader code that knows how to use this data.

Now that our mesh has multiple vertex attributes, we need to keep track of the order these attributes so that we don't try to read data from the wrong place, like trying to read vertex color from position data. The order of our vertex attributes is set by openFrameworks, so we don't need to worry about telling OpenGL about it (openFrameworks does that for us), but we will have to adjust our vertex shader so that it knows how to interpret the vertex data it receives. This can be done with GLSL's *layout* qualifier. This bit of syntax tells our shader what order our vertex data is in, and for our current use case it looks like Listing 2-14.

Listing 2-14. Reading in Vertex Color, and Passing It to Our Fragment Shader

```
#version 410

layout ( location = 0 ) in vec3 pos; ❶
layout ( location = 1 ) in vec4 color;

out vec4 fragCol;
```

```
void main(){
     gl_Position = vec4(pos, 1.0);
     fragCol = color; ❷
}
```

In this example, we're using the layout qualifier to specify that our vertices store their data with the position attribute first (❶), followed by the color attribute. Since this matches the vertex data layout that we just used to define our mesh, our shader will be able to parse our more complicated vertices correctly.

Listing 2-14 is also the first time our vertex shader has had an "out" variable. Until now, the only output in this shader was the built-in gl_Position variable. Now, we're outputting data that is specifically for use by our fragment shader, so we need to manually specify that we want it as an output.

Our fragment shader also is going to need a new variable. Since vertex shaders are earlier in the pipeline, our fragment shader's new variable needs to be marked "in," since the data in that variable will come from a previous pipeline step. The "in" variable in our fragment shader must have exactly the same name as the "out" variable in our vertex shader; otherwise our GPU won't know to connect them. With that new variable added, our fragment shader should look like Listing 2-15.

Listing 2-15. Receiving a Uniform from the Vertex Shader, and Outputting It as Color Data

```
#version 410

in vec4 fragCol; ❶
out vec4 outColor;

void main()
{
     outColor = fragCol; ❷
}
```

If you run our program with the shader change from listing 2-14 and 2-15, you'll see our rainbow triangle. This will probably seems a little bit weird, given that all we've done is define three colors on our vertices but are ending up with a whole lot of different colors on our screen. The process that makes this happen is called *fragment interpolation*.

Introducing Fragment Interpolation

In our example project, we only have three vertices in our mesh. This means that our vertex shader only sends three positions to our GPU: one for each point on the mesh. The GPU uses these three points to generate all the fragments needed to render a filled in triangle on our screen. Since these fragments are located between vertices, the GPU needs to decide which vertex's output data needs to be sent to what fragment. Instead of picking just one vertex, the GPU gets the data from all three vertices that make up the face that our fragment is from and blends the data from all three of them. This blend is always linear across the face of the mesh, and never uses information from vertices or fragments on more than one face at a time. The computer graphics term for this blending process is *fragment interpolation*. You can see an example of this in Figure 2-4.

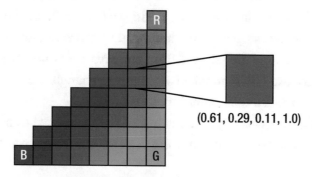

Figure 2-4. *An example of fragment interpolation*

When looking at Figure 2-4, assume that our vertices are located exactly in the center of the fragments marked R, G and B. You can see how the fragments generated for positions between these three vertex points end up with color values that are a combination of the three vertices that make up this mesh face. The highlighted fragment in Figure 2-4 isn't exactly in the middle of the triangle, it's closer to vertex R, and as such contains more of the red vertex's color. All of a fragment shader's "in" variables will be values that are interpolated from vertex data in this way.

Using vertex data and fragment interpolation is great for data that needs to change on a per vertex or per fragment basis, but what about data that doesn't need to change at all? It would have been incredibly wasteful for us to add color information to every vertex if we wanted each vertex to store the same color. This is why data that stays the same across all vertices and fragments gets handled in a different way, which we're going to cover before finishing off this chapter.

Introducing Uniform Variables

We've talked a lot about getting data into the rendering pipeline by using vertex attributes, but modifying vertex data is a very slow process and not something that you'd want to do every frame. For example, changing the color of a mesh whenever a player interacted with it would be incredibly cumbersome to do with vertex colors. For these kinds of use cases, there's another important way that we can get data from our C++ code into the pipeline: *uniform variables*. These variables can be set from C++ code without having to modify any vertex data and are generally the much easier and faster option for specifying data to use when rendering a mesh. Depending on the engine or graphics API you're using, you may also see uniform variables referred to as shader constants, shader properties, or shader parameters.

Uniform variables stay constant across every vertex and fragment in a mesh. Unlike the "in" and "out" variables that we've been using so far, which are different depending on data sent from previous stages of the pipeline, uniform variables are the same no matter where in the pipeline they're read from and are never interpolated. This means that we couldn't have used them to make our rainbow triangle, but they're perfect if we just want to be able to pick a solid color for our triangle.

Our next example does exactly that. Listing 2-16 shows what our fragment shader would look like if we wanted to use a uniform variable to render a solid color triangle.

Listing 2-16. Setting Fragment Color with a Uniform

```
#version 410

uniform vec4 fragCol;  ❶
out vec4 outColor;

void main(){
     outColor = fragCol;
}
```

The only difference between this new shader and the one we wrote for our rainbow triangle is the type of variable we used for fragCol (❶). Using the "uniform" keyword for this variable tells the GPU that this value will be the same for every fragment and that we're going to set its value from outside the rendering pipeline. This means that we don't need our vertex shader to pass color information to our fragment shader anymore,

so we'll go back and clean that shader up as well. When this is done, our vertex shader
should look like Listing 2-17.

Listing 2-17. Our Cleaned Up Vertex Shader

```
#version 410
layout ( location = 0 ) in vec3 pos;
void main()
{
     gl_Position = vec4(pos, 1.0);
}
```

We're only using the vertex attribute at location 0 now, so we don't technically need
to use the layout specifier in the preceding code. However, our mesh still has vertex color
information even if we aren't using it, and it doesn't hurt to be specific about what data
our shader is expecting.

Setting the value of a uniform variable in C++ is very simple; we just need to add a
new line of code to draw() in ofApp.cpp. This is shown in Listing 2-18.

Listing 2-18. Setting A Uniform Value in Our draw() Function

```
void ofApp::draw(){
     shader.begin();
     shader.setUniform4f("fragCol", glm::vec4(0, 1, 1, 1)); ❶

     triangle.draw();
     shader.end();
}
```

Our setUniform() function ends with the characters "4f." This is because the
uniform variable we're writing to is a vec4, meaning that it consists of four floating point
numbers. There are different setUniform() calls for each type of data we might want to
pass to shader code. For example, if we wanted to store a vec3 instead of a vec4, we could
use "setUniform3f()," and if we wanted that vec3 to contain integers instead of floats,
we could use "setUniform3i()." We'll use different versions of this function through the
book, so don't worry about needing to know all the different variations of it now. The last
important thing to learn from Listing 2-18 is that we need to make sure that any calls to

setUniform functions take place after we call shader.begin(). Otherwise, the GPU won't know what shader we're trying to send data to.

With that change, we can now change our triangle to any color that we want without needing to write a new shader to do so. We could even change the color of our triangle in response to keypresses, or other events. All we would need to do is change Listing 2-18 to use a variable for the vec4 argument at ❶ instead hardcoding a value there. We won't walk through the code changes to do that here, but I recommend giving it a shot before moving on to the next chapter. We've going to be using uniform variables a lot in subsequent chapters, and it will be important that you understand them moving forward.

Summary

We learned a lot in this chapter! Here's a quick summary of what we covered:

- openFrameworks is a creative coding framework that we're going to be using for most of the examples in this book. We walked through how to set up a new project using it.

- Creating a mesh in openFrameworks is done with the ofMesh class. We used this class to create a triangle mesh with both vertex positions and vertex colors.

- Normalized device coordinates are used to accommodate different screen sizes and resolutions. We saw how to write a vertex shader that converts screen pixel coordinates to normalized device coordinates.

- GLSL's "in" and "out" keywords allow us to send and receive data from different parts of the rendering pipeline. We used these keywords to create shaders that output a solid white triangle and a rainbow colored triangle.

- Uniform variables stay the same across all stages of the graphics pipeline. We used uniform values to create a shader that let us specify a color for our triangle from C++.

CHAPTER 3

Using Textures

While it's possible to make games with art assets that only use vertex colors, like our triangle in the last chapter, it would take millions of vertices to render an image as detailed as the parrot photo in Figure 3-1. This would not only mean that games needed very complicated meshes to display an image, it would also make it very difficult to swap images out if they needed to change later. For these reasons, most games don't use vertex colors, which can only vary on a per-vertex basis, to render detailed surfaces. Instead, they use image files to provide information that can vary on a per-fragment basis. In computer graphics these image files are referred to as *textures*, and this chapter is going to introduce the basics of working with them.

You can see examples of two textures in Figure 3-1. The left image is a texture that an artist created to wrap around a 3D barrel mesh, while the image on the right is intended to be viewed on a flat plane. Notice that textures used on 3D meshes don't usually look very much like the object that they're going to end up on. Luckily for us, no matter what mesh your texture is going to be applied to, the shader code is the same.

Textures are applied to meshes by a process called *texture mapping*, which is the process of taking a texture (which is usually 2D) and applying it to a 3D mesh. To do this, vertices on a mesh are assigned *texture coordinates* (also called *UV coordinates*). These per-vertex coordinates are interpolated across mesh faces just like the colors we worked with in the last chapter. This means that each fragment of a mesh ends up with a coordinate value in between the texture coordinates of the vertices that make up that mesh face. These coordinates map to a specific position in a texture, and fragment shaders can use these coordinates to determine the color value of the texture at that point. The process of looking up a color value in a texture for a given coordinate is called *texture sampling*.

This is all very abstract right now, so let's start getting our hands dirty. The first step to that is going to be to upgrade from our lowly triangle mesh to something a bit more useful, like a 2D plane. Once we have that mesh set up, we're going to use it to display a

© Kyle Halladay 2019
K. Halladay, *Practical Shader Development*, https://doi.org/10.1007/978-1-4842-4457-9_3

texture on our screen. If you're following along at home, a copy of the parrot texture from Figure 3-1 is available in the online sample code for this chapter (look in the "Assets" folder). Once that parrot is on our screen, we're going to see how to use shaders to adjust a texture's brightness, tint it different colors, and make it scroll across the screen.

Figure 3-1. *The left texture has been authored for use on a 3D mesh;, the right texture is meant to be displayed on a 2D plane*

Making a Quad

Our parrot texture is designed to be viewed on a 2D plane, so that's exactly what mesh we're going to create. To do that, we need to revisit setup() in ofApp.cpp and make what's known as a "quad," which means a square or rectangular mesh made up of two triangles. You can see an example of this in Figure 3-2.

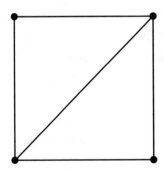

Figure 3-2. *A quad with both triangles outlined*

Remember that most game engines work with meshes that only have triangular faces. If we want a square mesh, we need to put two triangles together, which means we're going to create a mesh with two faces rather than one. Now that we want to add a second face, we have two options. We can define our second triangle by adding three new vertices, which means we need to add two of our existing vertices again, or we can add one new vertex and tell our mesh to reuse the vertices it already had. Obviously, the second option is much more space efficient, and it's how most video games store the complicated meshes that create the amazing characters and environments that you see on display in a modern video game. It's also the approach we're going to take in our example code.

The first thing we need to do is add a vertex to our mesh. Once we have our four vertices, the next step is to tell our GPU the order we want these vertices to be combined into triangles with. We can specify this order with a data structure called an index buffer. An index buffers is an array of integers that define the order of a mesh's vertices. We can create an index buffer for our ofMesh with the addIndices() function. You can see what this looks like in Listing 3-1. In the example, we changed our mesh's name to "quad," since it didn't make sense to keep calling it "triangle" now that it has four vertices.

Listing 3-1. Creating a Quad Mesh Using an Index Buffer

```
void ofApp::setup()
{
    quad.addVertex(glm::vec3(-1, -1, 0));
    quad.addVertex(glm::vec3(-1, 1, 0));
    quad.addVertex(glm::vec3(1, 1, 0));
    quad.addVertex(glm::vec3(1, -1, 0));

    quad.addColor(ofDefaultColorType(1, 0, 0, 1)); //red
    quad.addColor(ofDefaultColorType(0, 1, 0, 1)); //green
    quad.addColor(ofDefaultColorType(0, 0, 1, 1)); //blue
    quad.addColor(ofDefaultColorType(1, 1, 1, 1)); //white

    ofIndexType indices[6] = { 0,1,2,2,3,0 };
    quad.addIndices(indices, 6);
}
```

The addIndices() function takes an array of integers and assigns them to the ofMesh as its index buffer. You can see in Listing 3-1 that we're specifying two of our vertices twice. This is because our mesh's second triangular face will reuse those vertices as part of its mesh face, in addition to using the one new vertex that we've added. To help you get a feel for what the numbers in the index buffer refer to, Figure 3-3 has our quad mesh with the index of each vertex labelled according to how our example code is setting things up.

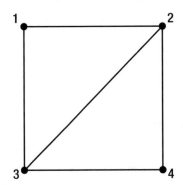

Figure 3-3. *Our quad mesh with each vertex's index labelled*

Even though the openFrameworks API separates colors and vertex positions from one another, when our index buffer references a vertex, it refers to all the vertex attributes for that mesh. In our case, this means that the first element of our index buffer is referring to our first vertex's position and color attributes. If we wanted a vertex at position (0, 0, 0) but with a different color, we'd still need to create a new vertex.

If you run Listing 3-1 with our shader from the last chapter, you should see your entire window filled with the same gradient of colors we saw on our triangle mesh. After doing so much work in a single triangle, it looks rather nice to see a pattern filling our window uniformly. However, we're not here to paint vertex colors, so let's add some UV coordinates to our mesh next.

Introducing UV Coordinates

As I mentioned very briefly in the introduction to this chapter: texture coordinates, or UV coordinates, are the positions used by fragment shaders to look up colors in a texture. Don't be fooled by the weird naming convention; UV coordinates are simply 2D coordinates. The only reason we don't call them "XY" coordinates is because we already use that terminology for position data and it would be even more confusing to also use that terminology for texture coordinates. Instead, convention is to call the X axis of texture coordinates the U axis, and the Y axis of texture coordinates the V axis. You can see our parrot texture overlaid with its UV coordinates in Figure 3-4.

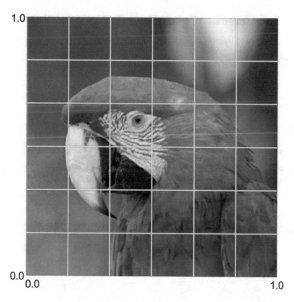

Figure 3-4. *Our parrot texture overlaid with UV coordinates*

UV coordinates start at the bottom left of an image and increase as you approach the top right. If we wanted a fragment to use a color from the parrot's feathers, we might give it a UV coordinate of (0.8, 0.3), which would grab a color from the bottom right section of the texture. For our first shader of this chapter, what we're going to do is give every fragment in our quad the UV coordinate that it needs to properly fill our window with the parrot texture, and then we'll output those coordinates as colors. This means the top left corner of our screen will be green, since its UV coordinates are (0.0, 1.0), and we'll output the color (0.0, 1.0, 0.0, 1.0). The bottom right corner of our window will similarly end up being red, since it will have the UV coordinate (1.0, 0.0).

Adding UV coordinates to our mesh is very similar to adding colors. The only difference is that we use the addTexCoord() function instead of addColor(). Remember that the V axis of our texture coordinates increases as you get to the top of the window, so we need to assign our texture coordinates in the order shown in Listing 3-2.

Listing 3-2. Adding UV Coordinates to the Quad Mesh

```
quad.addTexCoord(glm::vec2(0, 0));
quad.addTexCoord(glm::vec2(0, 1));
quad.addTexCoord(glm::vec2(1, 1));
quad.addTexCoord(glm::vec2(1, 0));
```

Now that we've added the texture coordinates, we can start writing our UV color shader. To start, make a new vertex and fragment shader in your project. I named mine "uv_passthrough.vert" and "uv_vis.frag" because our vertex shader will simply pass the UV coordinates to the fragment shader, and the fragment shader will output them for us to see.

Our vertex shader is going to be very similar to the one we wrote to pass vertex colors through to our fragment shader, except this time we're passing UV coordinates, which are stored in a vec2, instead of the vec4 we used for color data. You can see this in Listing 3-3.

Listing 3-3. passthrough.vert: A Shader That Sends UVs to the Fragment Shader

```
#version 410

layout (location = 0) in vec3 pos;
layout (location = 3) in vec2 uv;

out vec2 fragUV;

void main()
{
    gl_Position = vec4(pos, 1.0);
    fragUV = uv;
}
```

This is the second time that we've come across the layout specifier and used it to plug in locations for vertex attributes, so let's take a quick detour and look at how openFrameworks lays out vertex data. That way you can understand how I'm choosing the values for each vertex attribute's location. By default, openFrameworks assigns vertex attributes to the following locations:

1. Position

2. Color

3. Normal

4. UV Coordinates

If we wanted to change the order of these attributes, or supply vertex information that didn't fall into one of these four categories, we could manually set our vertex layout, but the code in Listing 3-3 is going to cover all the bases that we need for now, so we're just going to work with how openFrameworks sets everything up. Every engine sets up its vertex data layout a little bit differently, and there isn't any one right way to do it. Provided you end up with the right image on your screen, life is good.

Other than the attribute locations, not much else is different about this vertex shader than our previous ones. This will be a common theme for the rest of the book—vertex shaders are usually about getting data in the right form to have the pipeline interpolate the data for our fragment shaders later.

Speaking of our fragment shader, it's not going to be terribly complicated either. All we need to do is output the UV coordinates as the red and green channels of our fragment's color. It's very common to use a shader like this to help debug any problems with texturing objects in game. If all goes well, we should see a corner of our screen set to red, one set to green, one set to yellow (for the corner that is both 100% red and 100% green), and a corner that's black. In between our corners these colors should blend together, exactly like they did for our vertex color shader. You can see this in Listing 3-4.

Listing 3-4. uv_vis.frag: A Fragment Shader That Outputs UVs as Color Data

```
#version 410

in vec2 fragUV;
out vec4 outCol;

void main()
{
    outCol = vec4(fragUV, 0.0f, 1.0f);
}
```

This is almost identical to our vertex color fragment shader, and with good reason. Whether it's color data or texture coordinates, both are represented as vectors (which are just collections of floats), so there's no need to treat them differently. Running this shader gets us exactly the colors that we predicted earlier and should look like Figure 3-5.

Figure 3-5. *Visualizing UV coordinates on a full screen quad*

If your window looks like Figure 3-5, you've just successfully added UV coordinates to a mesh! As you may imagine, this process is quite a bit trickier when dealing with meshes that aren't flat squares. Most of the time, the process of assigning texture coordinates is handled by artists who have powerful tools to help them handle this process, rather than by code. As such, we don't really need to worry about handling anything more complex than a quad or triangle mesh in C++ for any of the examples in this book. If you're following along at home but haven't quite ended up with something like Figure 3-5, the code for this example is available in the Chapter 3 example code, in the "UV Quad" project.

Using Textures in Shaders

Now that our mesh has proper UV coordinates, we can use them to put our parrot texture on screen. The hardest part of working with textures in shaders is getting the texture data from our C++ code to the GPU, so let's start with that first. openFrameworks makes the first step in this process (loading our image from a file) very simple. The first step is declaring an ofImage object in our ofApp.h file. This is shown in Listing 3-5. We'll use this ofImage object to help us create an ofTexture object in a moment.

Listing 3-5. The Variables That We Need to Add to ofApp.h for This Example

```
class ofApp : public ofBaseApp{
    public:
            //functions omitted for brevity
            ofMesh quad;
            ofShader shader;
            ofImage img;
};
```

With that declared, we can add a line to load our image from disk using the ofImage class' load() function. We're also going to add a line of code that disables some extra openFrameworks functionality that we don't want to worry about in our shaders. For legacy reasons, openFrameworks enables support for a type of textures that use pixel coordinates rather than UV coordinates by default. We want to use the more standard type of texture, so we need to disable this bit of legacy functionality. The lines to both disable this functionality and load an image into our ofImage object are shown in Listing 3-6.

Listing 3-6. Loading an Image in openFrameworks

```
void ofApp::setup()
{
    //code omitted for brevity
    ofDisableArbTex();
    img.load("parrot.png");
}
```

Just like with ofShader objects, the file path that ofImage's load() function expects are relative to the application's bin/data folder. To make your life easier, put your image file in that folder so you can just load it by filename.

Once we have our image loaded, we still need to tell our shader about it. The coordinates we use to look up colors in our texture vary on a per-fragment basis but the texture will stay the same, so we're going to store it in a uniform variable. We can use the setUniformTexture() function to load our ofImage object into one of our shader's uniform variables. This call needs to be put in the draw() function after we've called shader.begin(). The version of setUniformTexture() that we're going to use right now will automatically convert our ofImage object into an ofTexture object, so we don't need to worry about doing that manually right now. You can see how to call this function in Listing 3-7.

Listing 3-7. Setting a Uniform Texture in openFrameworks. In Our Shader, the Texture Uniform Variable Is Going to be Named "parrotTex."

```
void ofApp::draw()
{
     shader.begin();
     shader.setUniformTexture("parrotTex", img, 0);
     quad.draw();
     shader.end();
}
```

The setUniformTexture() function takes three arguments. The first argument is the name of the uniform that we want our texture to use. The second argument is the ofImage that we're going to use as our texture, and the third argument is the "texture location." The texture location is important if your shader uses multiple textures. If we were setting multiple texture uniforms for our shader, we'd have to make sure that each texture was getting assigned a different texture location. This isn't a concern for us yet, since we're only using a single texture.

Now that we have all the C++ stuff out of the way, let's jump back to our shaders and put this all together. We don't need to modify our vertex shader, because we still want the same texture coordinates as we had before, but we need to make a new fragment shader to draw the colors of our texture. I called this new shader "texture.frag" in the example code, and Listing 3-8 shows what it should look like. Remember that you'll also have to update the setup() function to load this new shader on the quad mesh.

Listing 3-8. A Fragment Shader to Output Texture Data

```
#version 410

uniform sampler2D parrotTex;  ❶

in vec2 fragUV;
out vec4 outCol;

void main()
{
      outCol = texture(parrotTex, fragUV);  ❷
}
```

As you can see at ❶, the data type used for texture uniforms is "sampler2D." GLSL defines different sampler types for handling all kinds of textures, but the most common texture type by far is a 2D image, which makes the sampler2D the most common type of sampler that you'll use when writing shaders.

Getting a color value out of a sampler requires the use of the texture() function (❷). This is a built-in GLSL function that takes a sampler and a set of UV coordinates and returns the color at the point specified by those UVs. We want our fragments to be filled with the texture colors that match up to the fragment's position in our quad, so we can just output the return value of our texture() call.

With all that set up, running the program should give you a window filled with our friendly parrot. Unfortunately, our feathered friend is upside down! If we look at the output from earlier when we output UV coordinates as colors, we can see that everything is oriented correctly with our mesh, so what's going on? In this case, it's the result of a quirky bit of OpenGL. OpenGL expects that image data is stored starting from the bottom row of pixels, but almost every 2D image format stores things with the top row first. Having textures flipped upside down is a common problem you'll run into when writing graphics code. Luckily, flipping a texture vertically is as easy as adding a single subtract instruction in our vertex shader. You can see this in Listing 3-9.

Listing 3-9. Flipping a Texture Vertically in a Vertex Shader

```
void main()
{
      gl_Position = vec4(pos, 1.0);
      fragUV = vec2(uv.x, 1.0 - uv.y);  ❶
}
```

47

Since UV coordinates go from 0 to 1, all that's required to flip our image's UV coordinates is to subtract the Y component from 1.0. That means that the bottom of our image, which used to be Y coordinate 0, will now end up as Y coordinate 1, and vice versa. With that minor change, you should be finally looking at our handsome friend right side up:

Figure 3-6. *Our parrot texture displayed on a full screen quad*

If you're seeing something different (usually in computer graphics, "something different" means a blank screen), all the example code is located online in the "Fullscreen Texture" folder of Chapter 3. It's important to note that depending on the graphics API your program uses, you may not have to flip your textures like this. However, it's necessary for the examples in this book because we're always going to be using OpenGL. If you're with me so far, let's explore some simple ways we can modify our shader to make it a bit more interesting.

Scrolling UV Coordinates

One of the simplest ways we can make our shader more dynamic is to make something move, so let's make one that scrolls our parrot texture across the screen like a marquee. We can do this by manipulating the UV coordinates that our vertex shader passes to our fragment shader.

Our quad is using UV coordinates that exactly match up to the UV coordinates of our texture, but just because a texture's UV coordinates always have the range of 0-1 doesn't mean those are the only UV coordinates our shader can use. It's perfectly valid to sample a texture using coordinates that are outside of the 0-1 range, but what it looks like on the screen depends on how you've set up your texture. To see what our texture will look like with different UVs, we can start by creating a new vertex shader called "scrolling_uv.vert", copying in our "basic.vert" shader, and making a simple modification to the shader, as shown in Listing 3-10.

Listing 3-10. scrolling_uv.vert

```
void main()
{
     gl_Position = vec4(pos, 1.0);
     fragUV = vec2(uv.x, 1.0 - uv.y) + vec2(0.25, 0.0);   ❶
}
```

With the added vector addition at ❶, the UV coordinates that our quad's vertices use have been pushed beyond the 0-1 range of our texture. The vertices on the left side of the screen will use UV coordinates that start with an X component of 0.25, and the X component of our texture coordinates will hit 1.25 on the right side of the screen. This is going to make our window look like Figure 3-7.

Figure 3-7. *Our parrot texture displaying with offset UV coordinates*

The colors of the rightmost edge of our texture appear to be duplicated for fragments that are using horizontal UV coordinates greater than 1. Under the hood, what's happening is that the GPU is clamping our vertex coordinates to keep them in the proper range. This means that any fragment that was attempting to sample a texture coordinate with an X value greater than 1.0 was getting that value clamped to the maximum valid texture coordinate (1.0). In graphics terminology, how a texture responds to being sampled with non 0-1 coordinates is called a *wrap mode*, and we would say that our parrot texture's wrap mode is set to "clamp" in Figure 3-7.

Our stated goal for this shader was to have our parrot texture scroll as though it was on a marquee, which means that the clamp wrap mode isn't what we're after. What we want is for our texture to simply start over again when we start sampling outside of the texture. This requires that a UV coordinate of (1.25, 0.0) be translated to (0.25, 0.0). To do this, we need to change our texture's wrap mode to the "wrap" mode, which is a bit awkward to say but is easy to set in code. You can see how to do this in Listing 3-11.

Listing 3-11. Setting the Wrap Mode of Our Texture

```
void ofApp::setup()
{
    //rest of function omitted for brevity
    img.load("parrot.png");
    img.getTexture().setTextureWrap(GL_REPEAT, GL_REPEAT); ❶
}
```

The setTextureWrap() function takes two arguments so that we can set our vertical and horizontal wrapping mode separately. This time though, we're setting them to the same value (❶). If you wanted to set a texture to the clamp wrap mode instead, you'd pass in the value GL_CLAMP. One important thing to notice is that this is the first time we've needed to manually call getTexture() on our ofImage object. Earlier, we just passed the ofImage directly to setUniformTexture() and let that function handle calling this for us. Now that we want to modify the ofTexture that corresponds to our image, we need to call this function ourselves. With that change, rerunning our app will give us the repeating parrot shown in Figure 3-8.

Figure 3-8. *The parrot texture on a full screen quad, using the "wrap" wrap mode*

This is much closer to our target; however, we also said we wanted our parrot to scroll over time. This means we need to add support for a time-based animation to our vertex shader. You can see how this looks in Listing 3-12.

Listing 3-12. Changing Our Vertex Shader to Scroll Our UVs Over Time

```
#version 410

layout (location = 0) in vec3 pos;
layout (location = 3) in vec2 uv;
uniform float time;  ❶
out vec2 fragUV;

void main()
{
    gl_Position = vec4(pos, 1.0);
    fragUV = vec2(uv.x, 1.0-uv.y) + vec2(1.0, 0.0) * time;  ❷
}
```

Shaders have no concept of time, so we'll need to pass a time value into our shaders from our C++ code. What time it is will be the same no matter where in the pipeline we access it, which means we can store it in a uniform, which I'm calling "time" (❶). This value is going to be set to the number of seconds that have elapsed since our program started to run. We'll see how to set this value from our C++ code in a moment. Once we have that value, we're going to use it to scale the offset vector that we add to our UV coordinates (❷). To do this, we changed our offset vector from (0.25, 0) to (1.0, 0), which is a normalized vector. Since it's normalized, we can multiply that by any value—let's call that value N—to produce vector (N, 0). This means that when our application has been running for 2 seconds, we're going to add a vector of (2.0, 0) to our UV coordinates, and so on for every other time value.

With that change, all that's left is to add a line in our C++ draw function to pass time in to our shader, shown in Listing 3-13.

Listing 3-13. Using Time as a Uniform Value

```
void ofApp::draw()
{
        shader.begin();
        shader.setUniformTexture("parrot", img, 0);
        shader.setUniform1f("time", ofGetElapsedTimef());
        quad.draw();
        shader.end();
}
```

Running the application now should scroll the parrot image to the left, over time. Unfortunately, it's hard to provide an image in a book of a moving object, so you'll have to do the legwork yourself if you want to see what this looks like. The code for this example is provided online in Chapter 3's "Scrolling UVs" example project, so consult there if you get stuck along the way.

Manipulating UV coordinates over time is the basis for countless special FX shaders, and it's only the beginning of the tools we have at our disposal for manipulating texture information. We can do a lot with just some simple math.

Adjusting Brightness with a Uniform

Speaking of simple math, we can adjust the brightness of a texture using only multiplication. This is a technique that's used all over modern video games. Buttons might darken when they've been pressed down (or disabled), things in a game world might blink to indicate that the player should interact with them, or you might just want to make an image brighter. Whatever your use case, brightening or darkening a color value is very simple and we're going to see how to do it to our parrot texture.

In shader code, brightening or darkening a color means that we're going to increase or decrease that color's red, green, and blue (RGB) channels uniformly. This means that we need to multiply each of those channels by the same value. If we wanted to double the brightness of our parrot texture, for example, we could modify our shader to multiply everything by 2. In the example code, I created a new shader (called "brightness.frag") to show this off. The code for this new shader is shown in Listing 3-14.

Listing 3-14. brightness.frag: A Brightness-Modifying Fragment Shader

```
#version 410

uniform sampler2D parrotTex;

in vec2 fragUV;
out vec4 outCol;

void main()
{
    vec4 tex = texture(parrotTex, fragUV);
    tex.r *= 2.0f;  ❶
    tex.g *= 2.0f;
    tex.b *= 2.0f;
    tex.a *= 2.0f;
    outCol = tex;
}
```

This is the first time we've seen shader code access components of a vector using properties named "r,g,b,a" instead of "x,y,z,w." This is a bit of syntactical sugar that GLSL provides, since it's so common to use vectors to store color data in shaders. Both sets of accessors are the exact same. For example, we would get the exact same results at ❶ if instead of using ".r" we used ".x," since in either case we want the first float that's stored in our vec4.

Our shader works now, but it's an awful lot of code just to brighten a single color. The texture() call returns a vector, and we know that multiplying a vector by a scalar value is simply the act of multiplying each component of that vector by the scalar individually, so we can rewrite Listing 3-14 to do the multiplications in a single line. Listing 3-15 shows what this looks like, and is functionally identical to the code in Listing 3-14.

Listing 3-15. A Simpler Way to Multiply Every Component of a Vector by a Scalar

```
void main()
{
    outCol = texture(parrotTex, fragUV) * 2.0f;
}
```

Let's modify our shader so we can set the brightness multiplier from C++ code. Just like our texture, the brightness multiplier is going to be the same no matter what fragment is being processed, so we can pass it to our shader as a uniform variable. Listing 3-16 shows what this will look like in shader code.

Listing 3-16. Using a Uniform Variable to Control Brightness

```
uniform float brightness;
void main()
{
    outCol = texture(parrotTex, fragUV) * brightness;
}
```

In C++ we can set this just like how we've set any other uniform variable. First, declare a float variable called "brightness" in ofApp.h. The draw() function can then be modified to set the value of our brightness uniform using the same setUniform1f() call that we're using to tell our shader what time it is. You can see the full draw() function for our example project in Listing 3-17.

Listing 3-17. Setting Brightness as a Uniform Variable

```
void ofApp::draw()
{
    shader.begin();
    shader.setUniformTexture("parrot", img, 0);
    shader.setUniform1f("time", ofGetElapsedTimef());

    //declare brightness as a float in ofApp.h
    shader.setUniform1f("brightness", brightness);

    quad.draw();
    shader.end();
}
```

This is probably a good time to talk about what will happen if we forget to give a shader uniform a value. By default, all uniform values are initialized to a zero value when our shader is created. If you forget to supply a value to the brightness uniform in our example project, for example, you will end up with a black screen. This is because the brightness uniform will be set to 0 by default, and multiplying any color by 0 produces the color black.

Provided you don't forget to supply a value to the brightness variable, your code should now be able to use that variable to control the brightness of the parrot texture. However, if you set this brightness variable to lower than 1.0 (which should darken the image), you're going to see results you don't expect. This is because openFrameworks enables "alpha blending" by default. This means that as the alpha value of a fragment decreases, it gets more translucent. As our texture gets more translucent it will allow more of the background color of our window to be visible. Since our window's background is a bright gray, this will likely be very confusing, because it will look like the image is getting brighter rather than getting darker. You can see an example of this in Figure 3-9. We're going to talk a lot about alpha blending in a later chapter, but for now you can disable this by adding a call to ofDisableAlphaBlending() in your setup() function.

Figure 3-9. *The left image is what our image looks like if we multiply our texture color by 0.5 with alpha blending on. The right has alpha blending disabled.*

The code for this example is located in the "Brightness" example project in this chapter's example code. If you've hit any snags (and aren't seeing a dimly lit parrot), head there to see where your code differs from mine.

It's a short jump from adjusting brightness to being able to perform several different color-based modifications in our shader. So, let's talk about those before moving on.

Basic Color Math

In Chapter 1, we talked about how to add, subtract, multiply and divide vectors. We also looked at a few examples of what some of those operations would look like if our vectors were representing positions. Now that we're working with color information, it's also useful to see what those operations look like when our vectors are storing color data. Since the closer any one of our color channels gets to 1.0, the brighter it will be, any operation that increases the value of a component of a color value will make the color brighter, and vice versa. Figure 3-10 shows a few examples of what this looks like in practice, for addition and subtraction.

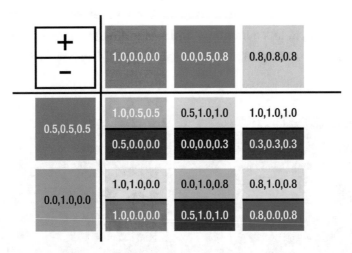

Figure 3-10. *Table of color addition/subtraction*

Modifying a color's components uniformly results in that color becoming brighter or darker uniformly. Modifying some color channels instead of others produces entirely new colors. One important thing to note about the preceding examples is that we can never increase a color's value past 1.0, so adding pure red (1.0,0.0,0.0) to itself would produce the same color as we had before. Color subtraction works in a very similar way: we can never reduce a color channel's value to less than 0.0.

If we were to apply some of these operations to our parrot texture, the results would look like Figure 3-11. Starting at the top left and going clockwise, this figure shows off the results of subtracting a flat gray (0.5,0.5,0.5,1.0), adding a blue (0.25,0.25,1.0,1.0), adding a solid red (1.0,0.0,0.0,1.0), and adding a flat gray (0.5,0.5,0.5,1.0) to all the fragments in our parrot texture uniformly.

Figure 3-11.   *Examples of adding and subtracting a color uniformly from our parrot texture*

It's important to note that while the examples on the left side of the figure might initially look like they're doing the same thing as our brightness multiplier did, there are some subtle differences in how the two approaches handle the dark areas of an image. When we multiplied our image, pixels that had darker colors were less affected by the multiplication than brighter pixels. When we're just performing an addition or subtraction, all pixel values are uniformly adjusted. There are times when you may get better results with one approach to modifying brightness than the other, so it's important to know the difference.

The previous section of this chapter showed us that multiplying each component of a color value by the same scalar value can be used to adjust that color's brightness. Multiplying a color by another color can also be used to tint or shade one color by another color. Figure 3-12 shows what our parrot would look like if instead of adding and subtracting colors like we saw in Figure 3-10, we multiplied by them instead. You'll see that the top left example in Figure 3-12 is a solid black square. This is because we were adding (-0.5,-0.5,-0.5,-1.0) to the example in Figure 3-11, and multiplying by the same value produces negative values in our fragments' color channels. As we saw in Figure 3-10, color channels that would have negative values are always simply clamped to 0.0, giving us a solid black square in Figure 3-12.

Figure 3-12. *Examples of multiplying our parrot texture by the same colors we used in Figure 3-11*

Figure 3-12 leaves out color division because it's not very common to see division being used to modify colors. This is partly because division is slightly slower than multiplication on some GPUs, and partly because most people can visualize what a color multiply will do much easier than they can with division. In either case, if you have a strong preference for division over multiplication, you are certainly free to take that approach.

Now that we know what adding, subtracting, and multiplying a color can do, let's modify our shader to use any combination of these basic operations at once. Listing 3-18 shows how to do this in a shader. You can see an example of how to use this shader in the "ColorMath" example project included in the Chapter 3 source code.

Listing 3-18. A Color Math Shader

```
#version 410

uniform sampler2D parrotTex;
uniform vec4 multiply;
uniform vec4 add;

in vec2 fragUV;
out vec4 outCol;

void main()
{
      outCol =  texture(parrotTex, fragUV) * multiply + add; ❶
}
```

The order of operations at ❶ is important. The multiplication is performed first, then the addition. This is a common optimization seen in shader code. GPUs can perform what's called "MAD" operations, which stands for "multiply, then add." MAD instructions allow us to perform these two operations in a single GPU instruction. When possible, it's good practice to keep math operations in this order. We'll return to this much later in the book when we look at optimization techniques, but it's a good thing to keep in mind as you start building your own shaders.

In addition to tinting or otherwise manipulating the color of a texture, it's also very common for shaders to combine two or more textures together to create visual effects. The last two shaders that we're going to cover in this chapter are going to show off how to do that.

Mixing Textures with the "Mix" Instruction

Mixing textures together is one of the most useful things that shaders can do, and the easiest way to accomplish it is with GLSL's "mix" instruction. The mix() function takes three arguments. The first two of these arguments are the values we want to mix together; when mixing textures, these values will be the colors retrieved from each of the texture's samplers. The last argument controls how much of each input value to use when mixing. If the third argument is 0, then the result of the mix will be 100% of the first argument, and 0% of the last. Similarly, a value of 1 will use 100% of the second argument, and none of the first.

This type of mixing is called a *linear interpolation*, and in some shader languages the mix function is called "lerp" instead of "mix."

We don't need to worry about what a linear interpolation is from a math point of view for this book, but there are a few things to note about using them. Probably the most important thing to be aware of is that a linear interpolation does not preserve vector normalization. If you're using the mix() function to blend between two normalized vectors, there is no guarantee that the resulting vector will also be normalized. It also might be worth noting that just because a linear interpolation smoothly blends between values does not mean that this blend always looks good, especially for colors. If the colors you're blending are very different (like red and cyan), the in-between colors may not be what you expect. Just like everything else in graphics code, it's always good to test things out on your specific assets to make sure things look how you expect.

With all those caveats out of the way, it's time for us to see the mix() function in action and build a shader that mixes textures together. This means we're going to need a second texture. The example code uses a simple black and white checkerboard texture, like the one you see in Figure 3-13. This texture is also included in the Assets directory for the Chapter 3 example code.

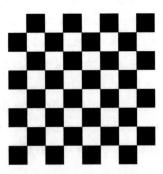

Figure 3-13. *The checkerboard texture that we'll use in the following examples*

Let's start by writing a shader that displays a 50/50 mix of both of our input textures. You can see an example of this in Listing 3-19.

Listing 3-19. A Fragment Shader That Blends Two Textures Together

```
#version 410

uniform sampler2D parrotTex;
uniform sampler2D checkerboardTex;

in vec2 fragUV;
out vec4 outCol;

void main()
{
    vec4 parrot = texture(parrotTex, fragUV);
    vec4 checker = texture(checkerboardTex, fragUV);

    outCol = mix(parrot, checker, 0.5);
}
```

I'm going to start skipping over the C++ code required to set up new textures and uniforms, since we've already looked at several examples of that. When things have been set up correctly, running our program with this shader should look like Figure 3-14.

Figure 3-14. *A 50/50 blend of a checkerboard texture and our parrot*

Each fragment in our window is being set to a value exactly halfway between the color of that point in the parrot texture and that point in our checkboard texture. While blending every fragment to be a 50/50 mix of two textures isn't very useful, having different fragments use different amounts of each texture has a ton of applications in games. For example, you could have a character's facial features be stored in one texture and have the eyes of the character be stored in a second texture, so that users could choose between one of several different eye shapes to customize their character. Then you could use a third texture's color value as the last argument in the mix(), to control which fragments use color data from the facial features texture and which get data from the eye texture.

For our next example, we're going to do just that. We'll use the value in one of our textures as the third argument to our mix() function. The example code uses our checkerboard texture to overlay black squares on our parrot photo but leaves the rest of the parrot texture unchanged (no blending between the parrot texture and the white squares). This is a simple 1-line change to our previous shader. Listing 3-20 shows the code change necessary.

Listing 3-20. The 1-Line Code Change to Our Mix Function

```
//change this
outCol = mix(parrot, checker, 0.5);
//Into this:
outCol = mix(checker, parrot, checker.r);
```

Let's break down what's happening here. We know that the mix function blends between our two inputs based on the third argument that it's given. When our checkerboard texture sample is from a white square, all the components of that color are going to be set to 1 (remember that the color white is (1.0f, 1.0f, 1.0f, 1.0f)). This means that when our checkerboard sample is white, the "r" component of its color vector will also be 1.0. Passing 1.0 as the third argument to mix() means that it will return 100% of the second input, which happens to be our parrot texture. You can see the results in Figure 3-15. The "Mixing Textures" example project shows how to set it up in code, in case you get stuck setting it up yourself.

Figure 3-15. *Blending between textures based on the red channel of the checkerboard texture*

The techniques we looked at in this chapter are some of the fundamental building blocks that are used to create the stunning visual effects seen in modern video games. We've only scratched the surface of all the different ways that a shader can manipulate texture data, but the foundations covered in this chapter should provide you a solid foundation to use when exploring tutorials and articles online.

Summary

Here's what we covered in this chapter:

- We can use index buffers to combine the vertex data for a mesh into mesh faces.

- Images rendered on meshes are referred to as "Textures."

- Retrieving the color value at a specific point in a texture is referred to as "sampling."

- Meshes use UV coordinates to allow fragments to sample colors from different parts of a texture. Textures are always set up to allow UV coordinates with the range 0–1, to be able to sample every point in the texture.

- The type of variable used to store a texture in GLSL is called a "sampler." For 2D textures, we use "sampler2D."

- A texture's wrap mode determines how it looks when we try to sample a point in the texture outside of this 0-1 range.

- Using only addition, subtraction, and multiplication, you can modify colors in a variety of ways. If you apply these operations to every pixel in a texture, they can be used to brighten, darken, tint, and shade the texture.

- Color values can be mixed together using GLSL's mix() function. Applying this to every fragment of a mesh lets you create effects that blend between the textures applied to that mesh.

CHAPTER 4

Translucency and Depth

We know from Chapter 1 that colors in computer graphics commonly are made up of red, green, blue, and alpha channels. We've mostly focused on ways that we can work with the red, green and blue channels, and we've mostly ignored the alpha channel. This chapter is going to remedy that. We're going to use the alpha channel to draw an entire scene's worth of differently shaped objects, render everything from aliens to sun beams, and wrap up by animating a character. How exciting!

We're going to start off by using the alpha channel of a texture to render something that isn't rectangular on a quad mesh. While 3D games commonly use complex meshes to render different shapes, many 2D games render everything in-game on quads. If you've played any of them however, you know that most 2D games don't look like a bunch of rectangles moving around the screen. To render shapes that aren't rectangles, 2D games use shaders that can make unused fragments on a quad invisible. You can see an example of this in Figure 4-1.

Figure 4-1. *A 2D Character rendered on a quad. The original texture is shown on the left. The black areas are pixels with an alpha of 0.*

K. Halladay, *Practical Shader Development*, https://doi.org/10.1007/978-1-4842-4457-9_4

Our little green friend in Figure 4-1 is a rectangular texture being rendered on a quad, just like our parrot texture was before. The difference this time is that some fragments of our quad have been made transparent, making it appear as though we aren't drawing a rectangle at all. This is all made possible by a process called *alpha testing* and is the first example that we're going to work through in this chapter. Before we get started though, we have a little bit of housekeeping to take care of.

Example Project Setup

I recommend creating a new openFrameworks project to start off this chapter. Remember to modify the main.cpp file in this new project just like we did in our previous examples, so that this new project is still using the correct version of OpenGL. Also remember to add the ofDisableArbTex() function call in the new ofApp's setup() function. Finally, our first example is going to require an ofMesh, ofShader, and ofImage object for our alien character. Listing 4-1 shows the declaration of these variables with the names used in the example code for this chapter.

Listing 4-1. Our New Project's ofApp's Member Variables

```
ofMesh charMesh;
ofShader charShader;
ofImage alienImg;
```

If you're following along in your own code, you'll want to head online to the book's website and grab the texture assets used in this chapter's examples and put them in your project's bin/data folder. With all that done, you should be all set!

Drawing Our Little Green Man

The first thing that we need to do to draw our alien is to adjust our quad mesh. Until now, we've been working with a full screen quad, but it would look very weird to see our character texture stretched across our whole window. To recreate Figure 4-1, we need to make our quad mesh much smaller and adjust its dimensions so that it's taller than it is wide. We'll also want to be able to position our mesh somewhere on screen that isn't perfectly centered. Since we haven't covered how to move meshes around yet, this means creating vertices that are already in the exact position we want them to be.

We're going to be creating a lot of different quads in this chapter, so the example code is going to move the logic for creating these quads into a buildMesh() function that you can see in Listing 4-2.

Listing 4-2. A Function for Creating Different Quads

```
void buildMesh(ofMesh& mesh, float w, float h, glm::vec3 pos)
{
    float verts[] = { -w + pos.x, -h + pos.y,  pos.z,
            -w + pos.x,  h + pos.y,  pos.z,
             w + pos.x,  h + pos.y,  pos.z,
             w + pos.x, -h + pos.y,  pos.z };

    float uvs[] = { 0,0, 0,1, 1,1, 1,0 };

    for (int i = 0; i < 4; ++i){
        int idx = i * 3;
        int uvIdx = i * 2;

        mesh.addVertex(glm::vec3(verts[idx], verts[idx + 1], verts[idx + 2]));
        mesh.addTexCoord(glm::vec2(uvs[uvIdx], uvs[uvIdx + 1]));
    }

    ofIndexType indices[6] = { 0,1,2,2,3,0 };
    mesh.addIndices(indices, 6);
}
```

With this function added to the project, the code for creating our alien character is very simple. Listing 4-3 shows the one-liner we can use to adjust our character mesh so that it will cover one quarter of the screen horizontally, and half the screen vertically. This will look much nicer than the full screen quad we had before.

Listing 4-3. Creating a Quad of Configurable Size and Screen Position

```
buildMesh(charMesh, 0.25, 0.5, vec3(0.0, 0.15, 0.0));
```

We're going to create two new shader files that we can use to render our alien with. The vertex shader that we'll start with will look identical to the "passthrough.vert" shader from the last chapter. Listing 4-4 shows the code for that again.

Listing 4-4. passthrough.vert, the Vertex Shader We'll Render the Alien With

```
#version 410

layout (location = 0) in vec3 pos;
layout (location = 3) in vec2 uv;

out vec2 fragUV;

void main()
{
    gl_Position = vec4(pos, 1.0);
    fragUV = vec2(uv.x, 1.0-uv.y);
}
```

The fragment shader that we're going to start with is the first bit of new shader code that we'll write in this chapter. It will hide the fragments of our alien quad that correspond to areas of the alien texture with an alpha value less than 1.0. The example code calls this file "alphaTest.frag," and Listing 4-5 shows what this looks like.

Listing 4-5. alphaTest.frag

```
#version 410
uniform sampler2D greenMan;
in vec2 fragUV;

out vec4 outCol;

void main()
{
    outCol = texture(greenMan, fragUV);
    if (outCol.a < 1.0) discard;  ❶
}
```

The shader in Listing 4-5 features the "discard" statement (❶), which we haven't seen before. This statement is essential for rendering our alien correctly, and it's the first way we're going to use our alpha channel. We've already seen lots of code for drawing meshes in the previous chapters, so I'm going to omit providing the setup() or draw() function here and dive directly into explaining how Listing 4-5 works. If you want to look at the full source code for what we've talked about so far, check out the "DrawCharacter" project in the Chapter 4 example code.

Alpha Testing with Discard

The first way we're going to use our texture's alpha channel is by doing what's called an *alpha test*. To do this, we'll define a cut-off threshold value for our alpha channel and then check the alpha value for each fragment against it. Fragments with an alpha value greater than our threshold will be rendered normally, while any fragments with an alpha below this value will be discarded. You can see this in Listing 4-5, at ❶. Our example's cut-off threshold is 1.0, so any fragments that aren't 100% opaque will be thrown away. The actual throwing away of the fragment is done with the discard keyword.

The discard keyword is unique among GLSL syntax in that it allows you to remove a fragment from the graphics pipeline. To understand this, it may be helpful to take another look at the diagram of the pipeline from Chapter 1 (included here as Figure 4-2 for convenience). After the fragment shader step is completed, the data for that fragment is usually passed to the fragment processing step of the pipeline. The discard keyword stops this flow and the fragment never advances to the next step.

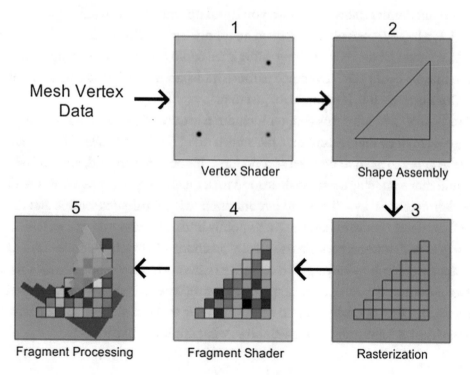

Figure 4-2. Our simplified view of the graphics pipeline

This chapter is going to be all about the "fragment processing" stage of our pipeline, since that's where a lot of alpha and depth calculations live. This first example showed us what happens if a fragment never reaches that stage, but the next example is going to start talking about what happens to the ones that do.

When setting up the new project for this chapter, you may have brought the line we added to disable alpha blending over from our previous examples (ofDisableAlphaBlending()). It might be surprising to learn our new shader still works how we would expect even if this statement is present. This is because discarding fragments doesn't require the GPU to do any actual alpha blending. Rather, it tells the GPU to simple stop processing some fragments. Most of our examples in this chapter won't work correctly if this function is called, but it's important to note that alpha testing is different from alpha blending from the point of view of the graphics pipeline.

Building a Scene with Depth Testing

If you run our demo project right now, you'll end up with exactly what we saw in Figure 4-1, a happy green alien drawn on an otherwise invisible quad. While this is nifty by itself, it would be much more interesting if we could position something behind our alien so that we could take advantage of those transparent fragments and see behind our quad. Our next example is going to do just that.

The "Assets" folder for this chapter includes a texture of a forest environment. We're going to draw that texture on a full screen quad behind our alien. This means that we're going to need to create a second mesh for our background, and probably resize and move our character mesh around to fit nicely in that scene. While creating our background mesh, we'll need to pay attention to Z coordinates for this first time. In normalized device coordinates, the Z axis points into our computer screen, which means that vertices with lower Z coordinates will be positioned in front of vertices with higher ones. Since we're still specifying all our vertices with normalized coordinates, this means that the background mesh we make must have vertices with Z values greater than 0. Otherwise, our program will have no way of knowing that our alien should be rendered in front of the background. Listing 4-6 shows what this looks like in code.

Listing 4-6. Creating a Background Mesh Behind Our Character

```
buildMesh(backgroundMesh, 1.0, 1.0, vec3(0.0, 0.0, 0.5));
```

Since we've already spent a lot of time creating quads with openFrameworks, I'm going to omit the rest of the code needed for us to set up this second quad and load its texture, and skip right to our new draw function. You can see this in Listing 4-7.

Listing 4-7. Drawing Our Background Mesh

```
void ofApp::draw()
{
        using namespace glm;
        shader.begin();

        shader.setUniformTexture("tex", img, 0);
        quad.draw();

        shader.setUniformTexture("tex", bgnd, 0);
        background.draw();  ❶

        shader.end();
}
```

This probably looks very unremarkable, but if you run the demo project so far, you'll notice that our character has disappeared! If you experiment a bit, you'll find that reversing the order that you submit the draw calls, so that the background mesh goes first, will make our character visible again. We've set our Z coordinates correctly, so what's going on?

It turns out that looking at the Z value of a vertex or fragment isn't something that happens by default. While a mesh is being processed by the graphics pipeline, the GPU doesn't normally have any information about the other things that have been drawn in the current frame. Without that information, there's no way to know whether any given set of vertices or fragments are located behind something that's already been drawn. To make it possible to position objects behind one another based on position, we need to create a *depth buffer*. This is a special texture, which the GPU can write information to and keep around as it draws all the objects in a frame.

The mechanics of how this depth buffer works aren't important for understanding the examples in this book. What is important to note is that any calculations that use this depth buffer are done in the fragment processing stage of the pipeline. If we discard a fragment before it reaches that stage, that fragment isn't considered in depth calculations either. This is a good thing, because it would be weird if our invisible fragments could occlude objects behind them. It's also important to know that GPUs won't create a depth buffer unless we tell them to. We can do this with a call to ofEnableDepthTest() in our setup function. Running the program with that line added should give you something like Figure 4-3.

Figure 4-3.   *What this chapter's example program looks like so far*

Unless you've adjusted the size and position of your alien quad, it's likely that your example isn't quite as pretty as Figure 4-9 (I'll leave that as an exercise to the reader). Regardless of how big your alien is, however, there are two important things that this example demonstrates. First, our depth buffer must be working correctly, since the alien mesh is being rendered in front of the background. Second, our alpha test shader must be working correctly, since we can see the background through the invisible parts of the alien quad.

Creating Clouds with Alpha Blending

While our scene is already looking great, we can do a lot more with alpha than just use it to discard pixels. You might recall from the book's introduction that we can also use alpha to create objects that are *translucent*. Translucent objects aren't 100% transparent, but we can still see through them. Examples of translucent objects in the real world include stained glass windows or a pair of sunglasses. Drawing translucent objects uses a process known as *alpha blending*, which works a bit differently than the alpha test shader we just wrote. With alpha testing, we have a binary choice: a fragment is visible or invisible. Alpha blending allows us to say things like "this fragment is 80% opaque," and have that draw correctly. Our next example is going to do exactly that and draw a low flying cloud at 80% opacity.

To create our cloud, we're going to need to create yet another quad mesh and put a new texture on it. This time we'll use the "cloud.png" texture from the chapter's Assets folder. This texture already has some alpha information in it, which is being used to define the shape of the cloud. Pixels that are within the cloud's shape have an alpha of 1. This means that we can draw the cloud with our alpha test shader and get most of the way to what we want. However, the cloud itself will be 100% opaque when drawn with the alpha test shader and our cloud is going to be translucent.

Drawing the cloud with our alpha test shader is a great way to let us position our cloud mesh how we want it though, so let's start with that. For the examples, I created a quad that was one quarter of the screen wide, and about 1/6th of the screen tall, and positioned it at (-0.55, 0, 0). If you do the same, and draw the quad using the alpha test shader, you should end up with something like Figure 4-4.

Figure 4-4. An alpha-tested cloud

Now that we know our cloud is being sized and positioned right, it's time to focus on making it more translucent. Create a new fragment shader just for the cloud; the example code calls this file "cloud.frag." We want this shader to be able to preserve the existing alpha of our texture so that we don't lose the shape of the cloud, but allow us to adjust the alpha on the fragments that are otherwise opaque. The simplest way to accomplish this is to use a conditional test just like we did in our alpha test shader. You can see what this looks like in Listing 4-8.

Listing 4-8. Using a Conditional to Test for Alpha

```
//lines above here omitted for brevity
void main()
{
    outCol = texture(tex, fragUV);
    if (outCol.a > 0.8) outCol.a = 0.8;
}
```

Running the example program now should give you something like Figure 4-5. If your cloud mesh is still 100% opaque, it might be that you still have the call to ofDisableAlphaBlending() somewhere in your code.

Figure 4-5. *An alpha-blended cloud*

Our shader is working now, but there's a better way to accomplish the same thing. For performance reasons, it's generally a good idea in shaders to avoid conditional branching where possible. While our small "if" statement in Listing 4-6 is certainly not going to slow our program to a halt, there's a built in GLSL function that can accomplish the same task without needing a branch. We're going rewrite our shader to use that function instead.

GLSL's min( ) and max( ) Functions

The min() and max() functions in GLSL are used to pick between two values based on how big the values are. Each of them takes two arguments and returns the argument that is the smaller or the larger of the two. For example, min() will return the smaller of the two arguments passed to it. Since that's the one we're going to be using right now, let's look at Listing 4-9, which shows two examples of how to use this function in a shader.

Listing 4-9. Using the min() Function

```
float a = 1.0;
float b = 0.0;
float c = min(a,b) // c == b  ❶

vec3 a = vec3(1, 0, 0);
vec3 b = vec3(0, 1, 1);
vec3 c = min(a,b); // c == vec3(0,0,0); ❷
```

The example at ❶ is exactly what we just described: two floats go in, the smallest comes out. Min() and max() aren't limited to working on single floats. As you can see at ❷, we can also use vectors as the arguments. When the arguments to these functions are vectors, what we get back is a vector that has the same number of components as the argument vectors, but with each component of the returned vector being a result of a min() or max() being performed on the components of the input vectors individually.

The max() function works the opposite way and will always return the largest value that was passed to it. Listing 4-10 shows what this looks like in code.

Listing 4-10. Using the max() Function

```
float a = 1.0;
float b = 0.0;
float c = max(a,b); // c == a

vec3 a = vec3(1, 0, 0);
vec3 b = vec3(0, 1, 1);
vec3 c = max(a,b); // c == vec3(1,1,1);
```

To render our cloud properly, we need to have our shader do two things. Fragments with a high alpha value should not be able to exceed 0.8, while any alpha value below 0.8 should be left intact. This is a textbook use case for min(), and we can rewrite Listing 4-8 to look like Listing 4-11.

Listing 4-11. Using a min() Instead of a Conditional

```
void main()
{
    outCol = texture(tex, fragUV);
    outCol.a = min(outCol.a, 0.8);
}
```

Running our application with the shader rewritten should yield the same result as before: a nice see-through cloud for our alien friend's forest. There's a lot of new stuff going on in this project, so if you want to see the entire code for rendering our scene with the cloud mesh added, look at the "AlphaClouds" project in the example code.

How Alpha Blending Works

Our cloud example probably made alpha blending seem trivial. We wanted an 80% opaque cloud, so we set some fragments' alpha to 0.8 and everything worked out exactly as we predicted. The reality is a bit more complicated. Remember that none of our shaders have any information about what else is in the scene by default, and we didn't need to provide any information about the scene to our cloud shader. Despite all of this, the pixels on screen that were covered by our cloud image also contained enough information about the background to appear as though we could see through the cloud.

This means that our GPU had to know to blend the colors from multiple fragments together in order to come up with a final on-screen pixel color.

This blending is handled by the "fragment processing" step of the pipeline, which takes place after our fragment shader has finished executing. We've already talked about the depth calculations that are performed in this step, but it's also where all alpha blending is done. Remember that our fragment shader is writing fragments, not screen pixels. In the case of our test scene, we have seen multiple fragments generated for every screen pixel that our cloud covers: one fragment for the cloud and one for the background behind it. It's the fragment processing step's job to figure out how to combine these fragments into what appears on screen.

When our cloud was opaque, the GPU could do a depth calculation and determine that the cloud fragment was in front of the background. Since the cloud was opaque, we could safely discard the fragment for the background and write only the cloud fragment to the screen. Now that our cloud is translucent, we can't simply discard background fragments, because we need to be able to see the background through the cloud. Instead, the final color that gets written to the screen must be a blend of the two fragments that occupy that single screen position. How this blend occurs is controlled by a *blend equation*, which is a bit of math that tells the GPU how to blend between two fragments.

Alpha blending is probably the most common blend equation in games, and here's what it looks like in some pseudocode:

```
vec4 finalColor = src * src.a + (1.0 - src.a) * dst;
```

In the preceding example, "src" and "dst" are the names given to the color values for the two fragments that are being blended together. The graphics pipeline executes for each mesh individually, so the first mesh that gets drawn to the screen will complete its fragment processing step before the next object's fragment shader is complete. The results from each pass of the graphics pipeline are stored in what's known as the *back buffer*, which is the image that will be presented on screen when the frame is completely done being rendered. The "dst" value in a blend equation refers to the current value of the back buffer when the blend takes place; "src" refers to the new fragment that needs to be blended with the value currently stored in the back buffer. As the alpha value of the "src" fragment increases, we end up with more of the color from the "src" fragment and less from the "dst" fragment.

Let's walk through what this looks like for a single pixel in our example scene. Assume that we're looking at one of the screen pixels that contains both the green from the leaves of a tree in our scene and the white cloud in front of it. The process that the GPU takes to put the correct color on screen for this pixel looks like this:

1. The background image is drawn to the screen. This generates an opaque green fragment for our screen pixel. We don't need to blend opaque fragments, so that color is written to the back buffer (which had no data in it before now).

2. The cloud is drawn next. Its fragment shader generates a fragment for the same screen pixel as the background, except that this fragment is translucent and white. After the shader is done, this fragment is sent to the fragment processing step of the pipeline.

3. The GPU sees that there is already a value in the back buffer for this screen pixel, and since the new fragment is translucent, needs to do a blend between the two fragments. It sets the fragment from the cloud as the "src" variable in the blend equation and reads the current value of the back buffer for this screen pixel into the "dst" variable.

4. The blend equation is then evaluated, and the result of this blend is stored at that screen pixel's position in the back buffer.

The order that fragments are written to the back buffer matters a lot. If we had written our cloud fragments to the back buffer first, the background would have drawn completely over the cloud, and we wouldn't have seen it at all. You can try this in your example project by reordering the code in the draw() function to draw the cloud first. This is why translucent objects need to be drawn after all the opaque objects in a scene have finished rendering. All major game engines take care of this for you, but it's a handy thing to know if you ever need to figure out when certain objects are drawn to the screen.

We just walked through how the standard "alpha blend" equation works, but there are many different blend equations used in games. The second most common of these is known as "additive blending," and we're going to use that next.

Adding Some Sun with Additive Blending

Alpha blending was great for translucent objects that obscure the things behind them, but what if we instead wanted our translucent object to brighten up part of the screen rather than obscure things behind it? We could also try to draw a white shape in front of things with alpha blending enabled but that would also wash out the colors on screen. Instead, what we need is a different blend equation.

This is where *additive blending* comes in. Additive blending is the name given to another common blend equation that games use, and it's much simpler than the alpha blending equation we just used. Here's what it looks like in pseudocode:

```
vec4 finalColor = src + dst;
```

Like its name implies, additive blending adds fragments together. This means that it's impossible to make something darker with an additive blend but it's great if you want to make things brighter. Unlike alpha blending, the additive blending equation doesn't use the alpha channel of a fragment to figure out how much of each fragment to blend together, it just adds 100% of each. In practice, this means that if you'd like a texture to only add a little bit of brightness with additive blending, you need it to use dark colors rather than a low alpha. We'll see this in our example.

For our additive blending example, I think it might be nice to give our alien friend some sunshine. The assets for this chapter have one more texture in them, which is an image of the sun and some rays. This texture is going to look very dark, since we're looking for subtle sun beams and not earth scorching sun rays. Using brighter colors would mean making our sun ray effect more pronounced. When we have this working, our forest scene should look like Figure 4-6.

Figure 4-6. *Our scene with sun rays added*

To match Figure 4-6, we need to put our sun texture on a full screen quad and then draw that quad in front of the background. Listing 4-12 shows the buildMesh() function call that the example code uses for this.

Listing 4-12. The buildMesh() Call for Our Sun Ray Quad

```
buildMesh(sunMesh, 1.0, 1.0, glm::vec3(0.0, 0.0, 0.4));
```

Funnily enough, we're going to be able to render our sun mesh with the same shader that we used for our clouds. Since the alpha values for our sun shader are so low, the logic we added to clamp the maximum alpha values for our cloud mesh won't apply to any fragments. This is going to save us some typing and demonstrate an important concept: the blend equation that a shader uses is separate from the shader code itself.

You may have noticed in our earlier cloud shader that we didn't specify the blend equation that we wanted to use anywhere in it. This is because the blend equation must be set from code before submitting a draw call. We didn't have to specify anything earlier because openFrameworks enables alpha blending by default. Now that we want to use different blend equations, we need to add some more code to our draw() function. Listing 4-13 shows the changes that we need to make.

Listing 4-13. Our New Draw Function

```
void ofApp::draw()
{
        ofDisableBlendMode(); ❶

        alphaTestShader.begin();
        alphaTestShader.setUniformTexture("tex", alienImg, 0);
        charMesh.draw();

        alphaTestShader.setUniformTexture("tex", backgroundImg, 0);
        backgroundMesh.draw();
        alphaTestShader.end();

        ofEnableBlendMode(ofBlendMode::OF_BLENDMODE_ALPHA); ❷

        cloudShader.begin();
        cloudShader.setUniformTexture("tex", cloudImg, 0);
        cloudMesh.draw();
```

```
ofEnableBlendMode(ofBlendMode::OF_BLENDMODE_ADD); ❸

cloudShader.setUniformTexture("tex", sunImg, 0);
cloudMesh.draw();
cloudShader.end();
}
```

In addition to the code to set a texture and issue a draw call for our sunMesh, which I assume are old hat to us by now, there are three new lines of code that we need to add to our draw() function to set things up. It makes the most sense to talk about them in the opposite order that they appear in our code, so let's start with line ❸. This is the line of code we need to add, to tell the GPU that the next draw call we issue—sunMesh.draw()— will use additive blending. Note that we're still using the same shader that our cloud did, so the only thing changing is this blend mode. We also added a line at ❷ to explicitly set the blend mode for our cloud to alpha blending. Once you set a blend mode, your GPU will remain in that mode until you change it. Now that we're changing between multiple blend equations, we need to explicitly specify the one we want before we draw the cloud.

Finally, ❶ disables blending for our character and background meshes. We didn't need to do this earlier because our alien and background meshes are drawn with fragments that are either fully opaque or fully transparent, meaning that alpha blending didn't need to do anything to render them correctly. Now that we end our draw() function with additive blending enabled, we need to do a bit of setup before we can render these first couple of meshes. It's also just good practice to only enable blending if you really need it, since it's a relatively performance-intensive process.

With these changes made to our draw() function, we're almost ready to call this example done! However, if you run things right now, you'll see that our cloud doesn't look quite right. You can see what I mean in Figure 4-7.

Figure 4-7. *What our example should look like right now, with some additive sun rays added to the scene*

The quad for the cloud is obscuring the rays of sun behind it! This is because even though we're using alpha blending to hide the quad, we're still submitting depth information for the entire cloud quad. Since our cloud mesh is being placed in front of the sun beams, the GPU is using this depth information to skip processing the fragments for the sun that are behind our cloud's quad. What we need to do is to disable sending depth information for our translucent meshes. Most translucent meshes in games don't write depth information for exactly this reason. To fix this, we need to add two more lines to our draw() function. Listing 4-14 shows the changes we need to make.

Listing 4-14. Our Updated Draw Function

```
void ofApp::draw()
{
      ofDisableBlendMode();
      ofEnableDepthTest(); ❶

      alphaTestShader.begin();
      alphaTestShader.setUniformTexture("tex", alienImg, 0);
      charMesh.draw();
      alphaTestShader.setUniformTexture("tex", backgroundImg, 0);
      backgroundMesh.draw();
      alphaTestShader.end();
```

```
ofDisableDepthTest(); ❷
ofEnableBlendMode(ofBlendMode::OF_BLENDMODE_ALPHA);

cloudShader.begin();
cloudShader.setUniformTexture("tex", cloudImg, 0);
cloudMesh.draw();

//rest of function omitted for brevity
}
```

Just like with blend modes, once you enable or disable depth testing, every draw call you make will keep that same setting until you tell the GPU to do something different. We're going to accomplish that by disabling depth testing before we start issuing draw calls for our translucent meshes (❷) and then enabling it again before our opaque meshes (❶). Depending on the Z positions you've given to your sun, character, and cloud meshes, you may see different depth problems than in Figure 4-7. No matter what order you've put them in, however, the answer to these problems is to only enable depth testing when writing out opaque meshes and disable depth testing on everything else. If your project has ended up in a state where adding these two lines of code doesn't fix everything, check out the code in the "AdditiveSun" project in this chapter's example code to see where your code differs from mine.

In some engines, there's a difference between enabling depth writing and depth testing, allowing you to tell the GPU to use the existing depth buffer to allow a mesh to be obscured by other meshes, but not to write out depth information for the mesh itself. This is very useful if you have translucent meshes (like a ghost character) that need to be able to hide behind opaque walls. It's possible to do this in openFrameworks by writing OpenGL code, but we're not going to dig into that in this book. Just keep this in mind for when you start working in other engines.

Animating with Sprite Sheets

Before we end this chapter, there's one more shader that I want us to write. Now that we have a handle on translucency and have seen how to draw a 2D character on a quad, we have almost all the pieces needed to render a 2D game. One important thing that we're missing though is the ability to animate anything. Now that we have a handle on blending and how to work with UV coordinates though, we have all the pieces we need to add some life to our scene.

Most 2D games animate characters as if they were a flipbook. Multiple images of the character in different stages of a motion are stored in what's known as a *sprite sheet*. The last texture included in this chapter's assets is a sprite sheet for our alien character, which you can see in Figure 4-8. Meshes animated with a sprite sheet still use a regular quad mesh, but use some additional values in their vertex shader to offset and scale that quad's UV coordinates so that it only displays one frame of animation at a time. The frame of animation that needs to be displayed in a given frame is chosen by a shader uniform and updated by C++ code. For our example, we're going to just loop a walking animation forever (the frames for this are shown in Figure 4-8). More complicated games would use a much more complicated sprite sheet, with frames for all the different actions that the character is able to perform.

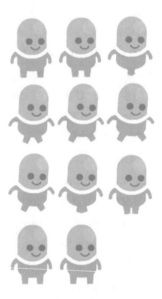

Figure 4-8. *The sprite sheet for our alien character*

Let's start by taking a quick look at the UV math that our vertex shader will have to do. The first thing that we're going to do is to scale our UV coordinates so that they select only the first frame of the sprite sheet. Texture coordinates start at $(0, 0)$, at the bottom left of a texture; however, as we saw earlier, we're going to invert our V coordinates to flip the image the right way up. This means that our $(0, 0)$ texture coordinate is functionally going to be the top left corner of the image, which makes life a lot easier for us because that's where the first frame of our animation is!

To select a single frame out of the sprite sheet, we first need to multiply our quad's UV coordinates by a 2D vector to scale them to the size of a single frame of animation in our sprite sheet texture. Once they're scaled correctly, we can then add another 2D vector to offset the coordinates so that they encompass the frame we want to draw. Figure 4-9 shows how this process looks visually. Don't worry if this sounds a bit confusing; we're going to walk through it all very slowly.

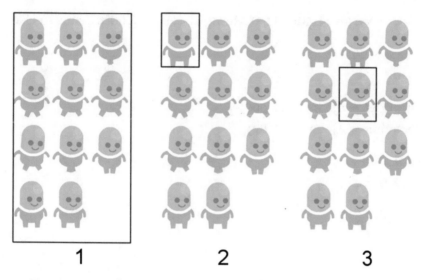

Figure 4-9. *How UV coordinates are adjusted to display a single frame of a sprite sheet*

We start with UV coordinates that cover the entirety of our sprite sheet texture; you can see this above the "1" in Figure 4-9. The size of a single sprite in our sprite sheet is (0.28, 0.19), so the first thing we do is multiply our UV coordinates by that size vector. This will give us a UV rectangle that is only big enough to cover one frame's area in our texture. The result of this is visible above the "2" in Figure 4-9. If we were to draw the mesh now, we would see it textured with only the frame of animation that our UVs are currently encompassing. Once our UVs are scaled accordingly, we need to add a vector to them to move our UV rectangle over the frame of animation we want. This last operation is shown in Figure 4-9, above the "3."

The shader code for this is all very simple, despite there being multiple steps involved. Let's set up our C++ code to pass in a vec2 for our sprite size, and a second one that chooses the frame we want. We will multiply those values together to get the translation vector that we need to apply to our vertex UV coordinates. Put together, the vertex shader for our character ends up looking like Listing 4-15. I created a new file for this code called "spritesheet.vert" and copied Listing 4-15 into it.

Listing 4-15. A Vertex Shader That Manipulates UV Coordinates to Use a Sprite Sheet

```
#version 410

layout (location = 0) in vec3 pos;
layout (location = 3) in vec2 uv;

uniform vec2 size;
uniform vec2 offset;

out vec2 fragUV;

void main()
{
    gl_Position = vec4(pos, 1.0);
    fragUV = vec2(uv.x, 1.0-uv.y) * size + (offset*size);
}
```

We can combine this new vertex shader with our existing alpha testing fragment shader to create a new ofShader object (which the example code calls the "spritesheetShader") to render our character. To do this, we need to modify the draw() function to submit the draw call for our alien using this new ofShader object, pass values for our two new uniforms in the vertex shader, and replace our alien texture with the sprite sheet texture. As before, I'm going to assume that we don't need examples of creating an ofShader object or using it to draw our character, but the online code examples for the chapter have all that code in case you get stuck (check out the "SpritesheetAnimation" project). Instead, Listing 4-16 only contains the code snippet that the example code uses to loop between sprite frames.

Listing 4-16. A Quick Way to Generate Values for the Uniform in Listing 4-15's Vertex Shader

```
static float frame = 0.0;
frame = (frame > 10) ? 0.0 : frame += 0.2;
glm::vec2 spriteSize = glm::vec2(0.28, 0.19);
glm::vec2 spriteFrame = glm::vec2((int)frame % 3, (int)frame/3);
```

While the preceding code snippet certainly won't scale for a full game, it's enough to get our alien moving! With only the code we've covered so far, you should be able to see your alien walking in place on screen when you run the program. This is cool, but our alien friend looks a little bit weird looping through the walk animation cycle without going anywhere. Our next chapter will help get him moving and talk about how to use vertex shaders to move meshes around the screen.

Summary

With what we covered in this chapter, we've almost covered enough to write all the shaders we would need to make simple 2D games. Here's a quick recap of what we've learned:

- Alpha testing is the process of checking whether a given fragment's alpha value is above or below a certain threshold, and discarding any fragments that are not.

- The "discard" statement is used to remove the current fragment from the pipeline.

- GPUs use a depth buffer to store the information needed to allow objects to occlude each other based on position. This process is called depth testing.

- Translucent fragments are blended with the current contents of the back buffer in the fragment processing step.

- How this blend occurs can be configured by specifying a blend equation. Two of the most common blend equations are the "alpha blend" equation and the "additive blend" equation.

- It's common to not submit depth information for translucent meshes.

- Flipbook style animations can be done using sprite sheets.

CHAPTER 5

Making Things Move

We've focused a lot so far on things we can do with a fragment shader: tinting, brightening, mixing—all that jazz. You'd be forgiven for thinking that vertex shaders exist only to pass information to the real stars of the show, but nothing could be further from the truth. While fragment shaders drive a lot of the visual effects that we're used to in modern games, vertex shaders are the unsung workhorse of modern video game graphics, and this chapter is going to focus on why.

We've created two different meshes for our projects so far, a triangle and a quad. Both meshes have been completely *static* (stationary), but meshes in games move around a lot and it's about time ours did too. The simplest possible way to do this is to modify the vertices of the mesh itself. For example, if an object needs to move five units forward on the X axis, you could add (5, 0, 0) to every vertex in the mesh. In our project, you can try this out yourself by adding the snippet from Listing 5-1 to our ofApp's onKeyPressed() function.

Listing 5-1. Moving a Mesh by Modifying its Vertices

```
int numVerts = charMesh.getNumVertices();
for (int i = 0; i < numVerts; ++i)
{
    charMesh.setVertex(i, charMesh.getVertex(i) + glm::vec3(0.2f, 0.0f,
    0.0f));
}
```

This works, but has some major drawbacks. First, updating a mesh's geometry is a relatively slow operation and not something that you want to do every frame if you can help it. Second, this requires that every object in our game get its own instance of a mesh, rather than being able to share one mesh in memory. This would be a total nightmare for games, since it would require much more memory to store a game's mesh data. Vertex shaders solve both problems in one fell swoop.

© Kyle Halladay 2019
K. Halladay, *Practical Shader Development*, https://doi.org/10.1007/978-1-4842-4457-9_5

Rather than modify mesh data, vertex shaders move objects around by modifying the positions that an object's vertices will be drawn to the screen. The same mesh can be submitted to the graphics pipeline repeatedly, and be positioned in different places depending on logic in the vertex shader. To see this in action, let's modify "spritesheet. vert" from the last chapter to move our character around. It will still pass the sprite sheet UVs to the fragment shader, so we only need to change the vertex shader that we're using. Listing 5-2 shows the changes that we need to make to our "spritesheet.vert" shader's main() function to start moving our character.

Listing 5-2. Translating a Mesh in a Vertex Shader

```
void main()
{
      vec3 translation = vec3(0.5, 0.0, 0.0);
      gl_Position = vec4(pos + translation, 1.0); ❶
      fragUV = vec2(uv.x, 1.0-uv.y) * size + (offset*size);
}
```

Moving our mesh to the right is as simple as adding a vector to the position of each vertex in our mesh (❶). Since normalized device coordinates go from -1 to +1, moving to the right by 0.5 means that this shader is going to move our entire mesh to the right by one quarter of our window's width. If you run the program with the preceding change, you should see our alien character still walking in place, but this time a bit more to the right of the screen. While this is cool, it would be a lot cooler if we could make the alien move around based on keyboard input, so let's do that next.

Making Our Character Walk Forward

We've already seen how to put a translation into our vertex shader. The next step is for us to move that translation vector into a uniform so that we can set it from C++ instead of hardcoding it. We've worked with vector uniforms in shaders enough now that I'm going to skip providing example code for that. As always, the full code for this example is available in the example code for this chapter (look for Chapter 5's "WalkingCharacter" example project).

In Listing 5-1 we wrote some code that made our character move whenever we pressed a key. However, that movement was very jumpy and didn't really match the walking animation on our character. Instead of doing that again, let's make our character smoothly walk forward while we hold down a key, and stop walking forward when we release that key. Once per frame we'll check to see if that key is still pressed. If it is, we'll modify the vector that gets passed to our character's vertex shader. This means that we're going to need two new variables, a vec3 for the character's translation, and a Boolean to store the state of the key that we're using to move the character. We'll be accessing these variables from multiple functions, so let's declare them as member variables in ofApp.h, like you see in Listing 5-3.

Listing 5-3. Two New Member Variables in ofApp.h

```
class ofApp : public ofBaseApp
{
      //rest of code omitted for brevity
      bool walkRight;
      glm::vec3 charPos;
}
```

Notice that I called our translation vector "charPos" instead of something like "charTranslation." We'll talk about why that is later in the chapter, but don't worry about it too much right now.

Now we need to write a bit of code to track the state of our key press. Since we're going to make our character walk forward, it makes sense to use the right arrow key to control this motion. Getting the state of that key is as easy as adding a few lines of code to our ofApp's keyPressed() and keyReleased() functions. You can see this in Listing 5-4.

Listing 5-4. Tracking the State of the Right Arrow Key, and Updating Our Translation

```
void ofApp::keyPressed(int key)
{
      if (key == ofKey::OF_KEY_RIGHT) {
            walkRight = true;
      }
}
```

```
void ofApp::keyReleased(int key)
{
     if (key == ofKey::OF_KEY_RIGHT){
          walkRight = false;
     }
}
```

Now we're ready to update our charPos vector and pass it to our shader. So far, we've been putting all the logic that we want to execute each frame into the draw() function for simplicity, but that's not usually where nonrendering logic goes. Instead, logic that needs to happen every frame that isn't directly related to creating draw calls should be put in the update() function, and that's where we're going to put the logic for moving our character. Listing 5-5 shows what our update function looks like with the logic for updating our position vector.

Listing 5-5. Updating the Character Position Vector Each Frame

```
void ofApp::update()
{
     if (walkRight)
     {
          float speed = 0.4 * ofGetLastFrameTime(); ❶
          charPos += glm::vec3(speed, 0, 0);
     }
}
```

One thing that might be confusing about Listing 5-5 is the use of the function ofGetLastFrameTime(). This function returns the amount of time that has elapsed since the beginning of the last frame to the beginning of this one. Most engines call this time interval "delta time." It's important to multiply the speed of our character by this value, so that the character moves at the same speed no matter how fast your computer renders each frame. Using delta time in this way is how games can make sure that no matter how fast the computer is that they're running on, the game play stays at a consistent speed.

Now that our update() function is set up, all we need to do is pass the charPos to the translation uniform in our character's vertex shader, just like the size and offset vectors for the sprite sheet. Since our charPos is a vec3, we'll need to use setUniform3f() to do this. If you've wired everything up correctly, pressing the right arrow key will make our alien friend walk to the right of the screen without modifying his mesh data! If your alien friend isn't walking around yet, check out the "WalkingCharacter" project in this chapter's example code to see what you may have missed.

Our alien isn't the only part of the scene that we're going to animate in this chapter. Next, let's see how we can scale and rotate our cloud mesh.

Scaling Our Cloud in Shader Code

Translating a mesh isn't all that vertex shaders can do. An object's place in a 3D scene is defined by three different properties. Our vertex shader now acts on the first of these three properties, position, which is that object's translation from the origin of our 3D world. The other two properties are rotation and scale. Operations that modify one or more of these properties are referred to as *transformation*s. Just by modifying these properties, we can describe virtually any position and orientation that an object might have in 3D space.

We've already seen translation in a shader, so let's move on to scale. Scaling a mesh in a vertex shader is as easy as adjusting position was. All we need to do is multiply our position by a vector, instead of adding to it.

Listing 5-6. Scaling a Mesh in a Vertex Shader

```
void main()
{
    vec3 scale = vec3(0.5, 0.75, 1.0);
    gl_Position = vec4( (pos * scale), 1.0); ❶
    fragUV = vec2(uv.x, 1.0-uv.y);
}
```

In Listing 5-6, the "scale" vector scales the size of the mesh by multiplying each component of the vertices' position by a component of the scale vector. To keep a mesh the same size it was originally, we could use a scaling vector of (1.0, 1.0, 1.0). Scaling by values above or below 1.0 will adjust the scale of the mesh in that dimension. The shader in Listing 5-6 will scale our mesh to be half its size in the X dimensions, and three quarters its size in the Y dimension. Figure 5-1 shows what this looks like if we modify the "passthrough.vert" shader to give our background mesh a scale of less than 1.0.

Figure 5-1. _Scaling a quad mesh in the X and Y dimensions_

Notice in Figure 5-1 that the background mesh is still centered on the screen despite being scaled. This is because the positions of our vertices are defined in normalized device coordinates, which means the origin of the coordinate system they're defined in is the center of the screen. The coordinate system that a mesh's vertices are defined in is called that mesh's _object space_. In this case, we could say that our background's object space is identical to normalized device space. You'll often hear the term _coordinate space_ in computer graphics, rather than coordinate system. They're basically interchangeable terms for our purposes; a coordinate system is just the way of describing something's position in a coordinate space.

When we scale a vertex position, we're either going to be moving that position toward or away from the origin of that mesh's object space. For scaling to work how we expect, the center of a mesh should be the (0, 0, 0) point—also called the _origin_—of whatever coordinate space was used to construct that mesh. Scaling produces weird results if the origin of a mesh's object space doesn't match up to the center of the mesh,

All our quads have been created with the same object space, but the buildMesh() function has allowed us to position them at different places on screen by offsetting their vertices from the origin of this space. This means that the origin of our cloud quad's object space is the center of our screen despite that mesh not being anywhere close to that point. Figure 5-2 shows what happens when we try to scale our cloud mesh instead of the background quad. You can see that it appears to move toward the center of screen, in addition to shrinking.

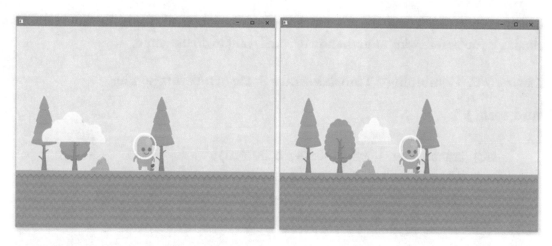

Figure 5-2. *The left image is our scene without the sun rays. The right is the same scene with the cloud mesh scaled to half size—(0.5, 0.5, 1.0). It appears to move toward the center of the screen, which is its object space origin.*

To fix this weirdness, we need to change our cloud mesh so that its vertices are centered on the origin of its object space. This means modifying our setup function to create a quad that has no position offsets supplied for our cloud and moving it into place using a vertex shader. Listing 5-7 shows what this change looks like.

Listing 5-7. Changing Out buildMesh() Function to Create a Centered Cloud

```
void ofApp::setup()
{
    //other code omitted for brevity
    buildMesh(cloudMesh, 0.25, 0.15, vec3(0.0, 0.0, 0.0));
}
```

We'll need to change the shader for our cloud to use a translation vector to position it where we want on screen. However, we're also going to want that shader to be able to scale the mesh without making it move around like we saw in Figure 5-2. The trick to this is to make sure that we scale our mesh before we translate it. That way, when the scaling operation occurs, all the vertices of the cloud mesh are still centered on the origin. Once the scaling is complete, we're free to translate the cloud to wherever it needs to be. We'll see this rule come up again when we add rotation to our shader as well: the scale always needs to happen first. You can see what this means for our shader code in Listing 5-8. I created a new vertex shader specifically for the cloud in this example, so that hardcoding in some values didn't scale the other meshes that were originally using the same vertex shader. If you're following along at home, you'll want to do the same.

Listing 5-8. Combining a Translate and a Scale in a Vertex Shader

```
void main()
{
    vec3 translation = vec3(-0.55, 0.0, 0.0);
    vec3 scale = vec3(0.5, 0.75, 1.0);
    gl_Position = vec4( (pos * scale) + translation, 1.0); ❶
    fragUV = vec2(uv.x, 1.0-uv.y);
}
```

First we multiply by the scale vector and then we add the translation (❶), just like we said we we're going to do before the code snippet. This also has the advantage of giving us another example of a MAD operation (a multiply followed by an add operation), which is something that GPUs can do very quickly. Rendering our cloud mesh with this shader should give us a scene with the cloud scaled down, but positioned in the same place as it was originally. You can see what this will look like in Figure 5-3.

Figure 5-3. *A properly scaled cloud*

That's looking much better! If you're seeing something different in your own project, all the code for positioning our cloud can be found in the "ScaledCloud" example project. Next, we're going to create a second cloud for our scene, so that we have a new mesh that we can use to see how to rotate things in a vertex shader.

Rotating Objects with a Vertex Shader

As I mentioned, rotation is a bit trickier than translation or scaling, especially when you're working with 3D objects. However, because we're working with just 2D quads in our scene, we can accomplish the rotation with a bit of trigonometry. This is shown in Listing 5-9.

Listing 5-9. A 2D Rotation in a Vertex Shader

```
void main()
{
        float radians = 1.0f;

        vec3 rotatedPos = pos;
        rotatedPos.x = (cos(radians)*pos.x)-(sin(radians)*pos.y);
        rotatedPos.y = (cos(radians)*pos.y)+(sin(radians)*pos.x);

        gl_Position = vec4( rotatedPos, 1.0);
        fragUV = vec2(uv.x, 1.0-uv.y);
}
```

We're not going to spend time walking through the math for this rotation, because in a minute I'm going to show you a much easier way to do all our transformations— translate, scale, and rotate—with one line of code. Before we get to that though, I want to use the preceding example code to talk about how to add a rotation operation to the vertex shader we wrote earlier that could scale and translate. Just like before, the order of operation matters. We know that scaling needs to be our first operation, so the rotation can be placed either before or after the translation. Figure 5-4 shows what each of these options looks like when applied to our cloud.

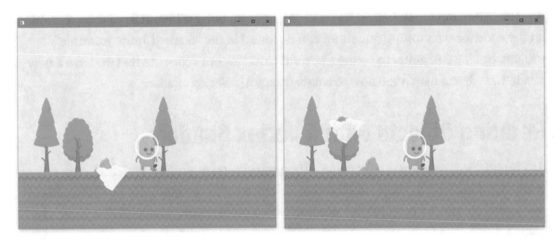

Figure 5-4. *The left screenshot shows the result of a rotation happening after the translation; the right screenshot shows what it looks like if the rotation happens prior to the translation*

If we put the rotation math before our translation, the cloud rotates in place and then moves in the direction that we would expect our translation to go. If we rotate after a translation, the mesh rotates around the origin of its coordinate space. This ends up looking as though the mesh has moved in the direction that it was pointed in by the rotation. While both options may at some point be what you're looking for, the most common use case is to put the translation after the rotation. This means that most vertex shaders perform a scale first, then a rotation, and then end with a translation. Combining our preceding examples together would give us a vertex shader for our clouds that looks like Listing 5-10.

Listing 5-10. Combining Our Scale, Rotation and Translation in a Single Vertex Shader

```
#version 410

layout (location = 0) in vec3 pos;
layout (location = 3) in vec2 uv;

uniform vec3 translation;
uniform float rotation;
uniform vec3 scale;

out vec2 fragUV;
```

```
void main()
{
    vec3 scaled = pos * scale;

    vec3 rotated;
    rotated.x = (cos(rotation)*scaled.x)-(sin(rotation)*scaled.y);
    rotated.y = (cos(rotation)*scaled.y)+(sin(rotation)*scaled.x);

    gl_Position = vec4( rotated + translation , 1.0);

    fragUV = vec2(uv.x, 1.0-uv.y);
}
```

While this isn't the most optimized way to move a mesh around, you could use something like it to build a 2D game using the preceding vertex shader. In fact, let's take this shader for a spin and draw a couple more clouds for our window. All we'll need to do is add a few more calls to setUniform() in our draw() function. Listing 5-11 shows what this looks like.

Listing 5-11. Passing Translation, Rotation, and Scale as Uniforms

```
void ofApp::draw() {

//beginning of function unchanged

    cloudShader.begin();
    cloudShader.setUniformTexture("tex", cloudImg, 0);
    cloudShader.setUniform1f("alpha", 1.0);

    cloudShader.setUniform3f("scale", glm::vec3(1.5, 1, 1));
    cloudShader.setUniform1f("rotation", 0.0f);
    cloudShader.setUniform3f("translation", glm::vec3(-0.55, 0, 0));
    cloudMesh.draw();

    cloudShader.setUniform3f("scale", glm::vec3(1, 1, 1));
    cloudShader.setUniform1f("rotation", 1.0f);
    cloudShader.setUniform3f("translation", glm::vec3(0.4, 0.2, 0));
    cloudMesh.draw();

    //we won't render the sun mesh to give us a better view of the cloud
}
```

This is the first time we've submitted multiple draw calls for the same mesh. In Listing 5-11, we're using the same quad mesh for both draw calls, but because we're setting up our uniforms differently, those two draw calls result in two very different quads drawn on screen. You can see both results in Figure 5-5.

Figure 5-5. Submitting multiple draw calls with different transformation uniforms

Reusing the same mesh data and adjusting it on an individual basis with transformation data—like we just did—is how games can draw a million of the same cloud in a game world without needing to store a million cloud meshes in memory. In general, games will only ever need one copy of a mesh in memory no matter how many different copies of it exist in game. If you want to take a look at the full code for this example, you can find it in the "RotatedCloud" project in the Chapter 5 example code.

Introducing Transformation Matrices

While the vertex shader that we've written so far is a perfectly capable shader, the vertex shaders most games use to orient and position meshes do things differently. Instead of handling each of our three transformation operations separately, most games combine all three operations into a matrix, called a *transformation matrix.*

A matrix is just an array of numbers, arranged in some sort of rectangle. Figure 5-6 shows a few examples of what matrices can look like.

$$\begin{bmatrix} 1 & 0 & 0 & 0 \\ 0 & 1 & 0 & 0 \\ 0 & 0 & 1 & 0 \\ 0 & 0 & 0 & 1 \end{bmatrix} \begin{bmatrix} -\cos\theta & \sin\theta \\ \sin\theta & \cos\theta \end{bmatrix} \begin{bmatrix} 0.5 \\ 0 \\ 0 \end{bmatrix}$$

Figure 5-6. Examples of matrices

While matrix math is a very deep subject, every modern game engine provides matrix classes that can do all the math we need for us already. This means that we only need to worry about how to use this math in our rendering. We're going to talk about matrix math in a few chapters but to get started, we really only need to know three things:

1. Matrices can be thought of as a data structure that's used to store any combination of a translation, rotation, and scale (in any order).

2. We can combine matrices by multiplying them together. If you combine two transformation matrices, you end up with a matrix that combines the operations stored in both.

3. If you multiply a vector by a transformation matrix, you apply that matrix's translation, rotation and scale operations to that vector.

We don't have to worry about how to build a matrix or multiply them by hand, but we do need to know how to get our code to do it for us. Let's start by creating a few matrices in our C++ code with GLM. Listing 5-12 shows how this is done.

Listing 5-12. A Function for Creating Different Transformation Matrices with GLM

```
using namespace glm;
mat4 translation = translate(vec3(0.5, 0.0, 0.0)); ❶
mat4 rotation = rotate((float)PI * 0.5f, vec3(0.0, 0.0, 1.0)); ❷
mat4 scaler = scale(vec3(0.5, 0.25, 1.0)); ❸
```

GLM provides a bunch of matrix types, but 3D transformation matrices are always 4×4 matrices. This means that they're composed of four rows of numbers, and each row contains four elements. The type name of a 4×4 matrix is a mat4, which you can see used in the example code. Making translation, rotation, and scaling matrices are very common tasks, and GLM provides functions to simplify this process. To create a translation matrix, we can use GLM's translate() function (❶). Similarly, we can use the rotate() and scale() functions (❷ and ❸, respectively) to create matrices that store rotation and scale operations.

The function for creating a rotation matrix is a bit less intuitive than the other two, so let's take a minute to dig into line ❷ a little bit more. Line ❷ is creating a rotation using an "axis/angle" style function. This means that we provide the vec3 axis that we want our object to rotate on, and how far we want it to rotate around it (in radians). In Listing 5-12 the axis being provided is (0.0, 0.0, 1.0), which is the Z axis. Since the Z axis points into the screen, you can think of this rotation like pushing a pin through the center of one of our meshes and spinning that mesh around the pin. The resulting rotation will look exactly like the rotations we've used in our vertex shaders earlier in this chapter.

Now let's talk about how to use these matrices to transform our mesh. If we only needed to do one of these operations—let's say that our mesh only needs to be scaled—we could pass the matrix at ❸ to our shaders and be on our way. However, the advantage of working with transformation matrices is that they can be combined. It would be a shame to not take advantage of that in our first example, so let's pass our shader a matrix that combines the operations in all three of our example matrices.

We can combine matrices by multiplying them together. Matrix multiplication is a little bit different from regular multiplication, because it matters what order the matrices are multiplied in. This means that the two lines of code in Listing 5-13 will produce different results.

Listing 5-13. Two Different Ways to Combine Transformation Matrices

```
mat4 transformA = translation * rotation * scaler; ❶
mat4 transformB = scaler * rotation * translation; ❷
```

Determining which multiplication order you need to use to get the results you expect is a more complicated question than you might expect, and has to do with how our math library stores matrices in memory. Although our transformation matrices are 4×4 square matrices, in computer memory they're stored as a linear array of values. There are two different ways to map values in this linear array to their 2D positions in our matrices. The first is to store values of our array row by row, so the first four values in our array correspond to the first row of data in our matrix, and so on. The second way is to store values column by column, so the first four values in the array correspond to the values from top to bottom in the first column of our matrix, and so on.

Figure 5-7 illustrates this difference. In memory, both matrices in Figure 5-7 would look like a linear array of the numbers 1 to 4 in order. Depending on whether we choose to interpret our array's data as rows or columns, we end up with two very different matrices.

$$\begin{bmatrix} 1 & 2 \\ 3 & 4 \end{bmatrix} \qquad \begin{bmatrix} 1 & 3 \\ 2 & 4 \end{bmatrix}$$

Figure 5-7. *The left matrix is an example of a row-major matrix, while the right is a column-major matrix*

If our data is laid out in rows, we would say that our matrix was *row-major,* which is the computer graphics term for that matrix memory layout. If our data was stored column by column, we would say that our matrix was *column-major.* While there is no benefit to choosing one memory layout over the other, that choice has implications for how we multiply matrices. If we're working with column-major matrices, we need to *post-multiply,* like line ❶ in Listing 5-13. This means that if we read our matrix multiplications from left to right, it will look like we're performing our operations backward. Row-major matrices are the reverse: we can write their multiplications in the order we want them to occur, like at ❷. The choice of what memory layout to use is purely one of preference. By default, GLM uses column major matrices, so that's what we'll use in this book. To that end, Listing 5-14 shows a simple function that I'm going to use in future examples to quickly create a transformation matrix for an object.

Listing 5-14. A Function for Creating Transform Matrices

```
glm::mat4 buildMatrix(glm::vec3 trans, float rot, glm::vec3 scale)
{
    using glm::mat4;
    mat4 translation = glm::translate(trans);
    mat4 rotation = glm::rotate(rot, glm::vec3(0.0, 0.0, 1.0));
    mat4 scaler = glm::scale(scale);
    return translation * rotation * scaler;
}
```

We're going to need to modify our draw function to pass matrices to our vertex shaders. Let's go ahead and set up the C++ code to store that matrix in a uniform, which we can do with the setUniformMatrix() function. Listing 5-15 shows what our cloud drawing code should look like now.

Listing 5-15. Drawing Clouds with Transformation Matrices

```
ofDisableDepthTest();
ofEnableBlendMode(ofBlendMode::OF_BLENDMODE_ALPHA);
using namespace glm;

mat4 transformA = buildMatrix(vec3(-0.55, 0.0, 0.0), 0.0f, vec3(1.5, 1, 1));
mat4 transformB = buildMatrix(vec3(0.4, 0.2, 0.0), 1.0f, vec3(1, 1, 1));

cloudShader.begin();
cloudShader.setUniformTexture("tex", cloudImg, 0);

cloudShader.setUniformMatrix4f("transform", transformA);
cloudMesh.draw();

cloudShader.setUniformMatrix4f("transform", transformB);
cloudMesh.draw();

cloudShader.end();
```

That's all the C++ work we need to do to, so it's time to revisit our vertex shader. Remember earlier when I promised that transformation matrices would let us compress all the translation, rotation, and scale math in our vertex shader to a single line of code? Listing 5-16 shows what that looks like.

Listing 5-16. A Vertex Shader That Uses a Transformation Matrix

```
#version 410

layout (location = 0) in vec3 pos;
layout (location = 3) in vec2 uv;

uniform mat4 transform;
out vec2 fragUV;

void main()
```

```
{
    gl_Position =  transform * vec4( pos, 1.0);
    fragUV = vec2(uv.x, 1.0-uv.y);
}
```

With this shader change made, you should be able to run your program and see the scene rendered exactly as it was before. If you're seeing something different, take a look at the "TransformMatrices" project in the example code for this chapter.

Switching to using transformation matrices in our shaders also means that, in addition to being simpler code, we also now can correctly handle 3D rotations. Using matrices for this sort of math is also a lot more optimized than our earlier shaders. GPUs are very good at doing matrix multiplications. Swapping out our earlier code, which used a lot of the slower trig functions (like sin() and cos()), and replacing it with a single matrix multiply is a gigantic win for our shader's runtime performance.

Animating a Transformation Matrix

Now that we know how to use matrices, let's use them to make one of our clouds rotate over time. The easy way to do this is to change our rotation angle each frame and use that to create a per-frame transformation matrix for our mesh. Listing 5-17 shows what creating our cloud's transformation matrix would look like if we just wanted to do that.

Listing 5-17. Updating a Rotation Matrix Every Frame

```
static float rotation = 0.0f;
rotation += 0.1f;
mat4 transformA = buildMatrix(vec3(-0.55, 0.0, 0.0), rotation,
vec3(1.5, 1, 1)); ❶
```

You can see that all we've really done in Listing 5-17 is to replace the constant rotation amount in our rotation matrix function with a value that we can update each frame (❶). This is close to how a modern video game would handle rotating a mesh. However, I want to use this example as an opportunity to demonstrate more ways that we can combine meshes together, so we're going to approach this problem a bit differently. We're going to create a transformation matrix to represent just the rotation that we want to apply to our cloud and then combine that cloud's initial transformation matrix by this new rotation matrix.

The first thing that you might be tempted to do when implementing this is to simply multiply the transformation matrix by a new rotation matrix. You can see in Listing 5-18.

Listing 5-18. Pre- and Post-multiplying by a Rotation Matrix

```
mat4 transformA = buildMatrix(vec3(-0.55, 0.0, 0.0), rotation, vec3(1.5, 1, 1));
mat4 ourRotation = rotate(rotation, vec3(0.0, 0.0, 1.0));
mat4 resultA = transformA * ourRotation; ❶
mat4 resultB = ourRotation * transformA; ❷
```

However, our cloud's matrix already has a scale, rotation, and translation stored in it. If all we do is multiply by a rotation matrix, we're just adding a rotation on to the beginning or end of the original operations. You can see this in Listing 5-18. Post-multiplying by our rotation matrix gives us resultA (❶), which is a matrix that performs our rotation immediately before the original scale, rotation, translation operations. Pre-multiplying gives us resultB (❷), which performs our rotation at the end of this sequence. You can see the results of this in Figure 5-8.

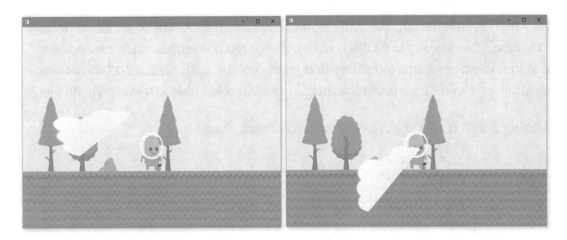

Figure 5-8. *The left screenshot shows the result of using matrix "resultA" in Listing 5-18 in our vertex shader. The right screenshot uses matrix "resultB."*

Neither of these results are exactly what we want. Either we end up skewing our mesh in weird ways because we're rotating it before a scaling operation, or we end up rotating our mesh around its origin because we rotate after we've translated everything. Remember that, ideally, we want all our rotation operations to happen in between the scale and translation operations applied to a mesh. What we really need to do is to find a way to insert our rotation into the middle of the original sequence of operations, so that we can rotate the object before the translation occurs but after the scale. Something like the following:

Scale -> Rotation -> **OUR ROTATION** -> Translation

That isn't technically possible, but we can add additional operations to our rotation matrix. Rather than just containing a rotation, our new matrix will perform the exact opposite translation that the original transformation matrix did, then perform a rotation, and then finally redo the original translation. In the end, it will look like this:

Scale -> Rotation -> Translation -> **-Translation** -> **OUR ROTATION** -> Translation**

We'll start by creating a matrix that contains the last two operations first. This matrix will contain the rotation we want to apply to our cloud mesh, followed by the translation already stored in that mesh's transformation matrix. Once we have that set up, all that will be left is to prepend this series of operations with the opposite translation.

To create this initial matrix, we need to multiply the per-frame rotation matrix by the original translation matrix. Remember that we need to multiply our matrices in the opposite order that we want the operations to be performed, which is why Listing 5-19 might look a bit backward at first glance.

Listing 5-19. Creating a Matrix That Performs a Translation After Our Rotation

```
mat4 ourRotation = rotate(radians, vec3(0.0, 0.0, 1.0));
mat4 newMatrix = originalTranslation * ourRotation;
```

Now all that's left is to come up with a matrix that represents the exact opposite translation from the original. This means that if the original translation was moving our object five units to the right, we need a matrix that moves five units to the left. Luckily for us, every transformation matrix, no matter how complicated, has an exact opposite matrix, called its *inverse matrix*. Inverting a matrix by hand is a rather involved process, but GLM can handle that for us with the inverse() function, which takes a matrix and return its inverse. All we need to know is what to do with the inverse matrix once we have it.

Listing 5-20. newMatrix Will Perform an Inverse Translation, Then Our
Rotation, Then Finally a Translation

```
mat4 ourRotation = rotate(radians, vec3(0.0, 0.0, 1.0));
mat4 newMatrix = translation * ourRotation * inverse(translation);
```

If we multiply the original matrix by "newMatrix," we will end up with the same result
as we had originally: our object will rotate in place! The idea of multiplying a matrix by
its inverse to undo a transformation is one that's going to come in very handy later when
we're working with 3D meshes. Put together, the code to draw both our clouds should
end up looking like Listing 5-21.

Listing 5-21. Our Final Cloud Drawing Code

```
static float rotation = 1.0f;
rotation += 1.0f * ofGetLastFrameTime();

//construct the transform for our un-rotated cloud
mat4 translationA = translate(vec3(-0.55, 0.0, 0.0));
mat4 scaleA = scale(vec3(1.5, 1, 1));
mat4 transformA = translationA * scaleA;

//apply a rotation to that
mat4 ourRotation = rotate(rotation, vec3(0.0, 0.0, 1.0));
mat4 newMatrix = translationA * ourRotation * inverse(translationA);
mat4 finalMatrixA = newMatrix * transformA;

mat4 transformB = buildMatrix(vec3(0.4, 0.2, 0.0), 1.0f, vec3(1, 1, 1));

cloudShader.begin();
cloudShader.setUniformTexture("tex", cloudImg, 0);

cloudShader.setUniformMatrix4f("transform", finalMatrixA);
cloudMesh.draw();

cloudShader.setUniformMatrix4f("transform", transformB);
cloudMesh.draw();

cloudShader.end();
```

After integrating the code in Listing 5-21 to your own project, you should be able to run the program and see one of the clouds rotating in place. The full code for this example is located in the "AnimatedTransform" project of the Chapter 5 example code, so take a look there if you're seeing something different.

As mentioned before, most games don't rotate objects by constructing matrices to untranslate->rotate->re-translate a mesh. It's much more common for games to store an object's translation, rotation, and scales as individual vectors, and then construct a new transformation matrix each frame (or whenever one of those vectors changes). We did things the hard way to give you some more practice with how matrices work together.

We're going to get a lot of use out of matrix multiplication in later chapters, so make sure that you take some time to really understand the examples that we just walked through. If this was your first time seeing matrix math, I recommend experimenting with making a few of your own transformation matrices and seeing what they look like in your project before moving on.

The Identity Matrix

We're almost at the end of the chapter now, but we're in a bit of a weird spot. Some of the meshes in our scene are being drawn with shaders that use transform matrices and some aren't. Games like to treat objects as uniformly as possible, so that they can reuse shaders in the most efficient way. For us, this means that we need to make sure that everything has a transform matrix, even the meshes that don't need to move anywhere. A matrix that doesn't do anything when it gets multiplied against another matrix or vector is called an *identity matrix*. We can already make an identity matrix with our buildMatrix() function by passing in a zero vector for translation, no rotation angle, and a scale vector of all 1's; but there's a much simpler way to do it. GLM's mat4 type starts out as an identity matrix, so we can skip the buildMatrix() function entirely and still end up at the same place. Listing 5-22 shows the one-liner that will do that for us.

Listing 5-22. Making an Identity Matrix

```
mat4 identity = glm::mat4();
```

This is going to come in handy for our background mesh, since we don't want to move it but want to be able to render it with the same vertex shader that we use elsewhere. Let's go ahead and change our program so that everything uses a vertex shader that expects a transformation matrix. When we're done, we should only have two vertex shaders in our project. The first vertex shader will be for our character and use a sprite sheet. The second will be for everything else.

We've already written the general purpose one (it's the shader we just used to position our cloud), so all we need to do there is to replace passthrough.vert with that cloud shader and then change our code to have all our non-alien mesh shaders use passthrough.vert. Since the sprite sheet shader has some additional logic in it, we need to modify it to support a transformation matrix separately, so that it still adjusts out UV coordinates properly. I'm going to leave out providing an example of that here (since we just did this for the cloud vertex shader), but if you get stuck, the full source is available in the "AllMatrices" example project.

Making all our vertex shaders use transform matrices has a few implications for our code, including our background mesh, which will need to use an identity matrix. Since this is the first time we'll use an identity matrix in our code, I've included Listing 5-23 here, which shows how to set up our background mesh with the correct matrix.

Listing 5-23. Drawing the Background Mesh with a Transform Matrix

```
opaqueShader.begin();
opaqueShader.setUniformTexture("tex", bgnd, 0);
opaqueShader.setUniformMatrix4f("transform", glm::mat4());
bgMesh.draw();
opaqueShader.end();
```

The second implication in switching to matrices has for our code is that it breaks our character's walking functionality. This is because we've removed the translation uniform from our sprite sheet shader in favor of a transformation matrix, the logic we wrote earlier. As a final exercise for this chapter, see if you can figure out how to modify ofApp. cpp to create a translation matrix for the alien that preserves the functionality we had before. If you get stuck, there is code in the "AllMatrices" project in the example code for this chapter that shows how to do this.

Summary

That wraps up our first foray into matrix math, and this chapter! This was, of course, just a small look at all the things that matrices can do (and can be used for). Here's a quick rundown of everything we learned in this chapter:

- Vertex shaders can be used to translate, rotate, and scale meshes. We saw several example shaders that demonstrated how to do this for 2D objects.

- A matrix is a data structure which can be used to store translation, rotation, and scaling operations. They can be combined by multiplying matrices together.

- Most video games use transformation matrices to handle all mesh movement and orientation. We saw how to do this in our example project.

- A matrix that doesn't change anything when multiplied by another matrix or vector is known as an identity matrix. We saw how to create and use an identity matrix when rendering our background mesh.

CHAPTER 6

Cameras and Coordinates

Way back in the first chapter, we briefly heard about the term *game camera*. This is the term used for the virtual camera in a game world that decides what goes on screen by looking in different directions and moving to different positions in the scene. Now that we're comfortable with using matrices to move things around our screen, it's time for us to see how we can use matrices to build a simple game camera.

Using a game camera to move things around a screen is a bit different from moving individual objects. When the game camera moves, everything on screen has to move at once. If this seems counterintuitive, think about what it looks like in a TV show when the camera is moving. Even though we know the camera is moving, what we see on screen is that everything on screen appears to be moving in a uniform direction at a uniform speed. This is how game cameras work. In games, the actual camera itself doesn't move or rotate at all, everything else in the game world moves or rotates around the camera.

Of course, we can't change the world positions of objects in our game world to accommodate a camera, because that would make it impossible for us to be able to support multiple cameras at different spots in the world. Instead, game cameras generate what's known as a *view matrix*, which is another transformation matrix, that stores the translation, rotation, and scale information to position an object where it would be in the camera's view. This matrix is then combined with each object's individual transformation matrix in a vertex shader. The result of this is a matrix that first moves a vertex to the location on screen where it would be if there was no camera, and then adjusts that position based on where the camera is.

This all probably feels a little bit abstract, so before we dig into any more theory, let's build a simple camera for our alien scene. We don't need to create any new shaders yet, but we're going to need to modify both vertex shaders that we've already written.

© Kyle Halladay 2019
K. Halladay, *Practical Shader Development*, https://doi.org/10.1007/978-1-4842-4457-9_6

Using a View Matrix

Let's start by writing some C++ code that sets up the data for a simple game camera. At its most basic, a game camera can be represented with just a transformation matrix, just like the matrices we used to position our meshes in the last chapter. Even though we won't see our camera on screen, the camera object will still have a position and rotation value that represents its place in the game scene. It doesn't make much sense to scale a camera, so our camera's scale will always be (1,1,1).

We're going to start by creating a new struct type for our camera data, which we'll add to as our camera becomes more complex over the next couple chapters. Listing 6-1 shows what this is going to look like right now. The example code for this chapter has this struct declaration in ofApp.h, so that we can have a member variable in our ofApp class to store a camera without needing to worry about including any new files.

Listing 6-1. The First Version of Our CameraData Struct

```
struct CameraData{
      glm::vec3 position;
      float rotation;
};

class ofApp : public ofBaseApp{
      //rest of header omitted for brevity
      CameraData cam;

}
```

I've chosen to store the raw position and rotation variable in this struct instead of a matrix, to make it easier to work with our camera data. Since our first camera will only be used with a 2D scene, we don't need to store an axis for our rotation because we'll always be rotating the camera on the Z axis. We're also going to need to write a new function to create a matrix from a CameraData struct. We can't simply reuse the buildMatrix() function that we wrote earlier, because the matrix for a game camera needs to store the inverse of the transformation operations that the camera is doing. This is because the view matrix isn't used to move the camera, it's used to move everything else. Think about it like a movie set, if the camera is slowly moving to the right, everything on screen looks like it's moving to the left. This means that we need a function to create the inverse of the camera's transform matrix. Listing 6-2 shows this function.

Listing 6-2. A Function to Create Our View Matrix

```
glm::mat4 buildViewMatrix(CameraData cam)
{
    using namespace glm;
    return inverse(buildMatrix(cam.position, cam.rotation, vec3(1, 1, 1)));
}
```

We can use this new function and our CameraData struct to move our camera and create the appropriate view matrix for wherever that is. If we use an identity matrix as our view matrix, our scene will render as though our camera is located at the origin of our world; but that's no fun, so let's move our camera about half a screen to the left. This is going to result in our game scene rendering as though everything has been shifted half a screen to the right. Listing 6-3 shows the few lines that we need to add to our draw function to set this up.

Listing 6-3. Our First View Matrix

```
void ofApp::draw()
{
    using namespace glm;
    cam.position = vec3(-1, 0, 0);
    mat4 view = buildViewMatrix(cam);
    //rest of function omitted
```

Now that we know what a view matrix is and how to create one, it's time to see how to modify our vertex shaders to use one. Our example project from the last chapter ended with two vertex shaders in it: passthrough.vert and spritesheet.vert. Since both shaders position the vertices that they act on using a transformation matrix, we can make the same modification to each of them to make them work with a view matrix. Listing 6-4 shows what spritesheet.vert will look like after this change.

Listing 6-4. spritesheet.vert Modified to Use a View Matrix

```
#version 410

layout (location = 0) in vec3 pos;
layout (location = 3) in vec2 uv;
```

```
uniform mat4 model;
uniform mat4 view;
uniform vec2 size;
uniform vec2 offset;

out vec2 fragUV;

void main()
{
    gl_Position =  view * model * vec4( pos, 1.0); ❶
    fragUV = vec2(uv.x, 1.0-uv.y) * size + (offset*size);
}
```

Updating a vertex shader to use a view matrix is just a matter of adding an extra matrix multiply to our position calculations (❶). Since we want to apply the view matrix after the mesh's transformation matrix has been applied, we need to pre-multiply it with the view matrix, just like when we were combining matrices in the last chapter. You may have noticed that I also changed the name of the transform matrix to "model." This is because the view matrix is technically also a transformation matrix, so it's a bit confusing to refer to one as "transform." In graphics terminology, the matrix that's used to position a mesh in the world is called its *model matrix*, which is how I chose that new variable name. We'll talk more about these matrix names after this example.

The last step in this process is to add some new code to our draw() function to pass this new view matrix to our shaders. In the interest of keeping our examples easy to follow along with, the examples for this chapter will only show the drawing code our alien character. All that's required for the other meshes is to pass the same view matrix to their shader's "view" uniform. You can see this in listing 6-5.

Listing 6-5. Drawing a Mesh With a View Matrix

```
spritesheetShader.begin();
spritesheetShader.setUniformMatrix4f("view",view); ❶
spritesheetShader.setUniform2f("size", spriteSize);
spritesheetShader.setUniform2f("offset", spriteFrame);
spritesheetShader.setUniformTexture("tex", alienImg, 0);
spritesheetShader.setUniformMatrix4f("model", glm::translate(charPos));
charMesh.draw();
spritesheetShader.end();
```

If you have everything set up correctly, when you run the program with our new view matrix, you'll see something like Figure 6-1. The full code for this example can be found in the "FirstViewMatrix" project in the Chapter 6 example code.

Figure 6-1. *Rendering the scene with a view matrix*

If you wanted to, you could make an entire 2D game with what we have now and create a game with moving and animating characters, translucent geometry elements, and a moving camera. However, most game cameras are a little bit more complicated than the one we have here, for a very good reason—most games don't work in normalized device coordinates.

You've probably noticed that in our current window, a perfectly square mesh will appear to be wider than it is tall, because normalized device coordinates go from -1 to 1 no matter what the dimensions of our window are. While this is very useful for the GPU, it makes life very difficult for us when we're trying to make games that don't look different on differently sized screens. To solve this problem, modern video games use a combination of different coordinate spaces to render meshes. To understand what this means, however, we need to take a quick detour from our examples and cover a bit more theory.

Transform Matrices and Coordinate Spaces

We've talked briefly about what a coordinate space is already, but we need to get much more familiar with them in order to understand what our view matrix is doing. Think about an empty cardboard box. Let's imagine that we want to be able to choose any point inside the box and assign it a 3D coordinate (like (0,5,0)). The easiest way to do this would be to use the sides of the box as the axes of a coordinate space and pick one corner of the box to be the origin point. You can see what this might look like in Figure 6-2. Once we have our axes defined and an origin point picked, we've defined a coordinate space that can be used to describe any point inside the box. We could call this coordinate space "box space."

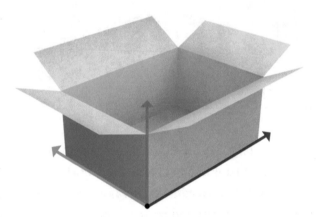

Figure 6-2. *Defining "box space" for a cardboard box*

I like the cardboard box example because it makes it easy to demonstrate that the same position can be described by different coordinate spaces while still being the same point in space. The origin point in box space (shown in Figure 6-2 as a black dot) can be described as point (0,0,0). Consider now what would happen if we defined a different coordinate space for our box, using the same axis directions but with a different corner as the origin. In this new space, our previous (0,0,0) point might be (10,10,0), or (5,5,5), or something else entirely. However, despite describing this position using a different coordinate space, the actual position of the box corner has remained the same.

You can see this same concept in our examples already. We define our mesh's vertex positions in model space, which for our examples so far look a lot like normalized device coordinates. However, when we multiply those positions by a view matrix, what we're really doing is converting those positions from model space into a new coordinate space that's defined by our camera. We'll talk about this new space in a moment, but what's important right now is to realize that even though our mesh appears to be moved to the right in view space (as shown in Figure 6-1), the actual position of our vertices hasn't changed; we've simply changed the coordinate space that we use to describe them.

Changing the coordinate space that's used to describe a position is known as "mapping" that position to a new coordinate space. When we multiplied our position by the view matrix in our last example, what we were really doing was mapping that position from world space to view space. Since we then passed the view space coordinate to the GPU (which interpreted it as normalized device coordinates), this had the net result of drawing our scene in a new location. Games typically use at least four different coordinate spaces when rendering a mesh, and transformation matrices are used to map mesh positions from one coordinate space to another. The rest of this section is going to describe what these spaces are, and how they're used.

The first coordinate space that a vertex exists in is model space. We've briefly talked about model space (also called object space) already. This is the coordinate space that a mesh's vertices are defined in. Each mesh's object space can be different, and artists generally use whatever coordinate space is used by their modeling programs. The origin of this space is also arbitrary, but because a mesh's vertices are defined in this space, their positions are all relative to this origin point. Figure 6-3 shows a quad in a modeling program, with its vertex positions shown in object space coordinates. Notice that the center of the quad is this mesh's origin of the modeling program's coordinate space, and all our mesh's vertices are defined relative to that.

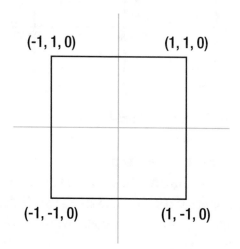

Figure 6-3. *A Quad Mesh with Object Space Vertex Positions Labeled*

This is great for artists who are working on individual meshes but makes life difficult for us. To place objects in a game scene, we need to create a shared coordinate space that all the meshes in our game can use. To accomplish this, game worlds define their own coordinate space, called *world space*. When a mesh is placed into a game world, its position is defined using the three axes of world space and are relative to the world origin point. This means that a mesh placed at position (0,0,0), will be positioned at the origin point of the game world. When we move this mesh in the game scene, what we're really doing is defining a translation from the world origin that we want to apply to the mesh.

When a mesh is sent to the graphics pipeline, the mesh data that our vertex shader receives is still in object space. This means that our vertex shader gets the exact positions that the artist originally authored each vertex to have. In order to place that vertex in the right location, we need to transform each individual vertex from model space to world space. We do this by multiplying a mesh's vertices by the model matrix, which as you might remember, consists of a translation, rotation, and scale. The result of this multiplication is where, in world space, that vertex exists. You can see an example of this in Figure 6-4, which shows our quad in world space, with the world space positions of each vertex displayed.

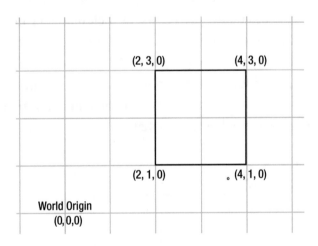

Figure 6-4. *The Quad Positioned in World Space*

World space is the coordinate space that most game developers think about first when creating a game scene, because it's the coordinate space that is commonly used to build levels. Since world space is a coordinate space that is shared by our entire game scene, it lets us say things like "this mesh is at position (100, 0, 0) and I want this second mesh next to it, so I'll put it at (110, 0, 0)."

The third coordinate space that games use is called *view space*. This is the coordinate space that our vertices are in after being multiplied by the view matrix. This is a bit different than going from object space to world space, because the axes of the coordinate system change direction, in addition to the origin point moving. View space is entirely relative to the camera, so the origin point is wherever the camera is—and the Z axis is pointing in whatever direction the camera is pointing. The X and Y axes are also adjusted to match the camera's view. Figure 6-5 shows a screenshot from the Unity game engine's editor, which clearly shows the axes of a camera's view space.

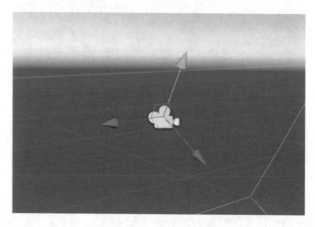

Figure 6-5. *The blue arrow is the Z axis in this camera's view space; it is pointing in the direction that the camera is looking, and not in the direction of the world space Z axis*

View space is useful for all kinds of shader effects, but more importantly, once a vertex is in view space, we can perform the last transformation that we're responsible for doing in our vertex shader: outputting a position in *clip space*, which is the name for the coordinate space that uses normalized device coordinates. We've been skipping straight to this coordinate space for most of the book, but in most games, getting a vertex into clip space requires the use of a *projection matrix*, which we'll talk about in a few pages. You might be wondering why this coordinate space isn't just called "normalized device space" instead of clip space. The answer is that because we know that any vertex that is outside of the -1 to +1 range of our screen in normalized device coordinates, those vertices can be "clipped" by the GPU and not processed directly. If only some of the vertices of a face are clipped (for example, a triangle that is halfway on screen), the GPU will automatically create smaller triangles to make sure that the right fragments still end up on screen. Figure 6-6 shows a frame rendered with the clip space axes labeled.

Once a vertex is in clip space, we can output the position from our vertex shader and let the GPU handle the last step in the process, which is converting from clip space to an actual position on our computer screen. This is the only coordinate space that we don't have to multiply by a matrix to get to; instead we can supply information about our viewport (the window or screen that we're rendering to), and the GPU will handle this for us. We've been setting this up in our main() function all along, when we specify how big our window needs to be.

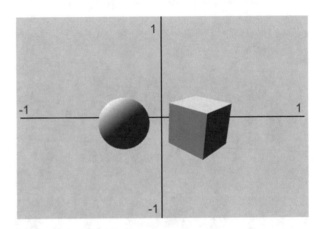

Figure 6-6. *A Frame with Clip Space Axes Labeled*

It's important to note that it's also possible to go backward in this order of coordinate spaces. For example, we can move a vertex from view space to world space with the inverse of the view matrix. Similarly, world space positions can be put back into object space by multiplying by the inverse of the model matrix.

We don't need to worry too much about the math implications of changing a coordinate space in this book. We simply need to make sure we're aware of what coordinate space a vertex position is in at any given time, and to keep a few simple things in mind:

- We can only compare positions, rotations, or scale between two objects or vertices that are in the same coordinate space.

- We can move from one coordinate space to the other by multiplying a mesh's vertices by a specific matrix.

- Multiplying by an inverse matrix always does the opposite of what multiplying by the non-inverted matrix will do.

This is all very abstract right now, so let's break down what coordinate spaces we're using in our new sprite sheet shader. Listing 6-6 has that shader's main() function again.

Listing 6-6. spritesheet.vert's Main Function

```
void main()
{
    gl_Position =  view * model * vec4( pos, 1.0); ❶
    fragUV = vec2(uv.x, 1.0-uv.y) * size + (offset*size);
}
```

All our coordinate space fun is happening on line ❶, and there's a lot going on there, so let's break it down step by step.

1. We get the "pos" data from our vertex. Since this is raw mesh data, pos starts off in object space.

2. We multiply by the model matrix to change our position from an object space position to a world space position.

3. We multiply by the view matrix, to go from world space to view space.

This is all great, but what about clip space? Our vertex positions started off in normalized device coordinates, which means we can cheat a bit here and pass them directly through to the fragment shader; but that's not exactly what we want, because of the screen size issue we talked about earlier. You can see this problem at work in our example project—our background is being rendered on a perfectly square quad, but is filling our nonsquare window perfectly.

To fix this, we need to add one more step to our shader and multiply our view space coordinates by a *projection matrix*. In geometry, a projection is a way to visualize 3D geometry on a 2D plane. A projection matrix projects our view space coordinates onto the 2D plane of whatever window we're rendering to. Listing 6-7 shows what that will look like in our sprite sheet vertex shader. Go ahead and make the same modification to the other vertex shader in our project, and then we'll dive into how to create a projection matrix in C++.

Listing 6-7. spritesheet.vert with a Projection Matrix

```
#version 410

layout (location = 0) in vec3 pos;
layout (location = 3) in vec2 uv;

uniform mat4 model;
uniform mat4 view;
uniform mat4 proj;
uniform vec2 size;
uniform vec2 offset;

out vec2 fragUV;

void main()
{
    gl_Position = proj * view * model * vec4( pos, 1.0);
    fragUV = vec2(uv.x, 1.0-uv.y) * size + (offset*size);
}
```

Writing the shader code to use a perspective matrix is the easy part. The harder part is figuring out how to create one at all, so let's jump back into our C++ code and figure this out next.

Camera Frustums and Projections

Unlike model and view matrices, projection matrices are not composed of translations, rotations, and scales. Instead, we build them using information about our game camera's *frustum*. A camera's frustum is the three-dimensional region that the camera can see, and is composed of the region between the two planes that represent the nearest and farthest that a camera can see. These are called the *near clip plane* and the *far clip plane*, respectively. Typically, a camera's frustum is one of two different shapes—a rectangular prism or a clipped pyramid—and each shape corresponds to a different kind of projection that we'll use to render our frame.

The first frustum shape we'll talk about is the rectangular prism, because it's the type most commonly used in 2D games. When a camera's frustum has this shape, it means that the camera will render the scene using an *orthographic projection.* Using an orthographic projection means that objects don't appear smaller as they get farther away. Put another way, parallel lines always appear parallel, no matter how far away from the camera they go. This is perfect when you need to use the Z axis to sort 2D objects, but don't want your art to grow or shrink when you're trying to put one thing in front of the other. Figure 6-7 shows what this looks like in a game scene.

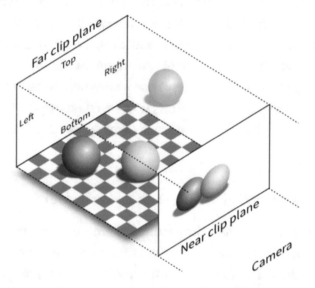

Figure 6-7. *An Orthographic projection. Figure from Nicolas P. Rougier, ERSF Code camp.*

In Figure 6-7, you can see that the frustum is defined as the area between the near and far clip planes. The green sphere that is located outside of this area isn't rendered to the final image, and the image that is rendered shows both red and yellow spheres as the same size, despite one being farther away from the camera than the other. We can create a matrix with this type of projection using the glm::ortho() function. This function takes six arguments that describe the frustum that our projection will use. Since we will be applying this projection to vertices that are already in view space, the arguments that we use to describe our frustum will also be in view coordinates.

Listing 6-8. The glm::ortho Function Declaration

```
mat4 ortho(float left, float right, float bottom, float top, float zNear,
float zFar);
```

The first two arguments describe the left and right planes of the frustum. If we wanted to create a projection matrix that matches what we've been doing so far, we would set the left argument to -1, and the right argument to 1, which would indicate that only vertex positions within that range in the X axis would appear on screen. Similarly, the next two arguments—bottom and top—would also be set to -1 and 1 to apply that same range to our screen's Y axis. The final two arguments define where on the Z axis our camera's near and far clip planes are. These planes define the range of the Z axis where our camera can see. Listing 6-9 shows how we could use this function to create a projection matrix that renders our scene exactly how we've been doing it all along.

Listing 6-9. Using glm::ortho

```
glm::mat4 proj = glm::ortho( -1.0f, 1.0f, -1.0f, 1.0f, 0.0f, 10.0f);
```

However, this still doesn't solve the problem of objects in our window appearing wider than they should. This is because we've still provided the same range of visible coordinates to both the X and Y axes. To fix this problem, we're going to have to modify the values that we pass to glm::ortho so that they match our window's *aspect ratio*, which is the ratio between its width and height. Our window is 1024 pixels wide and 768 pixels tall, which means our aspect ratio is 1024/768, or 1.33.

There are two different ways that we can use this value to modify our arguments: we can decide to keep the Y axis of our frustum in the -1 to +1 range and change the width, or we can leave the width alone and adjust the height. I chose to modify the width in the example code, but either choice is correct. Listing 6-10 shows what calling glm::ortho might look like if we want to take into account our window's aspect ratio.

Listing 6-10. Adjusting Our glm::ortho Arguments for Aspect Ratio

```
glm::mat4 proj = glm::ortho( -1.33f, 1.33f, -1.0f, 1.0f, 0.0f, 10.0f);
```

One thing to keep in mind when setting up an orthographic projection, is that the camera's frustum will be oriented so that it starts at the zNear value on the Z axis, and proceed along the negative z axis zFar units away. This means that our background mesh, which is positioned at 0.5 on the z axis, will be outside of the frustum using the code in Listing 6-9, since the frustum will start at 0.0 on the z axis, and end at -10.0. In order to make everything render correctly, you'll also need to adjust your background mesh's transform matrix to position it at -0.5 on the z axis, rather than 0.5.

Once that's all taken care of, the only thing left to do is to provide it to our shaders and see what our scene looks like once we correct for aspect ratio. Providing it to our shaders is done the same way that we handled the model and view matrices, so we don't really need any example code for that. Instead, let's jump straight to Figure 6-8, which shows our scene rendered with our shiny new projection matrix, and the view matrix set to an identity matrix. If your project looks different from Figure 6-8, all the code for this example is available in the "OrthoMatrix" project in the chapter's example code.

Figure 6-8. *our scene rendered with a projection matrix. Things look rather off, don't they?*

You can see in Figure 6-8 that our scene looks very different when we control for aspect ratio. The biggest change is that you can tell that our background is being rendered on a perfectly square quad, instead of one that is sized to the window. Our character and clouds also look a bit narrower than we might have expected. In fact, the entire scene looks significantly worse than when we didn't have a projection matrix at all! Remember that without a projection matrix, users on differently sized monitors would see our game scene stretched differently, so the projection matrix is at least solving that problem for us, but it does mean we have to do all the work of resizing our objects again if we want things to look like they did before. It's important to make sure that you have a projection matrix set up before you start sizing and positioning meshes in a game scene—otherwise you'll have to do all that work again once your camera is properly set up.

We don't have to worry about redoing our work though, because we're finished with this example program and it's time to move on to new and more exciting things. It's time for us to make the jump to 3D before we run out of pages in the book!

Summary

What we've accomplished is no small feat. With everything that we've covered so far, we could write all the shaders and graphics code needed for a simple 2D game! Here's what we covered in this chapter:

- Game cameras generate view matrices, which are then used in vertex shaders to adjust the position of vertices on screen based on the camera's position and orientation.

- Projection matrices are used to define the shape of our camera's frustum. This allows us to ensure that our content looks the same on differently sized screens.

- An orthographic projection is the type of projection used for most 2D games. With this projection, objects in the distance don't appear farther away. The glm::ortho() command can be used to generate an orthographic projection matrix.

- Writing shaders that use view and projection matrices is as simple as adding a few more matrix multiplications to our position calculations.

CHAPTER 7

Your First 3D Project

Rendering 3D games is a bit of a different animal than the 2D projects we've been doing so far. Unlike sprites drawn on quads, 3D meshes have a lot of information about their shape. 3D games can use this shape information to perform lighting calculations inside shader code, to make these objects appear to be lit in real time by the game world. We're going to see how some of these lighting calculations work in later chapters, but first we need to have a 3D project to work with. This chapter is going to walk through how to set one of those up. We're going to get a mesh loaded into a new project and set up a camera that can properly render 3D content.

This means that it's time to bid our alien friend goodbye and start a brand new openFrameworks project. We've done this a few times already, so this is hopefully starting to feel very routine. Make sure that your main() function is correctly setting the GL version, just like all our previous examples have done. If you go online to the book's website, you'll see that there is a folder of assets for this chapter. Download this folder and put the single file it contains in your new project's bin/data directory. This is the first 3D mesh that we're going to use. Once all that housekeeping is complete, we can dig into what makes a 3D project different from a 2D project.

Loading a Mesh

All our meshes from this point forward are going to be significantly more complex than a quad. Trying to make these new shapes by hand would be incredibly cumbersome, so instead we're going to load their data from mesh files. By default, openFrameworks comes with support for meshes in the "PLY" format. You can see that the assets folder for this chapter contains a single file that ends in ".ply." That's the mesh we're going to use for our first example.

Just like before, we're going to need to create an ofMesh object in ofApp.h to store our mesh data. The example code calls this object "torusMesh." A torus is the fancy

© Kyle Halladay 2019
K. Halladay, *Practical Shader Development*, https://doi.org/10.1007/978-1-4842-4457-9_7

computer graphics term for a donut shape. We'll also need to create an ofShader object in our header file. Our first shader is going to use the UV coordinates of our mesh as color data, so the example code calls it "uvShader." With all those objects created in our header, we can jump to ofApp.cpp and start writing our setup() function. This is going to look like Listing 7-1.

Listing 7-1. Our 3D Project's Setup Function

```
void ofApp::setup(){
    ofDisableArbTex();
    ofEnableDepthTest();

    torusMesh.load("torus.ply"); ❶
    uvShader.load("passthrough.vert", "uv_vis.frag");
}
```

The major difference between this project's setup() function and all our previous examples is how we're creating our mesh. This is the first time that we're loading a mesh from a file instead of making it ourselves. Luckily, openFrameworks makes this easy, with ofMesh's load() function (shown at ❶). Otherwise, this is a lot simpler than what we've been working with up to now.

Next, we need to write the shaders that we'll use to render our newly loaded mesh. The vertex shader that we need to write is going to look very similar to the "passthrough.vert" shader we've written before. However, this time we're going to combine our model, view, and projection matrices into a single uniform variable called "mvp," which is short for "model, view, projection." For optimization reasons, most games will combine those three matrices on the C++ side before sending the data to the GPU for rendering. This saves a lot of time because the matrix multiplication can be done once for the entire mesh, instead of once per vertex that gets processed by the pipeline. Listing 7-2 shows this off.

Listing 7-2. mesh.vert

```
#version 410

layout (location = 0) in vec3 pos;
layout (location = 3) in vec2 uv;
```

```
uniform mat4 mvp;

out vec2 fragUV;

void main()
{
        gl_Position = mvp * vec4(pos, 1.0);
        fragUV = uv;
}
```

The fragment shader that we'll use to visualize our mesh initially is identical to one we wrote way back in the third chapter to output UV coordinates as color values. Since we've written this already, and written many more fragment shaders since then, I'll leave out including the example code here. All the example code for this chapter can be found in the "PerspectiveTorus" project, so feel free to look there if you get stuck.

Finally, we need to write the draw() function that we'll use to see everything. This is going to look a little bit weird until we figure out what kind of projection matrix we want to use, but let's just roll with it and get something on screen. We'll pass an identity matrix to the shader as our "mvp" matrix to make sure everything except our matrix math is working as expected. Listing 7-3 has the initial source code for this draw() function.

Listing 7-3. Our Initial draw() Function

```
void ofApp::draw()
{
        using namespace glm;
        uvShader.begin();
        uvShader.setUniformMatrix4f("mvp", mat4());
        torusMesh.draw();
        uvShader.end();
}
```

Running the project right now should look like figure 7-1. Note that unlike our quad, the UVs for a 3D mesh aren't all uniformly even, so we don't get a nice gradient when outputting UV coordinates as colors. Things look a little weird without a view or projection matrix, but at least we know that our mesh is rendering correctly so that we can work on our matrix math in isolation.

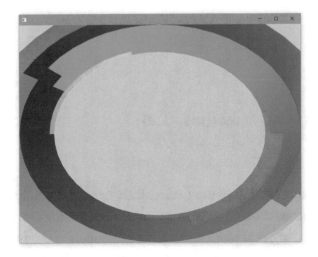

Figure 7-1. *What our 3D project should look like right now*

Making a Perspective Camera

Now that all the setup is complete, it's time to put together a game camera to render our new 3D scene. The obvious first choice is to set things up exactly like we did in the 2D example we just put together. While this would work, it wouldn't look exactly like how you might expect. This is because, as we mentioned before, orthographic projections don't make things in the distance appear smaller. This works with both 2D and 3D content, but it makes 3D meshes appear a bit odd and isn't how most 3D games choose to set things up. Figure 7-2 shows what our project would look like if we used the same orthographic projection that we used in the last chapter.

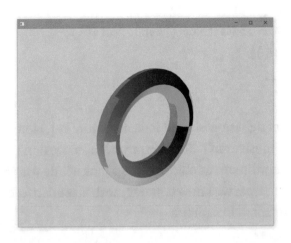

Figure 7-2. *Using an orthographic projection to render our torus*

There's nothing wrong with rendering our mesh like this, but it does make it difficult to judge depth. In the screenshot in Figure 7-2, the torus is rotated so that the left side of the torus is closer to the camera than the right. With an orthographic projection, both sides of the torus are the same width and this depth information isn't visible. For this reason, most 3D games use a *perspective projection* instead of an orthographic one. A good starting point for explaining how a perspective projection is different from what we've seen before is to show what the frustum of a camera looks like when it's set up to use this new type of projection. You can see this in figure 7-3.

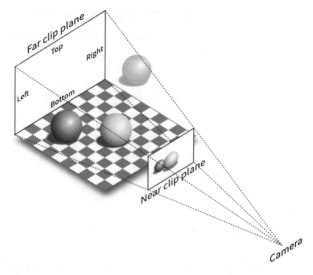

Figure 7-3. *This is what a perspective projection looks like. Figure from Nicolas P. Rougier, ERSF Code camp.*

Notice that the camera frustum is no longer a rectangular prism and is instead a pyramid shape that is clipped by the near and far clip planes. This type of frustum allows objects that are farther away to appear smaller. Put a different way, parallel lines will appear to move toward each other as the line moves away from the camera. This is why perspective projections are the most popular way to set up a game camera when working with meshes that aren't 2D shapes.

Setting up a perspective projection can be done with the glm:perspective() function. The function signature is shown in Listing 7-4. In addition to needing the aspect ratio of our window as an argument, this function has a new argument, called "fov." This stands for "field of view" and refers to the angle between the left and right planes of our camera's pyramid shaped frustum. The wider the field of view, the more of a game's scene is displayed on screen. Choosing the right fov angle for your project is beyond the scope of this book; we're going to use a 90-degree fov for all our examples, which is commonly used for PC games.

Listing 7-4. The Function Signature for glm::perspective

```
mat4 perspective(float fov, float aspect, float zNear, float zFar);
```

To set up our new 3D camera, start by first copying over the CameraData struct from the last chapter. Games sometimes need to support cameras with different fields of view, so we're going to add this value to CameraData for our 3D project. Make sure to also define a CameraData variable in ofApp.h. With that change made, we can modify our draw() function to build a perspective projection matrix based on our camera data. Listing 7-5 shows what that might look like.

Listing 7-5. Building a Perspective Projection in Our draw() Function

```
void ofApp::draw()
{
    using namespace glm;
    cam.pos = vec3(0, 0, 1);
    cam.fov = radians(100.0f);
    float aspect = 1024.0f / 768.0f;

    mat4 model = rotate(1.0f, vec3(1, 1, 1)) * scale(vec3(0.5, 0.5, 0.5));
    mat4 view = inverse(translate(cam.pos));
    mat4 proj = perspective(cam.fov, aspect, 0.01f, 10.0f);

    mat4 mvp = proj * view * model;

    uvShader.begin();
    uvShader.setUniformMatrix4f("mvp", mvp);
    torusMesh.draw();
    uvShader.end();
}
```

Listing 7-5 also includes an example of building the combined mvp matrix from some nonidentity matrices. With the preceding code set up, running the project should look like Figure 7-4. You can see that this new perspective matrix renders the left (closer) side of the torus mesh as much larger than the farther away right side.

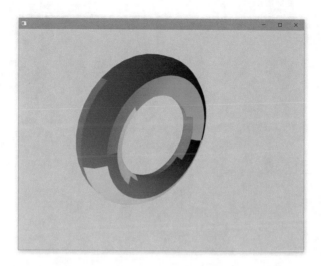

Figure 7-4. *Our 3D program rendering with a perspective projection*

That wraps up this chapter! Although the shader code that was needed to get through the examples was rather light, the underlying theory is essential to understanding the more complicated techniques that we're going to work through in later chapters. If you're stuck with anything in this chapter, or just want to peek at the full source code for our example, you can find it in the "PerspectiveTorus" project of the Chapter 7 example code.

Summary

Here's what we covered in this chapter:

- Complex meshes are usually loaded from a mesh file rather than created by code. openFrameworks supports the "PLT" mesh format by default. You can load a PLY mesh using ofMesh's load() function.

- For optimization reasons, many games combine the model, view, and projection matrices into a single "MVP" matrix that is then passed to vertex shaders.

- The type of projection most commonly used in 3D games is the perspective projection. You can create a perspective projection matrix using the glm::perspective() command.

- Outputting UV coordinates as color data is a common debugging technique. The UVs for a 3D mesh generally aren't a continuous gradient (like we saw on our quads). We walked through an example that rendered the UVs of a torus mesh as color data on our screen.

CHAPTER 8

Diffuse Lighting

In the last chapter we got our torus mesh rendering with perspective, but we still don't have a great way of coloring the surface of it. We can't take the easy way out and slap a texture on it, because we don't have a texture, and the UVs on our new mesh aren't really appealing to look at. Instead, we're going to do what every good shader developer does and throw some (simple) math at it to add some lighting to our mesh.

Our meshes so far have stored position, color, and texture coordinate information for each vertex in the mesh. Lighting calculations rely on a new vertex attribute called a *normal vector*. A "normal" is a vector that points outward from the mesh, perpendicular to the mesh's surface. This provides information about the shape of the face that each fragment belongs to. Just like UV coordinates, normal vectors are interpolated from the vertex shader to the fragment shader, so the normal vector for a single fragment is a combination of the normal vectors of the three vertices that make up that fragment's mesh face. You can see what our mesh's normals look like in Figure 8-1.

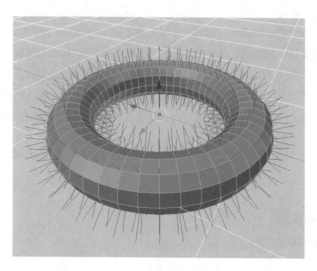

Figure 8-1. *Our torus mesh's normals—the blue lines show the normals of each vertex*

© Kyle Halladay 2019
K. Halladay, *Practical Shader Development*, https://doi.org/10.1007/978-1-4842-4457-9_8

It's sometimes helpful to use a shader to visualize a mesh's normals as color data for debugging purposes. The shader to do this is almost identical to our uv_vis.frag shader, except that we need to grab the normal vector from the vertex we're shading instead of the UV coordinate. This also means that we need a vertex shader that passes normals down the pipeline for any of this to work. Since all our shaders from now on will require use of normal vectors, we can make this change directly to the "mesh.vert" shader our meshes currently use. Listing 8-1 shows how this is done in the example code. The first example project that uses this modified vertex shader is the "NormalTorus" example project for this chapter.

Listing 8-1. Modifying mesh.vert to Pass Normals to the Fragment Shader

```
#version 410

layout (location = 0) in vec3 pos;
layout (location = 2) in vec3 nrm; ❶

uniform mat4 mvp;
out vec3 fragNrm;

void main(){
    gl_Position = mvp * vec4(pos, 1.0);
    fragNrm = nrm;
}
```

Notice that our mesh's normal vectors are stored at attribute location 2 (❶), instead of location 3 like our UV coordinates were. Remember that this order is set arbitrarily by openFrameworks. Different engines and frameworks will order their vertex attributes differently. Once we have our normal vector, writing a fragment shader to visualize it is as simple as outputting UV colors. You can see how it's done in Listing 8-2.

Listing 8-2. Visualizing Normal as Colors in a Fragment Shader – normal_vis.frag

```
#version 410

uniform vec3 lightDir;
uniform vec3 lightCol;

in vec3 fragNrm;
```

```
out vec4 outCol;

void main(){
    vec3 normal = normalize(fragNrm); ❶
    outCol = vec4(normal, 1.0);
}
```

This is the first time that we've seen the normalize function in a shader (❶), so let's take a moment to talk about it. Normalizing a vector is the process of lengthening or shortening a vector until it has a magnitude of 1 while preserving the direction of the vector. It's important to note that this doesn't mean that all the components of a vector are positive numbers, since that would change the direction of the vector. The vector (-1, 0, 0) and (1, 0, 0), both have a magnitude of 1, despite having opposite directions.

Most math that we'll do with normal vectors assumes that those vectors are normalized. The normal vectors on our mesh are already normalized, but the interpolation process that happens when we pass those vectors to the fragment shader isn't guaranteed to preserve vector length. It's very important to always renormalize any vectors that have been interpolated across a face, otherwise any calculations you do that require that a vector is normalized will be off.

If we throw our new shaders onto our torus mesh, your program should look like Figure 8-2. Notice that even with all the vectors normalized, some areas of the mesh are still black. This is telling us that the components of the normal vector for those fragments are all negative values. Since there's no such thing as negative color values, we end up with totally black fragments. If you're following along at home, the code to generate Figure 8-2 can be found in the "NormalTorus" project in the Chapter 8 example code.

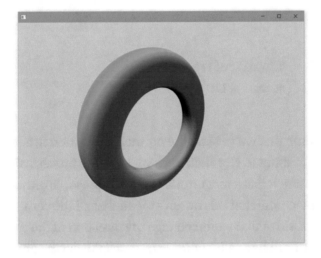

Figure 8-2. *Using mesh.vert and normal_vis.frag to Visualize the Normals on Our Torus Mesh*

Smooth vs. Flat Shading with Normals

The faces of our torus mesh are all uniformly curved surfaces. When the normal vectors for curved surfaces get interpolated, each fragment on a mesh face gets a normal vector that's slightly different from any other fragments on that face. The net result of this is that when we visualize these fragment normals as color data, we end up with the smooth gradient shown in Figure 8-2. This is great for curved surfaces but not ideal for flatter objects. For example, if we approached shading a cube the same way, we might end up with Figure 8-3, which shows both a set of normal vectors for a cube mesh, and how those vectors translate into fragment normals.

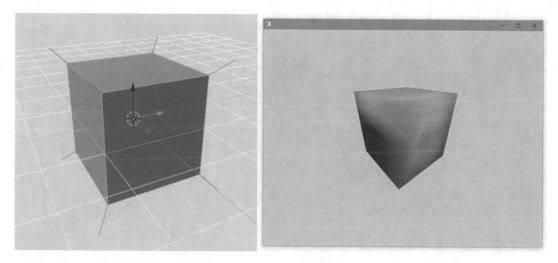

Figure 8-3. *Normals on a cube mesh. The left image shows a cube mesh in a modeling program with normals visible. On the right is the same cube rendered with our normal_vis shader.*

Figure 8-3 looks nice but isn't a great way to shade a cube. The smooth gradient of normal colors on the faces means that when we try to do any light calculations on our cube mesh, the mesh faces will be shaded as though they are curved. What we actually want to do is to give every fragment that belongs to a flat mesh face the same normal vector. Since a vertex can only have a single normal vector, this means that we can't share vertices across multiple faces. Instead, each face of our cube needs its own set of four vertices, with normal vectors pointing in the direction of that specific mesh face. You can see these normal vectors illustrated in Figure 8-4, which also shows off what the resulting fragment normals would look like when rendered by our "normal_vis.frag" shader.

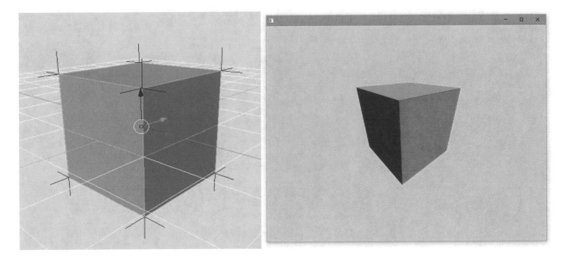

Figure 8-4. *Flat normals on a cube mesh. The left image shows a cube mesh in a modeling program with per-face normals visible. On the right is the same cube rendered with our normal_vis shader.*

In practice, deciding which vertices need to be duplicated to use flat normals and which can use smooth normals is a decision that's usually made by artists. 3D modeling programs provide powerful tools for setting up vertex normals to ensure that an object is shaded exactly how the artist intended. It's only important for us to understand how normals can be used to achieve different looks.

World Space Normals and Swizzling

One thing that you'll commonly want to do is to get the normal vector for a fragment in world space, instead of in object space like we're getting it now. This is going to make our lives much easier later when we're dealing with information about light positions in our scene. If you remember from the last chapter, we can use the model matrix to transform a vector from object space to world space. With this change, our "mesh.vert" shader might look like Listing 8-3.

Listing 8-3. Updating Our Vertex Shader to Pass World Space Normals to the Fragment Shader

```
#version 410

layout (location = 0) in vec3 pos;
layout (location = 2) in vec3 nrm;

uniform mat4 mvp;
uniform mat4 model;

out vec3 fragNrm;

void main(){
    gl_Position = mvp * vec4(pos, 1.0);
    fragNrm = (model * vec4(nrm, 0.0)).xyz; ❶
}
```

You may have noticed a weird bit of syntax in Listing 8-3 (at ❶). After we multiply our normal vector by the model matrix (which gives us a vec4), we're assigning it to our vec3 fragNrm variable with the .xyz operator. Until now, we've always accessed components of a vector one at a time, but vectors in GLSL can also be *swizzled* (yes, that's really what it's called) to select any combination of up to four components. This means that all of the examples in Listing 8-4 are actually valid GLSL.

Listing 8-4. Examples of Swizzling

```
vec2 uv = vec2(1,2);
vec2 a = uv.xy;            //(1,2)
vec2 b = uv.xx;            //(1,1)
vec3 c = uv.xyx;          //(1,2,1)

vec4 color = vec4(1,2,3,4);
vec2 rg = color.rg;        //(1,2)
vec3 allBlue = color.bbb;  //(3,3,3)
vec4 reversed = color.wzyx; //(4,3,2,1)
```

In the case of Listing 8-3, the swizzle operator was necessary because transform matrices need to be multiplied by vec4s, and the result of that multiplication is a vec4.

Our fragNrm variable is only a vec3, so we need to use the swizzle operator to choose which components of our vec4 to store in it.

For virtually any other type of vector, this would be all we needed to do to transform from one coordinate space to another. Normals are a bit of a special case though, and in some cases we need to take a few extra steps to make sure that these vectors are always correct when they get to the fragment shader.

The Normal Matrix

The tricky part of transforming normal vectors to world space occurs when we start using a mesh's model matrix to scale that mesh. If we always keep our mesh's scale uniform (that is, we always scale each dimension of our mesh the same amount), then the math we've already got will work just fine. However, any time we want to use a nonuniform scale, like (0.5, 1, 1) for example, this math starts to break down. This is because we want normals to always point away from our mesh's surface, and if we transform one of their dimensions more than another, we can influence the direction that they point in ways that don't hold up mathematically.

For example, let's say we had a sphere mesh with a model matrix that applied the scale (2.0, 0.5, 1.0) to it. If we also used that model matrix to transform our normal vectors, we would end up with normals that no longer pointed in the correct directions. It's the difference between the center sphere in Figure 8-5, and the one on the right.

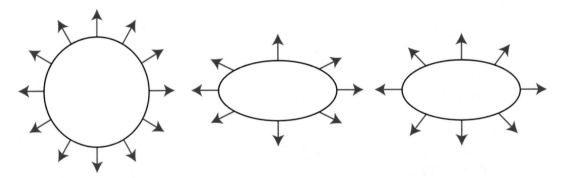

Figure 8-5. *Scaling normals nonuniformly. The center sphere has used the model matrix to transform its normals, while the right sphere has used the normal matrix.*

To deal with this, normals aren't usually transformed by the model matrix. Instead, we use the model matrix to create a new matrix (called the *normal matrix*), which can correctly transform our normal vectors without scaling them in funny ways. Instead of the model matrix, what we need is the "transpose of the inverse of the upper 3×3 of the model matrix." This is a mouthful, but for our purposes it just means a few more math operations in our C++ code. Listing 8-5 shows how we could create this matrix.

Listing 8-5. How to Create the Transpose of the Inverse Modelview Matrix. Add a Line Like This to Your draw() Function, so You Can Pass This Matrix as a Uniform

```
mat3 normalMatrix = (transpose(inverse(mat3(model))));
```

This matrix is a mat3 instead of a mat4 like all our other matrices have been so far. Creating a mat3 from a mat4 means making a 3×3 matrix composed of the top left 3×3 section in the larger matrix. This is a quick way to get a matrix that has no translation information, but keeps all the rotation and scaling data from our model matrix. The rest of the math in Listing 8-5 is simply doing exactly what the definition of the normal matrix tells us to do to create our normal matrix.

Again, all of this is only necessary if your object is scaled nonuniformly. It's not unheard of for engines to only support uniform scaling so that they can avoid having to worry about this. For our examples, however, we're going to use the normal matrix from now on. This way we can be sure that no matter how we set up our scene, we know our normal are correct. With this matrix being passed to our vertex shader, "mesh.vert" is going end up looking like Listing 8-6.

Listing 8-6. mesh.vert Using the Normal Matrix

```
#version 410
layout (location = 0) in vec3 pos;
layout (location = 2) in vec3 nrm;

uniform mat4 mvp;
uniform mat3 normal;

out vec3 fragNrm;

void main(){
    gl_Position = mvp * vec4(pos, 1.0);
    fragNrm = (normal * nrm).xyz;
}
```

Why Lighting Calculations Need Normals

Now that we have a better sense of what normals are and how we can access them in a shader, it's time to figure out how to use them to add some lighting to our mesh. Normals are essential to lighting calculations because they allow us to figure out the relationship between the direction of light that's hitting our mesh's surface and the orientation of that surface itself. We can think of every fragment on a mesh as being a tiny, completely flat point, regardless of the overall shape of the mesh. Using this mental model, light hitting a fragment can be thought about like Figure 8-6.

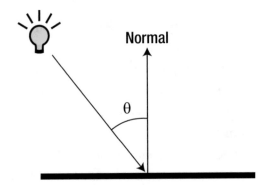

Figure 8-6. *Light hitting a fragment*

The more perpendicular our fragment is to the incoming light, the more light will hit that spot on the mesh, causing it to be brighter. Put more specifically, as the angle between our normal vector and the incoming light vector approaches 180 degrees, the amount of light that hits that specific point of our mesh increases. You can see the angle between the incoming light vector and our normal in Figure 8-6, labeled with the symbol theta (Θ). To calculate what theta is, we can use a specific bit of vector math called a *dot product*, which is a very handy piece of math that's used all over video game code.

What's a Dot Product?

A dot product is a math operation that takes two vectors and returns a single number that represents a relationship between the two vectors. Dot products themselves are very simple. They involve multiplying together the components of each vector (so the X component of vector A gets multiplied by the X component of vector B), and then adding up all the results. You can perform a dot product on vectors of any size, as long as both vectors have the same number of components. Listing 8-7 shows what this might look like in code.

Listing 8-7. A Simple Implementation of a Dot Product

```
float dot(vec3 a, vec3 b){
      float x = a.x * b.x;
      float y = a.y * b.y;
      float z = a.z * b.z;
      return x + y + z;
}
```

The value of a dot product can tell you a lot about the two vectors that were used to create it. Even whether that value is positive or negative can give us valuable information:

1. If the dot product is 0, it means that the two vectors are perpendicular to one another.

2. A positive dot product means that the angle between the two vectors is less than 90 degrees.

3. A negative dot product means that the angle between the two vectors is greater than 90 degrees.

Dot products can also be used to find the exact angle between the two vectors. This is done all the time in game code and only takes a few lines of code to do. You can see these few lines in Listing 8-8. Our lighting calculations won't be converting dot product values into actual angles. However, knowing how to get degrees from dot product values is a handy technique that's worth taking a minute to learn.

Listing 8-8. Using Dot Product to Find the Angle Between Two Vectors. The Returned Value Will Be in Radians

```
float angleBetween(vec3 a, vec3 b){
      float d = dot(a,b);
      float len = length(a) * length(b);   ❶
      float cosAngle = d / len;    ❷
```

```
        float angle = acos(cosAngle);
        return angle;
}
```

As you can see in Listing 8-8, once you divide the dot product of two vectors by the product of their two vector lengths (also called magnitudes), you end up with the cosine of the angle between the two of them. In shader code, our vectors are usually going to already be normalized, which means that the both their lengths are already 1. This means that we can omit lines ❶ and ❷ and still end up with the cosine of the angle between them, which is the value we'll need for our lighting calculations.

Shading with Dot Products

The first type of lighting that we're going to build is known as *diffuse*—or Lambertian— lighting. This is the type of lighting that you expect to see on nonshiny objects, like a dry, unpolished piece of wood. Diffuse lighting simulates what happens when light hits the surfaces of a rough object. This means that rather than reflecting light in a certain direction (like a mirror would), light hitting our object will scatter in all directions, and give our object a matte appearance. Figure 8-7 shows some examples of meshes being shaded with diffuse lighting.

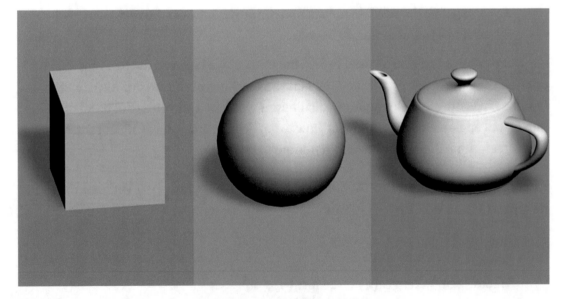

Figure 8-7. *Three meshes rendered with diffuse lighting*

Diffuse lighting works by comparing the normal for a given fragment with the direction that light is coming from. The smaller an angle there is between these two vectors, the more perpendicular we know the mesh surface is at that point. Dot products approach 1 as the angle between two vectors goes to zero, so we can use the dot product of the normal and light direction vector to determine how much light we need to use to shade each fragment. In shader code, this might look like Listing 8-9, which can be found in the "DiffuseLighting" example project and is called "diffuse.frag."

Listing 8-9. diffuse.frag - Diffuse Lighting in Shader Code

```
#version 410

uniform vec3 lightDir;
uniform vec3 lightCol;
uniform vec3 meshCol;

in vec3 fragNrm;
out vec4 outCol;

void main(){
    vec3 normal = normalize(fragNrm);
    float lightAmt = dot(normal, lightDir); ❶
    vec3 fragLight = lightCol * lightAmt;

    outCol = vec4(meshCol * fragLight, 1.0); ❷
}
```

After all that build up, the shader for diffuse lighting hopefully seems very straightforward. The only new bit of syntax is the dot() function at ❶, which is, as you might have guessed, how to calculate a dot product in GLSL. Once we have the dot product, we can use it to determine how much light our fragment will get by multiplying the incoming light's color by the dot product value. If our dot product is 1, this means that our fragment will receive the full intensity of the light, while any fragment with a normal pointing greater than 90 degrees away from the light will receive none. Multiplying the color of the fragment itself by our dot product/light color vector will give us the final color of that fragment. This final multiplication is shown at ❷.

You may have noticed that the math in Listing 8-9 is actually backward. The normal vector for our fragment points away from the mesh surface, while the incoming light vector points toward it. This would usually mean that the preceding calculations make the areas that face the incoming light darker, except that we're going to cheat a bit and store our light's direction backward in C++ code. This saves us having to multiply in our shader code to invert the light direction and makes all the math work out how we intend. If this is a bit confusing, look back at Figure 8-6, and see that the two vectors in the diagram are pointing different directions, and then compare it to Figure 8-8, which shows this light direction vector reversed.

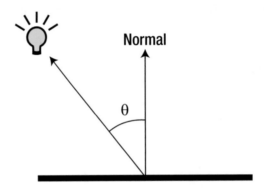

Figure 8-8. *How light data is sent to shader code. Notice that the light direction has been reversed, and is now pointing toward the light source.*

One other oddity in the math we have so far is that if we get a negative dot product value, we end up with a negative color for our light when we multiply those two values together. This doesn't matter to us right now because there's only one source of light in our scene. However, in scenes with multiple lights, this could end up with us making parts of our mesh darker than they need to be. To fix this, all we need to do is wrap our dot product in a max() call to make sure that the smallest possible value we can get is 0. With that change, line ❶ looks like Listing 8-10.

Listing 8-10. Using max() to Make Sure We Don't End Up with Negative Brightness

```
float lightAmt = max(0.0, dot(normal, lightDir)); ❶
```

Your First Directional Light

This is the first time that any shader we've written has worked with light information. To make things simpler, this shader has been written to work with a very specific type of light, which games commonly refer to as a *directional light*. Directional lights are used to represent light sources that are very far away (like the sun) and work by casting light uniformly in a single direction. This means that no matter where in our scene a mesh is positioned, it will receive the same amount of light, coming from the same direction, as every other object in the scene.

Setting up a directional light in C++ code is very simple, since we can represent all the data we need about that light in a few variables. Listing 8-11 shows a struct containing data for a directional light's color, direction, and intensity.

Listing 8-11. The Data Needed to Represent a Directional Light

```
struct DirectionalLight{
    glm::vec3 direction;
    glm::vec3 color;
    float intensity;
};
```

Our shader didn't have a separate uniform for light intensity, but the struct for our light does. Games commonly multiply the color of a light by its brightness before passing that data to the graphics pipeline. This is done for optimization reasons. It's much cheaper to do that math once, before any shader executes, than it is to do that math for every fragment that you need to shade. For the same reason, we're going to normalize the direction of our light in C++ code too. Listing 8-12 shows a few helper functions that we're going to use to make sure the data we send to our shader uses these optimizations.

Listing 8-12. Some Light Data Helper Functions

```
glm::vec3 getLightDirection(DirectionalLight& l){
    return glm::normalize(l.direction * -1.0f);
}

glm::vec3 getLightColor(DirectionalLight& l){
    return l.color * l.intensity;
}
```

In getLightColor(), we aren't clamping our light color to the standard 0–1 range that color data would usually be stored in. This is because the light color that we pass to our shader is pre-multiplied by that light's brightness, and therefore needs to be able to exceed the standard range of a color for lights with brightness greater than 1.0. We still can't write a value greater than (1.0, 1.0, 1.0, 1.0) to a fragment, so no matter how bright we set our light to, we still can only go as bright as white on our screen.

With these functions ready to go, we're ready to set up our light and use it in our draw function. Normally we'd want to set up the light in our setup() function, but for the purposes of a smaller amount of example code, Listing 8-13 is going to put the light setup logic into the draw() function. We're also going to adjust our model matrix so that our mesh faces upward. This is going to give us a better angle to see the lighting on our mesh.

Listing 8-13. Setting Up and Using Our New Light Data

```
void ofApp::draw(){
     using namespace glm;
     DirectionalLight dirLight;

     dirLight.direction = normalize(vec3(0, -1, 0));
     dirLight.color = vec3(1, 1, 1);
     dirLight.intensity = 1.0f;

     //code to set up mvp matrix omitted for brevity

     diffuseShader.begin();
     diffuseShader.setUniformMatrix4f("mvp", mvp);
     diffuseShader.setUniform3f("meshCol", glm::vec3(1, 0, 0));  ❶
     diffuseShader.setUniform3f("lightDir", getLightDirection(dirLight));
     diffuseShader.setUniform3f("lightCol", getLightColor(dirLight));
     torusMesh.draw();
     diffuseShader.end();
}
```

The other new thing, both in our shader from earlier and Listing 8-8, is that we're specifying a mesh color as one of our shader uniforms (❶). This lets us set a solid color for our mesh and gives you a value play with to get a feel for how different light colors interact with mesh surface colors. Passing in red to our mesh color and white to the light color uniforms will look like the left screenshot in Figure 8-9. You'll notice that the angle that we were originally viewing our torus from made it difficult to see what was going on with our lighting. To remedy that, I changed the example code's draw function to rotate our mesh so it was facing upward, and then positioned the camera so it was overhead, looking down. The code changes for this are shown in Listing 8-14, and the result is the right screenshot in Figure 8-9. The code to generate this screenshot can be found in the "DiffuseTorus" project of the Chapter 8 example code.

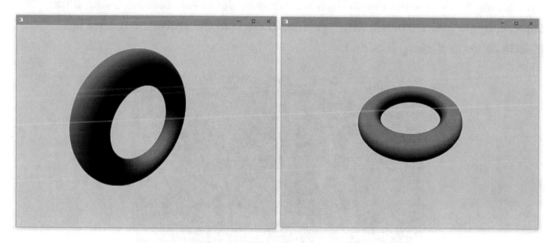

Figure 8-9. *Diffuse lighting on our torus mesh*

Listing 8-14. Code Changes to Get a Better Angle to See Lighting

```
void ofApp::draw(){
    //only the changed lines of code are shown, for brevity
    cam.pos = vec3(0, 0.75f, 1.0f);
    float cAngle = radians(-45.0f);
    vec3 right = vec3(1, 0, 0);
    mat4 view = inverse( translate(cam.pos) * rotate(cAngle, right) );
    mat4 model = rotate(radians(90.0f), right) * scale(vec3(0.5, 0.5, 0.5));

    //rest of function continues unchanged
}
```

Lighting in shaders is a big topic, and we're going to spend the next few chapters talking about all of it. However, before we end this chapter, I want to walk through one more simple lighting effect that can be built with just the math we've covered so far.

Creating a Rim Light Effect

One lighting technique commonly employed in games is known as *rim light*. This technique adds light (or color) around the edges of a mesh's shape, making them appear as though they are being back lit by a light that is invisible to the player. Figure 8-10 shows what our torus mesh would look like if we rendered it with only rim lighting applied to the mesh. To make things easier to see, I set the background color of my program to black, which you can do in your own program using the ofSetBackgroundColor() function.

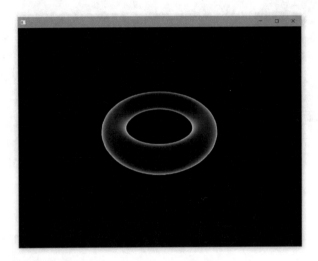

Figure 8-10. *Rendering our torus with rim light*

Rim light works very similarly to how our directional light did in the last section. The only real difference is that instead of using the light's direction vector in our calculations, we'll be using a vector that goes from each fragment to the camera. The result of this dot product will be how much extra light we need to add to each fragment in order to get a rim light. Listing 8-15 shows what a rim light only shader would look like. This is the shader used to render Figure 8-10.

Listing 8-15. A Rim Light Only Shader

```
#version 410

uniform vec3 meshCol;
uniform vec3 cameraPos; ❶
```

```
in vec3 fragNrm;
in vec3 fragWorldPos; ❷
out vec4 outCol;

void main()
{
        vec3 normal = normalize(fragNrm);
        vec3 toCam = normalize(cameraPos - fragWorldPos); ❸

        float rimAmt = 1.0-max(0.0,dot(normal, toCam)); ❹
        rimAmt = pow(rimAmt, 2); ❺

        vec3 rimLightCol = vec3(1,1,1);

        outCol = vec4(rimLightCol * rimAmt, 1.0);
}
```

The first differences between this shader and the directional light shader we wrote earlier in the chapter are the new variables that we need to make the rim light effect work. First, we need the position of the camera in world space (❶). Since we'll be calculating the vector from each individual fragment to the camera, we can't pass a single direction vector from C++ code. Instead, we pass the camera position so we can calculate this vector in our shader code. Additionally, we need the world position of our fragment. To calculate this, we need our vertex shader to calculate world space vertex positions, which we can then interpolate to get fragment positions. In Listing 8-15, this data comes from the vertex shader and is read into the fragWorldPos variable (❷). We'll discuss the changes we need to make to the vertex shader in a moment, but let's keep walking through the fragment shader first.

The rim light calculations start in earnest at ❸. As mentioned, this involves calculating the vector from the current fragment to the camera, and then using those vectors to calculate a dot product (❹). Notice that we then subtract this value from 1.0 before writing it to our rimAmt variable. Since our dot product value is being clamped to the range 0-1, this has the effect of inverting the dot product that we calculate. If you don't do this, you end up with an effect that lights the center of the mesh instead of the rim. You can see what this looks like in Figure 8-11.

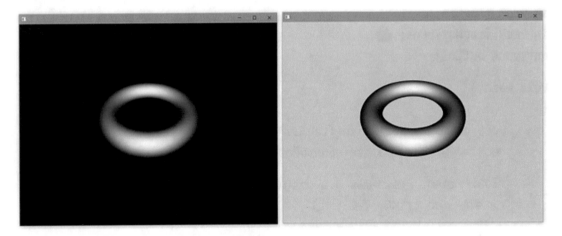

Figure 8-11. *What rim light looks like if you forget to invert your dot product value. If your background is black, like the left image, this gives your meshes a ghostly look.*

After we invert the dot product value, there's one last bit of math that we need to do in order to get our final rimAmt value. In order to control how "tight" the rim is on an object, we can raise our rimAmt value to a power (**❺**). This is the first time we've seen the pow() function used in GLSL, but it's the same as the pow function that you're probably used to in C++. All it does is return the first argument, raised to the power specified by the second argument. If you're confused as to why this will concentrate our rim effect, think about what happens when you raise a value that's less than 1 to a power. Values closer to 1 will stay relatively close to 1—for example, 0.95 raised to the 4th power is 0.81. However, as values get smaller, this operation is going to have a greater impact—0.25 to the 4th power is 0.004, for example. Figure 8-12 shows examples of what our rim effect looks like with different powers used for our rim calculation.

Figure 8-12. *What our rim shader looks like if we raise our rimAmt variable to different powers. From left to right, these screenshots show the result of not using a pow() at all, raising to the 2nd power, and raising to the 4th power.*

That wraps up all the new stuff in our fragment shader, but remember that we also need to modify our vertex shader to pass world space position information for our rim calculations. Listing 8-16 shows what the vertex shader looks like to support the rim light effect we just walked through.

Listing 8-16. The Vertex Shader That Supports rimlight.frag

```
#version 410
layout (location = 0) in vec3 pos;
layout (location = 2) in vec3 nrm;

uniform mat4 mvp;
uniform mat3 normal;
uniform mat4 model;

out vec3 fragNrm;
out vec3 fragWorldPos;

void main(){
    gl_Position = mvp * vec4(pos, 1.0);
    fragNrm = (normal * nrm).xyz;
    fragWorldPos = (model * vec4(pos, 1.0)).xyz; ❶
}
```

Just as we talked about earlier, in order to get the world space position of an individual fragment, the vertex shader needs to output world space positions of each vertex. These vertex positions are interpolated just like our other "out" variables, and the result of this interpolation is that we wind up with a perfragment position vector. Transforming vertex positions to world space is done by multiplying them by the model matrix for our mesh (❶). This also means that our C++ code will need to provide both the mvp matrix and the model matrix to our vertex shader.

Now that we've walked through what a rim light only shader looks like, it's time for us to combine our rim light effect with the directional lighting math we wrote earlier. We're going to use our existing directional light shader in the next chapter and don't want it to have rim light in it when we do, so create a new fragment shader in your example project and copy Listing 8-17 into it. Chapter 9 will use fragment world position calculations, so it's safe to add that to "mesh.vert."

Listing 8-17. Adding Rim Light to Our Directional Light Shader

```
#version 410

uniform vec3 lightDir;
uniform vec3 lightCol;
uniform vec3 meshCol;
uniform vec3 cameraPos;

in vec3 fragNrm;
in vec3 fragWorldPos;
out vec4 outCol;

void main()
{
    vec3 normal = normalize(fragNrm);

    vec3 toCam = normalize(cameraPos - fragWorldPos);
    float rimAmt = 1.0-max(0.0,dot(normal, toCam));
    rimAmt = pow(rimAmt, 2);

    float lightAmt = max(0.0,dot(normal, lightDir));
    vec3 fragLight = lightCol * lightAmt;

    outCol = vec4(meshCol * fragLight + rimAmt, 1.0); ❶
}
```

For the most part, this is just copying and pasting parts of our rim light shader into our existing directional light one. The only real thing to note is how to incorporate the rim light value with the rest of the fragment's color. Since we want the rim light to add on to the existing lighting of our mesh, we need to add the rim light's contribution to our fragment's color after all the other lighting has been done. You can see this at line ❶. In this example, we're adding a pure white rim light to our mesh, but many games will choose to use different colors instead.

After you've made these changes to our shader and modified your draw() function to pass the new uniform data we need about our camera position, your program should look like Figure 8-13. The code for this can be found in the "RimLight" project in the example code for this chapter if you're stuck.

Figure 8-13. *Our torus mesh rendered with a white rim light*

While it looks cool, the lighting calculations that are most commonly used by games don't include rim light by default. This is because rim light isn't based on how light works, it's a purely artistic effect. The next few chapters are concerned with how to model real-world lighting effects in our shader code, so we won't be using rim light again. This doesn't mean that you shouldn't use rim light in your projects. Rather, think of it as a technique to add to your shaders after all the other lighting for that object has been correctly set up, to add some unrealistic visual flair to your rendering.

Summary

That wraps up our first chapter about lighting! Here's a quick rundown of what we covered:

- Normal vectors are vectors that point outward from the surface of a mesh. These are stored on each vertex of a mesh to help provide information about the shape of each mesh face.

- If your game supports nonuniform scaling, normal vectors need a special matrix (called the normal matrix) to transform them from object to world space.

- A dot product is a scalar value that represents a relationship between two vectors. Calculating a dot product can be done with the GLSL dot() function.

- Diffuse lighting is the name for the type of lighting found on nonshiny surfaces. The amount of diffuse light a fragment receives is equivalent to the dot product between that fragment's normal vector and the incoming light's direction vector.

- Rim Light is the name of a shading technique that makes a mesh appear as though it's being lit from behind. It can be calculated by taking the dot product of a fragment's normal vector and a vector from that fragment to the game camera.

CHAPTER 9

Your First Lighting Model

Diffuse lighting is great for rendering matte (nonshiny) objects, but we need a few more tools in our toolbox if we want to be able to properly render all the objects that a game might have. For example, plastics, metals, mirrors, and wet surfaces are all impossible to render well with just diffuse lighting. Instead, we need to learn some new lighting math to handle shininess. Almost nothing is entirely shiny, or entirely matte, so we'll have to combine our diffuse lighting calculations with these new ones in order to be able to render everything well.

Games commonly combine several different bits of lighting math to create a single equation that they can use to calculate the lighting on every object in their game. This unified equation is commonly known as a *lighting model.* In this chapter we're going to combine three different types of lighting calculations. We've already looked at the first of these three: diffuse lighting. We'll cover the new two, specular and ambient lighting, and talk about how to combine them with our existing shaders. The result of this combination is going to be the Blinn-Phong lighting model, which is one of the most common lighting models to find in games. By the end of the chapter, we'll be able to render a whole range of different objects.

Specular Lighting

We walked through diffuse lighting in the last chapter, so we're going to start this chapter off with a look at *specular lighting.* This is the type of lighting we'll use to render those shiny materials we were just talking about. Specular lighting is what happens when light interacts with a smooth surface. Remember that diffuse light, which models a rough surface, simulates the appearance of light hitting an object and scattering in all directions. With a smoother surface, light that hits the surface of an object will be

© Kyle Halladay 2019
K. Halladay, *Practical Shader Development*, https://doi.org/10.1007/978-1-4842-4457-9_9

reflected away at a specific angle, known as the *angle of reflection*. The smoother the surface of the mesh, the more light gets reflected like this and the less light gets scattered in random directions. This results in a shiny appearance. Figure 9-1 shows off what specular lighting looks like on three example meshes.

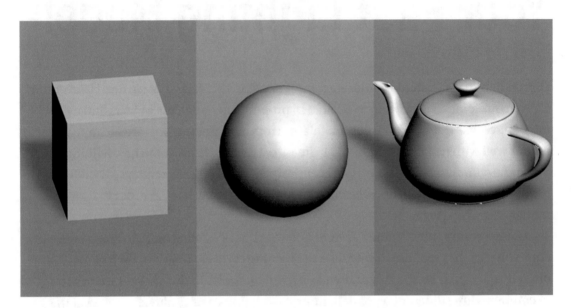

***Figure 9-1.** Specular lighting on three different example meshes*

Notice that the cube on the left doesn't appear any different from a diffusely lit cube. This is because no light is hitting the cube at the right angle to be reflected into the game camera, so we don't see any of the specular lighting on that mesh.

If you happen to be looking at a specular object from the direction that light is being reflected off it, you end up seeing a very bright *specular highlight,* which goes away as your viewing angle gets less parallel to that direction. This is different from diffuse lighting, which was completely independent of the viewing angle. You can see the specular highlight on the center and rightmost spheres in Figure 9-2; it's the bright white "hot spot" on the top right of the mesh. The center sphere in this figure is being lit only by specular light. You'll notice that it looks a bit odd compared with the other two examples. This is because—other than mirrors—almost every kind of object gets at least some diffuse light, and very smooth objects like mirrors don't look right without us also rendering reflections (which we'll do in a later chapter). So once we have our specular shader working, we're going to have to combine it with the diffuse shader we wrote in the last chapter.

Figure 9-2. *The left sphere is lit only with diffuse light, the center sphere is just lit with specular light, and the right sphere combines both types of lighting*

It's worth it to mention that in some more modern lighting models, metals are also treated differently with regard to diffuse lighting. However, the Blinn-Phong lighting model that we're building here treats metallic and nonmetallic surfaces the same.

Your First Specular Shader

To start off, let's create a brand new fragment shader to work with, and call it "specular. frag." We're going to have to modify our vertex shader as well, but it will be easier to do that once we know what information our fragment shader needs. The math for specular lighting is a bit more complicated than for diffuse lighting, but at its heart is still mostly about getting a dot product between two direction vectors. The hard part is getting these direction vectors in the first place.

The first direction vector we need is the direction at which a perfectly reflected ray of light would bounce off our fragment. We can calculate this from the normal vector of our fragment and the normalized light direction vector, and GLSL has a handy reflect() function that will do the math for us. Using it is going to look like Listing 9-1.

Listing 9-1. Using GLSL's reflect() Function

```
vec3 refl = reflect(-lightDir,normalVec);
```

It's important that you specify the arguments in the correct order. The first vector that gets passed in is the incoming light vector, and the second argument is the normal vector for the current fragment. Just like many of GLSL's functions, the reflect function can be used with vectors of any dimensionality, as long as both arguments are the same. Also notice that we're using the reverse of the light direction vector. This is because the reflect() function expects the vector that is being reflected to be pointing toward the mesh surface, and we have been manually flipping the light direction to point from our surface to the light in order to make our diffuse lighting math simpler. Now that we aren't just writing a diffuse light shader, we could modify our C++ code to not flip the light direction vector, but the examples have left it as is to maintain compatibility with shaders we've written previously.

Once we have our reflection vector, the second vector we need is the direction vector that points from our fragment's position to the camera position. We calculated this in the last chapter when we built our rim light effect, and we're going to do the exact same bit of math here. Just like before, our vertex shader is going to output the fragWorldPos data for us, and we'll pass the camera position from C++ code to the "camPos" uniform. Once this data is available to our fragment shader, calculating the vector between the camera and our fragment looks like Listing 9-2.

Listing 9-2. Calculating the toCam Vector

```
vec3 toCam = normalize(camPos - fragWorldPos);
```

With these two vectors in hand, the next step is to calculate the dot product between them. We can raise this dot product value to a power to control the appearance of the specular highlight. The higher the exponent, the smoother our surface is, and the tighter the specular highlight will be. Figure 9-3 shows what a shiny sphere would look like using a few different shininess powers.

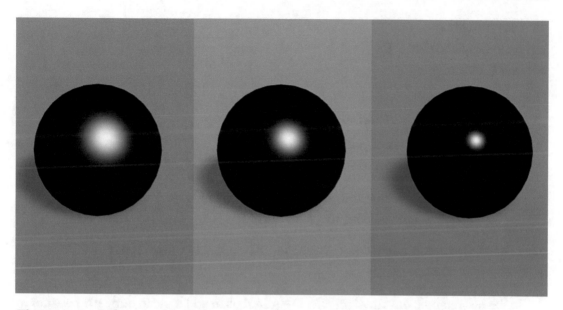

Figure 9-3. *Spheres with differently sized hotspots, achieved by raising the dot product of our toCam and reflection vectors to the 4th, 16th, and 32nd powers (from left to right)*

The exponent that we raise the dot product to is commonly referred to as the "shininess" value. Listing 9-3 shows how this last bit of math will look in shader code.

Listing 9-3. Calculating Specular Light Brightness

```
float specAmt = max(0.0, dot(refl, viewDir));
float specBrightness = pow(specAmt, 16.0); ❶
```

Finally, we can multiply this specBrightness against the color of our light (since it would make no sense for a red light to produce a white specular highlight) and the specular color of our mesh. This will give us the final color of our highlight. Put together, a specular only fragment shader might look like Listing 9-4.

Listing 9-4. specular.frag, A Specular Only Fragment Shader

```
#version 410

uniform vec3 lightDir;
uniform vec3 lightCol;
uniform vec3 meshCol;
uniform vec3 meshSpecCol;
uniform vec3 cameraPos;
```

```
in vec3 fragNrm;
in vec3 fragWorldPos; ❶
out vec4 outCol;

void main(){
    vec3 nrm = normalize(fragNrm);
    vec3 refl = reflect(-lightDir,nrm);
    vec3 viewDir = normalize( cameraPos - fragWorldPos);

    float specAmt = max(0.0, dot(refl, viewDir));
    float specBright = pow(specAmt, 16.0);

    outCol = vec4(lightCol * meshSpecCol * specBright, 1.0);
}
```

In the last chapter, our rim light effect required us to add logic to our vertex shader to calculate and output the fragWorldPos vector for us. If you haven't yet made that change to "mesh.vert," you'll need to make it now for our specular shader to work correctly. Since we covered how to do this in the last chapter, I'm going to omit providing the vertex shader source here. Flip back a few pages if you need to refresh your memory.

Once you have that set up you should be able to run the program and see something like Figure 9-4. If you hit any snags, the source code used to generate this figure is in the "SpecularTorus" project in this chapter's example code.

Figure 9-4. *Our torus mesh with a specular shader*

Combining Diffuse and Specular Light

Adding diffuse lighting to our specular shader is simple. All we need to do is add the diffuse calculations from our earlier shader to our specular fragment shader. Listing 9-5 shows how specular.frag's main function will look with diffuse calculations added back in.

Listing 9-5. specular.frag with Diffuse Lighting Added In

```
void main(){
    vec3 nrm = normalize(fragNrm);
    vec3 refl = reflect(-lightDir,nrm);
    vec3 viewDir = normalize( cameraPos - fragWorldPos);

    float diffAmt = max(0.0, dot(nrm, lightDir));
    vec3 diffCol = meshCol * lightCol * diffAmt;

    float specAmt = max(0.0, dot(refl, viewDir));
    float specBright = pow(specAmt, 16.0);
    vec3 specCol = meshSpecCol * lightCol * specBright;

    outCol = vec4(diffCol + specCol, 1.0);
}
```

If you render the preceding code, you'll see a delightfully shiny, red, torus mesh. Figure 9-5 shows what this should look like.

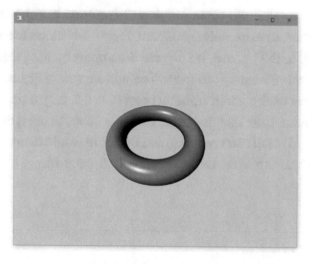

Figure 9-5. *Our torus rendered with diffuse and specular lighting*

Ambient Lighting

In the real world, a light doesn't have to be directly shining on an object for it to be illuminated. This is because light bounces off objects, onto other objects, which in turn reflect light onto other objects. In graphics, this is referred to as *global illumination*, and game developers are constantly inventing new ways to more accurately model lighting caused by these kinds of object to object light bounces.

The last type of lighting that we're going to implement is the simplest possible approximation of global illumination and is known as *ambient lighting*. Ambient lighting works by simply adding a color to every fragment in a mesh. This keeps any fragment from being completely black and is meant to represent light bouncing around the environment. This is extremely simple to add to our combined light shader. All we need to do is add a uniform for the ambient color of the scene, multiply that color by our mesh's surface color, and change the last line of our shader's main() function to use that value. Listing 9-6 shows the change that we'll need. The key thing to keep in mind is that no matter what color the lights are in a scene, a red object will only ever reflect red light. Thus, we need to multiply our ambient light color by the color of our fragment in order to make sure we're not adding colors that shouldn't be there.

Listing 9-6. Combining Diffuse, Specular, and Ambient Light

```
vec3 ambient = ambientCol * meshCol;
outCol = vec4(diffCol + specCol + ambient, 1.0);
```

Depending on the value we set our ambientCol uniform to, the impact of this light type can be very subtle, or extremely significant. Figure 9-6 shows two different use cases for ambient lighting. In the top row, we can see the impact of using a grey ambient color (0.5, 0.5, 0.5) to really brighten up our torus. The bottom row of Figure 9-6 shows what it might look like if we used a green ambient color (0.0, 0.3, 0.0) to simulate the lighting in a green environment. Note that the green example needs to use a different colored torus, since a pure red mesh can't reflect green light and would be unaffected by a green ambient color. The blue torus has a mesh color of (0.0, 0.5, 1.0).

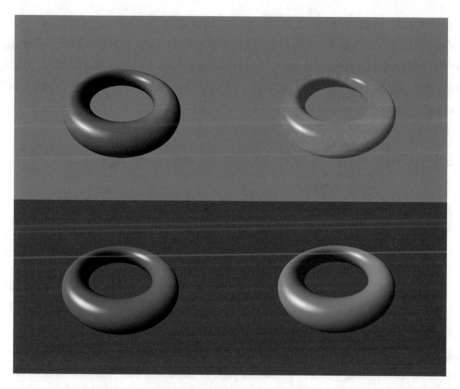

Figure 9-6. *Using ambient lighting. The left column shows our mesh with no ambient lighting. Meshes in the right column have an ambient color that matches the background color.*

If you want to look at the full source code for rendering a torus mesh using diffuse, specular, and ambient lighting, you can find it in the "PhongTorus" example project. The name "Phong" refers to the lighting model that we just implemented, which you're about to read a lot more about.

The Phong Lighting Model

We've now implemented three different types of lighting, but we haven't talked at all about where the math for them came from. As mentioned in the intro to this chapter, a collection of lighting calculations used together is commonly called a lighting model. The three bits of lighting math we're using right now (diffuse, specular and ambient) combine to form the Phong lighting model, which is one of the most common lighting models found in games.

If you look up Phong lighting online, you'll probably end up staring at a complicated mess of math that looks something like Figure 9-7. Don't worry if this looks alien to you, the math notation makes it seem much scarier than it is. We've actually already implemented all the complicated parts, so let's unpack what this equation is actually trying to say.

$$I_\mathrm{p} = k_\mathrm{a} i_\mathrm{a} + \sum_{m \,\in\, \text{lights}} (k_\mathrm{d}(\hat{L}_m \cdot \hat{N}) i_{m,\mathrm{d}} + k_\mathrm{s}(\hat{R}_m \cdot \hat{V})^\alpha i_{m,\mathrm{s}}).$$

Figure 9-7. The Phong lighting model in math notation

The equation in Figure 9-7 is the mathy way of describing how Phong shading calculates the illumination at a point on our mesh. This illumination value is called I_p and can be found on the left side of the equals sign in the Phong equation. The right side of the equals sign tells us what our shader needs to do to calculate it. As we know, Phong lighting is made up of a combination of ambient, diffuse, and specular lighting. As per the equation, these three values are scaled by constant values that control how much of each of these types of lighting a fragment receives. These constants are called K_a, K_d, and K_s, which are all vec3s that describe the colors of each of these three lighting types for the point on our mesh. In our shader, K_a and K_d have been defined as the mesh color, and K_s has been represented by the "meshSpecCol" uniform. We'll talk about alternate values these constants could have in a moment

According to the Phong equation, the lights in the scene also define their own constants that say how much of each light type they emit. These are the i_a, i_d, and i_s terms in the preceding equation. In practice, most games simply have light sources emit a single color value and use that color for both the i_d and i_s terms. The i_a term is defined separately for the entire game scene.

With these constants defined, the rest of the equation tells us how to use them. We just implemented all this math in our shader code, but it's a bit harder to read in equation form. Figure 9-8 breaks down the right side of the equation into sections to make things easier to talk about.

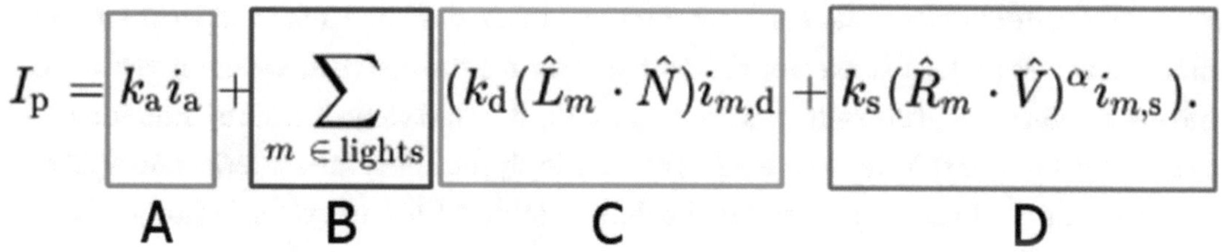

$$I_{\mathrm{p}} = \boxed{k_{\mathrm{a}} i_{\mathrm{a}}} + \boxed{\sum_{m \,\in\, \text{lights}}} \boxed{(k_{\mathrm{d}}(\hat{L}_m \cdot \hat{N}) i_{m,\mathrm{d}}} + \boxed{k_{\mathrm{s}}(\hat{R}_m \cdot \hat{V})^{\alpha} i_{m,\mathrm{s}})}.$$

A   B   C   D

Figure 9-8. *Isolating parts of the Phong lighting equation*

The "A" section of the equation is the math we used for ambient lighting. You'll notice that the full Phong equation specifies that a material can define its own color for ambient lighting (k_a), but it's common to assume that every fragment's k_a is the color of the mesh surface at that point. As already mentioned, the i_a term is usually defined for an entire game scene at once, rather than being set by a particular light. Regardless of how you want to handle these terms, however, once you know their values, you simply multiply them together and then add them to the rest of the lighting, just like we did earlier in our shader.

After the ambient lighting, we come to the meat of the lighting equation: handling diffuse and specular light for all the lights in the scene. The bit of notation marked as "B" simply means that we're going to perform the diffuse and specular calculations for each light that contributes to the lighting of our current mesh point and add them all together. We'll talk more about working with multiple lights a bit later in the book. For now, it's enough to know that when we get there, all we're going to do is add the lighting calculations for each light hitting our fragment together.

Immediately next to this is the "C" section, which is the math for diffuse lighting. We already know that the k_d term is the diffuse color for the point on the mesh we're lighting, and that the i_d term is the color of the incoming light. Inside the parentheses we can see two other values, L_m and N. Since we've already written diffuse shaders, it should come as no surprise that these are the light direction vector and the mesh normal. With all the terms defined, the C section of the equation simply says to multiply the mesh color and the light color with the dot product of these two vectors to get diffuse lighting, just like we did earlier.

Finally, we come to the specular lighting math (the "D" section). We know that k_s is the specular color for point on our mesh that we're currently lighting, and i_s is the color of incoming specular light. These two light colors control the color of the specular highlight on an object. In our shaders so far, k_s has been defined as white, making our specular highlight color be whatever our light color (i_s) has been. Some materials might look better if you manually choose a specular color for them instead, so feel free to experiment with different values for k_s. Just like our shader math earlier, the rest of this section says to get the dot product of R_m (the reflected light vector) and V (the view direction), raise this to the power α (our shininess constant), and multiply it against the material and light's specular colors. This is then added to the diffuse lighting term to get the lighting for a single light. All of this put together gives us the final color for our lit fragment.

Phong shading is far from the only lighting model that games use. You may have heard that many games are moving toward "physically based shading," which involves a much more complex lighting equation to render things in a much more realistic fashion. However, Phong shading is still used very widely in the games industry. Mobile games, for example, may choose Phong lighting rather than a physically based model because they need to run on a wide variety of hardware and need the extra performance gains that come from using a less realistic lighting model.

Blinn-Phong Lighting

Phong shading is a very capable shading model, but there are some lighting scenarios that it doesn't handle very well. Most notably, some viewing angles can result in some weird specular shading on objects that have a low shininess value. Figure 9-9 shows off what this looks like; notice that the lighting appears to have a hard edge to it, which isn't how things should look. In this example I've set the shininess exponent in our shader to 0.5.

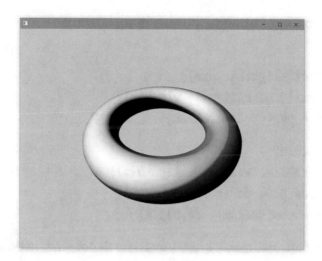

Figure 9-9. *An example of specular problems Phong shading has when working with a low shininess exponent*

This happens because the Phong shading model doesn't account for times when the angle between the reflected light vector and the camera vector exceeds 90 degrees. In most cases this isn't a problem because the specular highlight is so small that by the time you would see this lighting edge, the specular lighting has already gone to zero. However, for objects with a low shininess value (and thus, a really big specular highlight), these sorts of issues can creep up. To solve this problem, most games that use the Phong lighting model use a variation known as Blinn-Phong lighting. This variation changes the math used to calculate specular lighting. Blinn-Phong lighting also has the advantage of being more accurate to the real world than Phong specular is.

The main implementation difference between Phong and Blinn-Phong specular is that Blinn-Phong replaces the reflected light vector in our specular calculations with a new vector known as the *half vector*. Listing 9-7 shows how to calculate this in shader code.

Listing 9-7. Calculating the Half Vector

```
vec3 halfVec = normalize(viewDir + lightDir);
```

With this new half vector in hand, we then need to change our dot product calculation to give us the dot product between our normal vector and this new half vector. After that, we continue with our pow() function as usual. Listing 9-8 shows both Phong and Blinn-Phong specular calculations so that you can see the differences clearly.

Listing 9-8. Comparing Phong vs. Blinn-Phong Specular

```
//phong specular
vec3 refl = reflect(-lightDir,nrm);
float specAmt = max(0.0, dot(refl, viewDir));
float specBright = pow(specAmt, 16.0);

//blinn-phong specular
vec3 halfVec = normalize(viewDir + lightDir);
float specAmt = max(0.0, dot(halfVec, nrm));
float specBright = pow(specAmt, 64.0); ❶
```

Other than the math changes, it's also important to note that in order to get the same size of specular highlight, you'll need to set your Blinn-Phong shininess exponent to between 2 and 4 times the value that you would need for regular Phong specular lighting (you can see this at ❶).

Those few lines of changes are all that's needed to switch us over to using Blinn-Phong shading. If we throw that on our torus mesh—and set our shininess exponent to 2.0 instead of 0.5—we end up with Figure 9-10. Notice that the appearance of hard edges around our specular highlight has been greatly diminished (although not entirely eliminated), and things look a bit more natural. The code for rendering Figure 9-10 can be found in the "BlinnPhong" example project in the Chapter 9 example code.

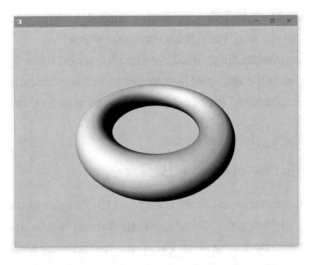

Figure 9-10. *Our torus with low shininess and Blinn-Phong specular lighting*

Using Textures to Control Lighting

Up until now, our mesh's surface has been completely uniform, that is, every fragment on our mesh had the same amount of shininess, was the same color, and reflected the same color of specular light. I probably don't need to tell you that this isn't typically how games do things. Instead, games use textures to vary this information across the surface of a mesh. We've already seen how a texture can be used to change the color of a mesh on a per-fragment basis, but games commonly use textures to store other information as well.

One common texture that's used to help vary the lighting across a mesh's surface is known as a *specular map* (often shortened to *spec map*). The data in this type of texture is used to control how shiny different parts of the mesh's surface are. There are lots of ways a texture like this can be used, but one of the simpler ways is to multiply the specular lighting on a fragment by the value in the spec map for the fragment's UV coordinates. This allows us to control which fragments are shiny, but requires that we set a fixed shininess value for all the shiny parts of the mesh.

To see this in action, let's leave our torus mesh behind and start using a mesh that you might see in a game. The assets folder for this chapter contains a mesh called "shield.ply", and two textures called "shield_diffuse.png" and "shield_spec.png." Grab those files and put them in your bin/data directory; we're going to use them for the rest of the examples in the book. The mesh itself is a low poly shield mesh and comes with all the normal and UV vectors that we'll need to texture it. As you may have guessed from the names of the textures, each of them is designed to provide information for a different lighting type. The diffuse texture is what provides the main colors for our mesh surface, and the color data from that will be multiplied against our diffuse lighting values. The specular texture will, similarly, be multiplied against our specular lighting contribution. You can see each of these textures in Figure 9-11.

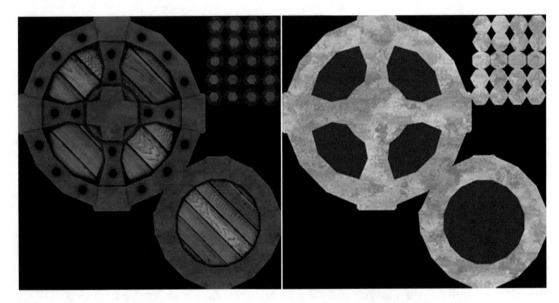

Figure 9-11. *The two textures we'll use to render our shield mesh*

Notice that only the metal areas of the shield have any color in the specular map. This means that the wooden areas of the mesh will not receive any specular light, as we'll be multiplying the specular lighting on the wooden fragments by pure black. You can also see that the metal areas aren't receiving a uniform amount of specular lighting. Instead, there's a bit of variance in how bright the specular areas are, to give the appearance of scratched up metal.

Since we're using a different mesh, you may want to play around with the model matrix for your mesh and the camera position in the scene to get a good view of the mesh when your program runs. Listing 9-9 shows the code that I used to position things for the screenshots in this chapter.

Listing 9-9. Setting Up the Camera and Mesh Transforms for the Example Screenshots

```
//building the view matrix - camera rotated to look down at mesh
float cAngle = radians(-45.0f);
vec3 right = vec3(1, 0, 0);
cam.pos = glm::vec3(0, 0.85f, 1.0f);
mat4 view = inverse(translate(cam.pos) *  rotate(cAngle, right));
```

```
//building model matrix - rotating to point up, and scaling larger
mat4 model = rotate(radians(-45.0f), right) * scale(vec3(1.5, 1.5, 1.5));
```

We've already set up lots of textures in our C++ code in previous chapters, so let's skip right to the changes we need to make to our fragment shader to use the diffuse and spec maps for this mesh. First off, we need to declare two new uniforms for our textures, and a new "in" variable for our UVs, as shown in Listing 9-10.

Listing 9-10. New Variables for Our specular.frag

```
uniform sampler2D diffuseTex;
uniform sampler2D specTex;
in vec2 fragUV;
```

After setting up these new variables, the only other change we need is to replace the meshCol and meshSpecCol variables in our main function with the colors in our textures. Listing 9-11 shows the two lines we need to change to finish off our shader modifications.

Listing 9-11. Changing Our Lighting Calculations to Use Texture Maps

```
//old
vec3 diffCol = meshCol * lightCol * diffAmt;
vec3 specCol = meshSpecCol * lightCol * specBright;

//new
vec3 meshCol = texture(diffuseTex, fragUV).xyz;
vec3 diffCol = meshCol * lightCol * diffAmt;
vec3 specCol = texture(specTex, fragUV).x * lightCol * specBright;
```

With these changes made, we'll also need to modify our vertex shader to pass UV coordinates to the fragUV variable in our fragment shader, but that's nothing we haven't seen before. Once it's all set up, your scene should look like Figure 9-12. The code used to render that figure can be found in the "BlinnShield" project of the Chapter 9 example code.

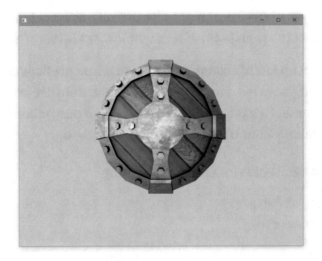

Figure 9-12. *Our shield mesh rendered with a diffuse and spec map*

If you look closely at Figure 9-12, you might be able to see the specular lighting that's hitting just the metal parts of the mesh. It's a bit difficult to really see the impact of a spec map with a completely static mesh though, since specular shading is very view dependent. We really need a moving mesh to see the full impact of our lighting, so to that end I added a few more lines to the example to make the mesh rotate at runtime. Listing 9-12 show off this simple change that makes a huge difference.

Listing 9-12. Making Our Shield Mesh Spin at Runtime

```
//building model matrix - rotating to point up, and scaling larger
static float rotAngle = 0.0f;
rotAngle += 0.01f;
vec3 up = vec3(0, 1, 0);
mat4 rotation = rotate(radians(-45.0f), right) * rotate(rotAngle, up);
mat4 model = rotation * scale(vec3(1.5, 1.5, 1.5));
```

With that change, the impact of our spec map is much more visible, and our Blinn-Phong lighting model implementation is looking good. There's a lot more to rendering meshes than just the diffuse and specular lighting though, and our next few chapters are going to keep expanding on our shader to make this shield really shine.

Summary

Here's a quick summary of what we covered in this chapter:

- Different types of lighting require different calculations in shader code. A "lighting model" is a combination of these calculations used to render an object.

- The Phong lighting model is a popular bit of lighting math, which models light hitting a mesh's surface as a combination of diffuse, specular, and ambient lighting.

- Games that want Phong style lighting commonly use a related lighting model called the "Blinn-Phong" lighting model. This variation looks more realistic and fixes visual artifacts on objects with very low shininess values.

- In order to vary lighting characteristics across the surface of a mesh, shaders use different types of textures to provide information about different types of lighting. On our shield mesh, we used a diffuse map to provide information about diffuse color, and a spec map to tell us how much specular lighting each fragment should receive.

CHAPTER 10

Normal Mapping

In the last chapter, we saw our first example of using a texture to store non-color data. In this chapter we're going to expand on that idea, except rather than store information about our mesh surface's shininess, we're going to store information about bumpiness. We'll do this with a special texture that stores normal vectors instead of colors. Until now, all our normal vectors have come directly from the geometry of our mesh. However, vertex normals can only provide information about the overall shape of a mesh face. If we want to render smaller details, like bumps or scratches, we need another source of normal data. This is much easier to explain visually, so Figure 10-1 has a close-up shot of the center of our shield mesh with vertex normal drawn as white lines.

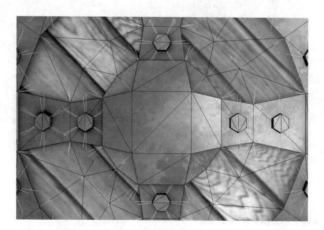

Figure 10-1. *The center of our shield mesh, with normal vectors displayed. Notice that the largest section of the center metal piece is modeled with only four vertices.*

Notice that the very center metal portion of our shield mesh consists of very few vertices. What would happen if we wanted that area to be covered with small scratches, or bumps, like you might expect from a shield made of unpolished metal? The central square of the shield is made up of only four vertices total, which means that without

K. Halladay, *Practical Shader Development*, https://doi.org/10.1007/978-1-4842-4457-9_10

adding more vertices to our mesh, we're incapable of adding these sorts of small details in actual mesh geometry. We could add more vertices to let us model more detail, but the more vertices a mesh has, the more vertex shader calculations need to be performed to render the mesh and the more memory the mesh takes up. Most games can't afford to add thousands of vertices to every object just for bumps and scratches.

To get around this problem, games use a special kind of texture map, called a *normal map*, to store normal vectors in the same way that our spec map texture stores information about our surface's shininess. Since there are many more pixels in our normal map texture than there are vertices in our mesh, this gives us a way to store many more normal vectors than we can with just our geometry. When this works correctly, it looks like the right-hand side screenshot of Figure 10-2, which is what we're going to build in this chapter.

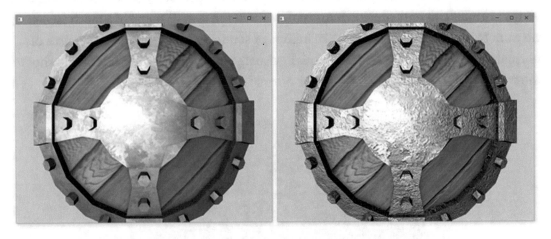

Figure 10-2. *Our shield without normal mapping (left), and with normal mapping (right)*

What Is a Normal Map?

Now that we've seen what they can do, let's spend some time talking about what a normal map is exactly. A normal map is a texture that stores normalized vectors instead of colors in each pixel. This means that the RGB value of each pixel in a normal map texture is really the XYZ value of a normal vector that we can use in our lighting calculations.

However, textures have no way to represent values less than 0, since there's no such thing as a negative color. This would normally mean that we would only be able to store vectors with positive components, but this would make normal maps almost useless for storing normal vectors, since it would severely limit the directions that could be stored. To work around this, normal maps treat the value 0.5 as 0.0. This means that a pixel with the color (0, 0.5, 1) represents the vector (-1, 0, 1). The side effect of this is that we have to do some additional shader math after sampling a normal map, to convert the color value to the desired vector direction. You can see an example of how this is done in Listing 10-1.

Listing 10-1. Unpacking a Normal from a Normal Map Sample

```
vec3 nrm = texture(normTex, fragUV).rgb;
nrm = normalize(nrm * 2.0 - 1.0);
```

You may have seen normal maps before; they usually have a blueish tint to them. For instance, the normal map we're going to use on our shield is shown in Figure 10-3. This blue tint is because the blue channel of every pixel in a normal map corresponds to the Z value of the vectors being stored in the texture. Normal mapping uses a special coordinate space called *tangent space*, which is defined relative to the surface of our mesh. For any given point, the Z axis in tangent space points in the direction of the mesh geometry's normal vector. Since the normal that we provide in a normal map will also point away from the surface of the mesh, this means that every normal vector we store will have a positive Z value, resulting in every pixel having a blue value greater than 0.5.

Figure 10-3 shows the kinds of surface details that normal mapping is commonly used to provide. If you look closely, you can see the bumpy surface of the metal areas of our mesh, and the grain of the wood. These kinds of small details would take thousands of triangles to render convincingly, but are handled easily by normal mapping.

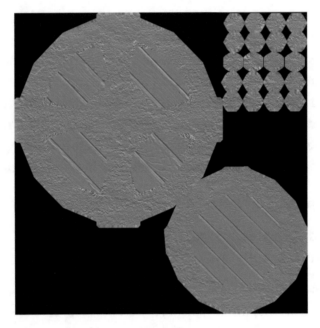

Figure 10-3. *The normal map for our shield*

Introducing Tangent Space

Now that we know how normal maps store vectors and how to unpack them in our shader, we need to talk about the coordinate space that those vectors are defined in. Tangent space is one of the weirder coordinate spaces out there, because it's a per-fragment coordinate space. Rather than being based on the orientation of the camera or the position of an object, it's defined relative to the surface of the mesh that each fragment is from.

We already know that the Z axis in tangent space always points in the direction of the normal vector that we get from our mesh's geometry, so all that's left is for us to figure out what the other two axes are. The X axis of tangent space comes from our mesh's *tangent vectors*. Tangent vectors are stored on each vertex of our mesh, just like vertex colors or normal vectors, and store the direction of the U axis of our mesh's UV coordinates. The Y axis of tangent space is known as the *bitangent*, which is a vector that is perpendicular to both the tangent and normal vectors. The bitangent is usually calculated in shader code, rather than stored in mesh memory. Put together, these three vectors create the axes of a coordinate space that is oriented to the current fragment being processed. Figure 10-4 shows what this might look like for a single fragment on a sphere.

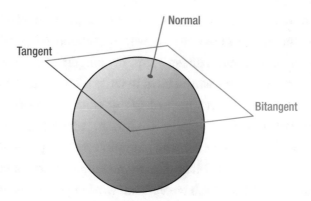

Figure 10-4. *What the tangent space axis vectors might look like for a point on a sphere mesh*

From the diagram, it may look as though we could use any set of perpendicular vectors for the tangent and bitangent directions, but it's important that they are aligned with our UV coordinate directions so that our normal mapping calculations match up with the texture samples for a given fragment.

You might be wondering why we're storing our normal vectors in this weird coordinate space at all, rather than just storing the vectors in a normal map in object space. Some games do choose to work with object space normal maps, rather than the more typical tangent space ones that we've seen so far. However, object space normal maps have several limitations, like not supporting mesh animations, and not allowing artists to reuse UV coordinates for different parts of a mesh. These limitations have led most games to opt for tangent space normal maps despite the increased complexity, so that normal mapping can be applied to the widest range of meshes possible.

Working with Tangent Vectors

Now that we know that we need tangent vectors, it's time to talk about how to get them. Tangent vectors aren't usually created by 3D artists, since they're simply a function of the UV coordinates on a mesh, so most meshes that you'll work with won't have these vectors in their data by default. Instead, many game engines will calculate tangent vectors for the meshes when that mesh is imported into the project. Once these vectors have been generated, however, accessing them is identical to how we've accessed any other vertex attribute so far.

Unfortunately, openFrameworks doesn't support tangent vectors by default. This means both that we don't have an easy to use way to calculate tangent vectors for our mesh, and that the ofMesh class doesn't support tangent vectors out of the box. Normally this would mean that we would have to write our own mesh class, and our own mesh import functions. However, the purpose of this chapter is to explain how to write a shader that implements normal mapping, not how to calculate tangents ourselves, or write our own mesh class (both of which can get rather hairy if you want to do it right). Instead, we're going to cheat a little bit and store the tangent vectors in the vertex color attribute of our mesh. The shield mesh we've been working with has been set up this way already, so we can access the shield's tangent vectors the same way we got vertex colors way back in Chapter 2, like you can see in Listing 10-2 below.

Listing 10-2. accessing our shield mesh's tangent vectors

```
layout (location = 0) in vec3 pos;
layout (location = 1) in vec4 tan;
layout (location = 2) in vec3 nrm;
layout (location = 3) in vec2 uv;
```

If you'd like to test out normal mapping on your own meshes in openFrameworks, code to generate tangents for an ofMesh and store them in that mesh's vertex color attribute is available in Appendix A and in the example code online. We won't talk about it here because normal mapping is already complex enough to wrap your head around without worrying about calculating tangent vectors, and you can usually count on your game engine to provide these vectors for you.

That covers what we need to get access to our mesh's tangent vectors, but I mentioned earlier that it's normal for shaders to calculate the bitangent vector in shader code. To do this, we need to learn a new bit of vector math, which I want to cover before we start writing shader code.

Introducing Cross Products

The bitangent vector is a vector that is perpendicular to both the normal and tangent vector of our fragment. You can see an example of this in Figure 10-5. Assuming the two original vectors are the normal and tangent vectors for our fragment, the green vector that is added in the right image is the vector we want.

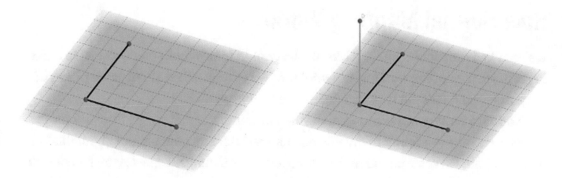

Figure 10-5. *If we calculate the cross product of the two vectors in the left image, the result is the green vector In the right image*

We can calculate this vector using a bit of math known as a *cross product*. A cross product is a mathematical operation that takes two vectors and returns a third one that is perpendicular to both of the input vectors. There are a few restrictions on this. First, your two input vectors can't both be part of the same line. Second, the cross product only works for 3D vectors.

Calculating a cross product is relatively straightforward. Listing 10-3 shows a function in GLSL that could be used to calculate it. However, just like the dot product, GLSL has a function built into the language that will perform this calculation for us as well, so the sample code here is just for reference.

Listing 10-3. An Example Implementation of a Function That Performs a Cross Product

```
vec3 cross(vec3 a, vec3 b){
    return a.yzx * b.zxy - a.zxy * b.yzx;
}
```

One thing to watch out for is that the cross product of two normalized vectors is not guaranteed to be a normalized vector itself. Make sure that if your math requires that a vector created by a cross product be normalized, that you're doing that explicitly in code.

The cross product is what we'll use to calculate the bitangent vector, given a vertex normal and a tangent vector. We'll then pass all three of our vectors (normal, tangent, and bitangent) from the vertex shader to the fragment shader. The resulting set of interpolated vectors received by the fragment shader will be what we use in our normal mapping calculations.

187

How Normal Mapping Works

We've talked a lot about different bits of background information that we need to know to get normal mapping working, but until now we've only talked about small pieces of the puzzle. Now, let's put it all together to see the big picture.

Normal mapping works by replacing the normal vector that we get from our mesh vertices with a vector found in the normal map texture. The difficult part about this is that the vector we get from the normal map texture is in tangent space, which means that we need to convert it to a different coordinate space to use it in our lighting calculations. To do that, we use the normal, tangent, and bitangent vectors to create a matrix that can transform a vector from tangent space to world space, which is where all our other lighting vectors are defined. Once we have this matrix, we transform the normal we get out of the normal map shader to world space and continue with our lighting calculations with our new normal vector.

The first step in this process is to create our tangent, bitangent, normal matrix (commonly referred to as a TBN matrix). This is done in the vertex shader and passed to the fragment shader. The first step in this process is to get these three vectors into variables we can work with. Listing 10-4 is a snippet that shows how this is done.

Listing 10-4. Getting the TBN Vectors in Our Vertex Shader

```
layout (location = 0) in vec3 pos;
layout (location = 1) in vec4 tan;
layout (location = 2) in vec3 nrm;
layout (location = 3) in vec2 uv;

void main(){
        vec3 T = tan.xyz;
        vec3 N = nrm.xyz;
        vec3 B = cross(T, N);

        //rest of function omitted
}
```

With these vectors in hand, the next step is to get each of these three vectors in world space. Even though the vectors we get out of our normal map will be in tangent space, the actual tangent vectors that are stored on our mesh are specified in object space. This means that for each of these vectors, we need to transform them from object space to world space. Just like with our normal vector, we can accomplish this by multiplying by either the model matrix or the normal matrix, but our example code is going to opt for the normal matrix to make sure that we properly account for nonuniform mesh scaling (even though our shield mesh is being scaled uniformly in our examples). Listing 10-5 shows what this looks like.

Listing 10-5. Converting Our TBN Vectors from Object to World Space

```
vec3 T = normalize(normal * tan.xyz);
vec3 B = normalize(normal * cross(tan.xyz,nrm));
vec3 N = normalize(normal * nrm);
```

Notice in the preceding code that we have to explicitly grab the xyz coordinates of our tangent vector because we've stored that vector in our vertex color attribute, which is a vec4 by default. Once we have these three vectors in world space though, all that's left for our vertex shader is to package them up into a 3×3 matrix and send it to the fragment shader. This is the first time we've passed a matrix to a fragment shader, but it works the same as passing vector data. Listing 10-6 has an example snippet. The order of vectors in this matrix matters, so make sure that your code matches the example.

Listing 10-6. Outputting a mat3 from Our Vertex Shader

```
out mat3 TBN;

void main(){
        vec3 T = normalize(normal * tan.xyz);
        vec3 B = normalize(normal * cross(tan.xyz,nrm.xyz));
        vec3 N = normalize(normal * nrm.xyz);
        TBN = mat3(T, B, N);
        //rest of function omitted
}
```

That's all that needs to be added to our vertex shader, so it's time to look at our fragment shader. The only part of our lighting calculations that normal mapping impacts is the direction of our normal vector, so the only part of our shader that we're modifying is the line where we're currently writing the normalized normal direction to a variable. You can see this in Listing 10-7.

Listing 10-7. The Line in Our Blinn-Phong Shader That We're Going to Replace

```
vec3 nrm = normalize(fragNrm);
```

Since we've replaced the normal vector that we were passing to our fragment shader with a TBN matrix, we don't have a fragNrm value to read from anymore. Instead, we need to start our fragment shader by getting the tangent space normal vector out of our normal map texture. We saw this earlier in Listing 10-1, but I'll put the same example code here again so that you don't have to start flipping between pages. Remember that after we sample the normal map, we then need to do a quick bit of math to convert the values from a 0 to 1 range back to the -1 to +1 range we need.

Listing 10-8. Unpacking a Normal Vector from a Normal Map

```
vec3 nrm = texture(normTex, fragUV).rgb;
nrm = normalize(nrm * 2.0 - 1.0);
```

After properly unpacking this vector, the last step in our normal mapping process is to convert this vector to world space. Until now we've always done these sorts of matrix multiplications in our vertex shader, but it looks the exact same in a fragment shader. Listing 10-9 shows how to use the TBN matrix to convert our normal into world space.

Listing 10-9. Converting a Tangent Space Normal to World Space

```
nrm = normalize(TBN * nrm);
```

With that change, the rest of your shader logic can proceed completely unchanged from how it was before. The new normal vector will fit into our lighting calculations exactly the same way as the old one. To finish off our example, Listing 10-10 has the new main() function for our Blinn-Phong shader.

Listing 10-10. The main() Function for our Fragment Shader, with Normal Mapping

```
void main(){
        vec3 nrm = texture(normTex, fragUV).rgb;
        nrm = normalize(nrm * 2.0 - 1.0);
        nrm = normalize(TBN * nrm);

        vec3 viewDir = normalize(cameraPos - fragWorldPos);
        vec3 halfVec = normalize(viewDir + lightDir);
```

```
float diffAmt = max(0.0, dot(nrm, lightDir));
vec3 diffCol = texture(diffuseTex, fragUV).xyz * lightCol * diffAmt;

float specAmt = max(0.0, dot(halfVec, nrm));
float specBright = pow(specAmt, 4.0);
vec3 specCol = texture(specTex, fragUV).x * lightCol * specBright;

outCol = vec4(diffCol + specCol + ambientCol, 1.0);
}
```

All our shader changes are done now, but as always, there's a bit of work to be done on the C++ side of things. In order for any of this to work, you'll have to create an ofImage to hold the normal map texture, and then pass that texture to your shaders as a uniform. Once that's set up, your shield mesh should be looking much bumpier than before. The example project "NormalMap" in this chapter's example code has all the code required to generate Figure 10-2 (our shield rendered with a normal map), so check it out if things aren't looking right in your own project.

Normal mapping really shines with objects that move, so make sure to try this out with the rotation code from the last chapter. The coolest part about this technique is how well it integrates with all our other lighting calculations and makes everything look more detailed. However, making meshes look more detailed isn't the only use for normal mapping, so before we finish off this chapter, let's use what we've learned to do something a bit different with it.

Writing a Water Shader

Another common use for normal mapping is creating simple water effects. In addition to making objects look bumpier, normal mapping is often combined with scrolling UV coordinates to make the surface of a mesh appear to ripple like water. It's a pretty fun effect to play around with, so we're going to build it. You'll find a plane mesh with tangents on it, and a texture called "water_normals.png" in the assets folder for this chapter online if you want to follow along in your own project.

This effect is going to combine concepts from a bunch of previous chapters. We're going to combine scrolling UVs (from way back in Chapter 3!), with a very high shininess exponent, and normal mapping to produce a very decent water effect. Figure 10-6 shows what this will look like when we're done.

Figure 10-6. *Our water effect*

To get things kicked off, let's create two new shaders for this effect; in the example code, these are called "water.vert" and "water.frag." The vertex shader is going to be similar to the one we used for our shield mesh, with some important additions. To have the effect animate over time, we need a uniform for us to pass a time value to, just like we did with our sprite sheet shader earlier. We're also going to need to make two different sets of UV coordinates, and have both of them scroll in different directions over time. For this example, I started by copying and pasting the code from our shield mesh's vertex shader, and then made the changes shown in Listing 10-11.

Listing 10-11. The Changes Made to water.vert After Copying from Our Earlier Vertex Shader

```
//prior declarations omitted
out vec2 fragUV;
out vec2 fragUV2;
uniform float time;

void main()
{
        float t = time * 0.05;
        float t2 = time * 0.02;  ❶
        fragUV = vec2(uv.x+t, uv.y) * 3.0f;  ❷
        fragUV2 = vec2(uv.x+t2, uv.y-t2) * 2.0;
        //rest of code omitted
```

In addition to the new variables that we said we were going to add, there's a bit of logic in the preceding code that might look a bit weird. First off, we are multiplying our time values by different constants (❶). This allows us to scroll our two sets of output UV coordinates at different rates. You can see at ❷ that we are simply adding these time variables to the UV coordinates that we get from our mesh geometry. Since we want to scroll two normal maps over top of one another in different directions, we need to add different values to the two sets of UV coordinates. There's no magic about why the preceding example is choosing to add a time value to some UVs and subtract from others; you can simply try different combinations until you find something that looks good.

The other bit of logic that might be confusing is also seen at ❷, and it's the multiplication that we're doing to our newly scrolled UV values. Since our normal maps are going to be set to the "repeat" wrap mode, we are free to have our UVs go beyond the 0-1 range in our vertex shader. Multiplying by a number larger than 1 has the effect of tiling our normal map texture across the plane. This is shown in Figure 10-7.

Figure 10-7. *The left image shows a plane textured with our normal map. The right image shows the same plane and normal map, but textured with UV coordinates that have been multiplied by 4.*

Multiplying each set of UVs by a different scalar value helps to limit the appearance of repetition on our water's surface as the two sets of coordinates scroll. To really limit this repetition, we're multiplying our UV coordinates by two numbers that are relatively prime. Saying two numbers are "relatively prime" means that there is no integer value greater than one that divides evenly into both numbers. Two and three are relatively prime with one another, which makes them excellent choices for scaling our UV coordinates.

The rest of this shader should look identical to the one we were using for our Blinn-Phong shader earlier, so it's time to move on to our fragment shader. Again, start this shader by copying and pasting the Blinn-Phong shader code from before, since most of the shader logic will stay the same. Before we dig into the scrolling water normals part of this shader, we need to make a few simple tweaks to the lighting calculations we have now in order to really get a convincing looking water effect. Listing 10-12 shows these minor changes.

Listing 10-12. Changes to the Lighting Calculations for water.frag

```
float diffAmt = max(0.0, dot(nrm, lightDir));
vec3 diffCol = vec3(0.3,0.3,0.4) * lightCol * diffAmt; ❶

float specAmt = max(0.0, dot(halfVec, nrm));
float specBright = pow(specAmt, 512.0); ❷
vec3 specCol = lightCol * specBright; ❸
```

The changes we need to make are all trivial changes to values used to control the appearance of our mesh surface. In a full game, these values are the things that would be exposed as uniforms so that C++ code could set these on a per object basis, but since we only have two objects, we're going to do this the quick and dirty way and hardcode things right in our shader. First, rather than use a diffuse texture, we're going to simply provide a blue color for our water's diffuse lighting (❶). Second, we need to raise the shininess exponent in our specular calculation to a very high value. Since water is very mirror-like, we need a very high value, like 512.0 (❷). Finally, since we don't have a specular texture for our water, we can remove that texture sample from the "specCol" calculation (❸). The rest of the lighting math stays exactly the same, so we're still working with Blinn-Phong lighting, just with different inputs.

With those changes out of the way, it's time to dig into the meat of the water effect: scrolling two normal maps over top of one another. Listing 10-13 shows how this is done.

Listing 10-13. The Changes Made to water.frag After Copying from Our Other Blinn-Phong Shader

```
in vec2 fragUV2;
void main()
{
        vec3 nrm = texture(normTex, fragUV).rgb;
        nrm = (nrm * 2.0 - 1.0);

        vec3 nrm2 = texture(normTex, fragUV2).rgb;
        nrm2 = (nrm2 * 2.0 - 1.0);

        nrm = normalize(TBN * (nrm + nrm2));
        //rest of shader omitted
```

You may recognize the technique of adding two vectors together and then normalizing the sum to get a combination of the two from when we calculated the half vector for our Blinn-Phong specular lighting in the last chapter. We're using the same idea here to allow us to blend between two different normal map texture samples. In the example code presented in this chapter, I'm reusing the same normal map texture for both texture samples, but this technique is also commonly done using two different normal map textures as well. Whether you use a single normal map or blend between multiple, however, the real trick to making your water look good comes from choosing normal map textures that work for this sort of technique. In general, you want to avoid normal maps with very strong vertical or horizontal shapes to them, since those are very noticeable when tiled across a water plane. You also need normal maps that are seamless—meaning that when you tile them, you can't tell where the edges of the texture are. Figure 10-8 shows an example of a normal map that exhibits some of these problems, compared with the normal map that we'll be using in our examples.

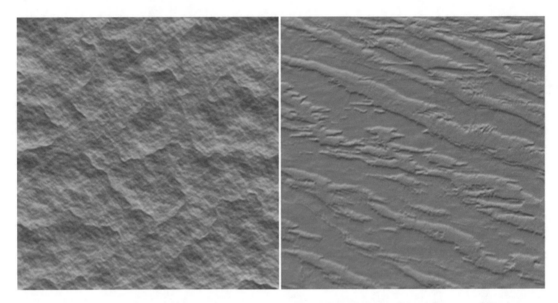

Figure 10-8. *On the left you can see the normal map that we're using for our water. On the right you can see a normal map with strong horizontal features, which would be very noticeable when tiled across a water plane.*

In C++ land there's a bit of setup required for our example code to look like our target screenshot from earlier. For one, we need to create a new ofImage object to hold our water normal map. Since we're going to be tiling this texture, we need to make sure that we set its wrap mode to repeat, like we did in Chapter 3 when we wanted to tile our parrot texture. Listing 10-14 shows the code snippet needed to do that, in case you've forgotten.

Listing 10-14. Loading a Normal Map and Setting the Wrap Mode to Repeat

```
waterNrm.load("water_nrm.png");
waterNrm.getTexture().setTextureWrap(GL_REPEAT, GL_REPEAT);
```

In the next chapter we're going to work with a technique that will lend itself well to both our shield mesh and the water mesh that we're about to render, so rather than replace the shield mesh that we've been working with, create a different ofMesh object to load the plane.ply mesh for our water into. We're also not going to overwrite the drawing code for our shield object, since we'll want to render both at the same time. Instead, let's split the drawing code into two functions, drawShield() and drawMesh(), and adjust the view and model matrices in the scene so that everything works well together. Listing 10-15 shows what the draw() function for the example looks like now.

Listing 10-15. Our New Draw Function

```
void ofApp::draw(){
        using namespace glm;

        DirectionalLight dirLight;
        dirLight.direction = glm::normalize(glm::vec3(0.5, -1, -1));
        dirLight.color = glm::vec3(1, 1, 1);
        dirLight.intensity = 1.0f;

        DirectionalLight waterLight;
        waterLight.direction = glm::normalize(glm::vec3(0.5, -1, 1));
        waterLight.color = glm::vec3(1, 1, 1);
        waterLight.intensity = 1.0f;

        mat4 proj = perspective(cam.fov, 1024.0f / 768.0f, 0.01f, 10.0f);

        cam.pos = glm::vec3(0, 0.75f, 1.0);
        mat4 view = inverse(translate(cam.pos));

        drawShield(dirLight, proj, view);
        drawWater(waterLight, proj, view);
}
```

One bit of weirdness in Listing 10-15 is that we're providing a different light direction for our water mesh, rather than using it to light the shield mesh. This is because in order to see our specular highlight on our water mesh, light has to be reflecting off of the plane toward the camera, but we want light going the opposite way (from the camera, toward the scene) to light the front of our shield. This is a hack, but it makes our example scene look a lot better. The drawWater() and drawShield() functions are very similar to one another, and mostly are used to simply set uniforms on their respective shaders and draw the mesh they need. However, if you're following along at home and don't want to look online for source code, it might be helpful to see how the example scene is setting up the model matrices for each object. Listing 10-16 shows the snipped in each function that sets up the matrices and values that then are set up as shader uniforms.

Listing 10-16. Snippets of the drawWater() and drawShield() Functions

```
void ofApp::drawWater(DirectionalLight& dirLight, glm::mat4& proj,
glm::mat4& view)
{
        using namespace glm;

        static float t = 0.0f;
        t += ofGetLastFrameTime();

        vec3 right = vec3(1, 0, 0);
        mat4 rotation = rotate(radians(-90.0f), right);
        mat4 model =  rotation * scale(vec3(5.0,4.0,4.0));
        mat4 mvp = proj * view * model;
        mat3 normalMatrix = mat3(transpose(inverse(model)));

        //code to set uniforms up and issue draw call omitted
```

```
void ofApp::drawShield(DirectionalLight& dirLight, glm::mat4& proj,
glm::mat4& view)
{
        using namespace glm;

        mat4 model = translate(vec3(0.0, 0.75, 0.0f));
        mat4 mvp = proj * view * model;
        mat3 normalMatrix = mat3(transpose(inverse(model)));

        //code to set uniforms and issue draw call omitted
```

When everything is put together, you should be able to run the example program and see both your shield mesh and water mesh rendered on screen, like Figure 10-9. I really like this example because it combines so much of what we've done in previous chapters of the book, and we're going to expand on it even more in the next chapter when we talk about reflections. So if you're following along at home, it's worth it to spend some time making sure that everything is working how you'd expect before moving on. Remember that you can always compare your code to the example code provided online. The "Water" example project has all the code required to render Figure 10-9.

Figure 10-9. *The final output of our water example, which unintentionally ended up very viking-esque*

There's More to Normal Mapping

The normal mapping implementation that we've built in this chapter isn't the only way that games implement this technique. Programmers sometimes opt to rearrange their math so that rather than convert the normal vector from tangent to world space, they instead convert their other vectors from world to tangent space. In other cases, you may see some shaders transform all these vectors into view space and perform the math there. In general, decisions like this are made because they allow more work to be done in the vertex shader, which as we'll see in our optimization chapter, is a very good idea. We're going to stick with our world space normal mapping implementation for the rest of the book because I find that it's the easiest version of this technique to wrap your head around, but if you find yourself wanting to squeeze a bit of extra performance out of your shaders, you might have luck investigating an alternative way to structure your normal mapping math.

Summary

Here's a brief list of what we covered in this chapter:

- A normal map is a texture that stores direction vectors instead of color data in each pixel. Games use them to provide information about small surface details when rendering objects.

- Normal maps commonly store their direction vectors in tangent space, which is a coordinate space that is defined by the UV coordinates and geometry normal of any given point on a mesh's surface.

- Normal mapping works by replacing the normal vector provided by a mesh's geometry with one stored in a normal map.

- Tangent vectors are special direction vectors stored on each vertex of a mesh. These vectors point in the direction of the U axis of the texture coordinates at that point on the mesh.

- A cross product is a mathematical operation that creates a new vector that is perpendicular to two input vectors. We can calculate a cross product in shader code using GLSL's cross() function.

- You can build a water effect by scrolling two different sets of UV coordinates across the surface of a mesh and using these coordinates to look up normal vector directions in the fragment shader.

CHAPTER 11

Cubemaps And Skyboxes

Our project now has two great examples of different types of shiny surfaces (water and metal), but there's still something decidedly fake about how they look. One major reason for this is that real shiny surfaces don't just reflect light coming from a single direct lighting source, they also reflect light that bounces off the world around them. If they didn't, we'd never be able to see reflections in anything! For this reason, the more complex lighting models used by game engines today include lighting calculations that take environment reflections into account when calculating the lighting on a fragment. The classic Blinn-Phong lighting that we're using for our examples isn't this complex, but there's no reason why we can't fake it anyway!

This chapter is going to be all about how to add simple static reflections to our shaders. We're going to be providing an image of what our world looks like in a special texture called a cubemap, and we'll sample that texture in our shader to figure out what colors our shiny objects should be reflecting. Our reflections won't be able to properly reflect moving objects, but they'll still go a long way toward making our scene look more convincing. We'll also use a cubemap to render a skybox in our example scene, giving the entire scene a seamless, 360-degree background texture.

What Is a Cubemap?

A cubemap is a special kind of texture, and what makes it special is that it's made up of a combination of six individual textures stored in memory in a way that lets us treat them as though they're a single object. Cubemaps get their name because each of these six textures is treated as though they are one of the faces of a cube, like you can see illustrated in Figure 11-1.

© Kyle Halladay 2019

K. Halladay, *Practical Shader Development*, https://doi.org/10.1007/978-1-4842-4457-9_11

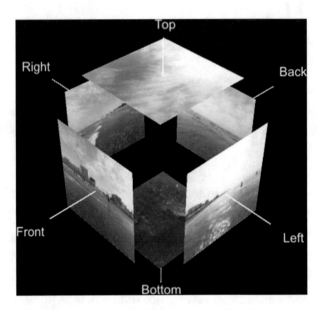

Figure 11-1. *The faces of our cubemap laid out in the shape of a cube*

Sampling a cubemap is different from sampling a 2D texture as well. Rather than using a UV coordinate vector, cubemap sampling requires a direction vector. To understand why this is, imagine that you are sitting in the center of the cubemap's imaginary cube. If you were looking at a pixel immediately in front of you, you would be able to draw a vector going from you, in the direction (0, 0, 1), until it hit the pixel on the cube that you were looking at. This is exactly how cubemap sampling works, and you can see an example of what that might look like in code in Listing 11-1. Every fragment assumes that it is located in the exact center of the cubemap's cube and is looking at a face of the cubemap.

Listing 11-1. Sampling a Cubemap

```
vec3 nrm = normalize(fragNrm);
vec4 cubemap = textureCube(cubemap, nrm);
```

In Listing 11-1's snippet, we're using a normal vector to get cubemap colors. We'll use a technique very similar to this on our shield mesh later in the chapter. Before we get to that though, we should probably figure out how to load a cubemap in our program at all.

Loading a Cubemap in openFrameworks

Unfortunately, just like tangent vectors, openFrameworks doesn't have support for cubemaps out of the box. This time, however, we can't cheat and simply store our data somewhere else; we need to add support for OpenGL cubemaps to our project. Since this book is explicitly not about the nitty gritty of OpenGL, I've written a simple class for us to work with that will handle all the work of loading cubemaps for us. The code is available both online and in Appendix A, but it's a bit too long to reproduce here in its entirety, so Listing 11-2 just shows off an example of how to use it.

Listing 11-2. How to Use the ofxEasyCubemap Class

```
ofxEasyCubemap cubemap;
cubemap.load("cube_front.jpg", "cube_back.jpg",
             "cube_right.jpg", "cube_left.jpg",
             "cube_top.jpg", "cube_bottom.jpg");

//some time later, when we need to use this as a shader uniform
shd.setUniformTexture("name", cubemap.getTexture(), 1); ❶
```

As shown, the class is called "ofxEasyCubemap," and for the most part we can use it exactly like we've been using ofImages so far. The constructor takes the paths to each of the six textures that will make up the faces of our cubemap and will handle all the details of loading each of them. The only functional difference for us is that we need to call getTexture() explicitly when we want to use the cubemap as a shader uniform, rather than just passing an ofImage reference like we have been (shown at a ❶).

Just like Listing 11-2, our first example (and all our examples) are going to require that we load six new images, and the assets folder for this chapter contains the files that you can see referenced in the example code. If you're following along at home, grab those files and the ofxEasyCubemap class, and add them to your project. You'll also want to grab the cube mesh in that folder for use in a few of our examples.

Rendering a Cubemap on a Cube

Given that cubemaps store the faces of an imaginary cube, it makes sense that the first object we texture using a cubemap is an actual cube. Our first shaders of the chapter are simply going to paint the faces of a cube mesh with the six textures that are in our cubemap. This is more than just an amusing first place to start: rendering the faces of the cubemap out to something we can see gives us an easy way to make sure that our textures are loading in correctly and look how we expect. It also gives us an excellent excuse to write some very simple shaders that work with this new type of texture.

We'll start with the vertex shader, so create a new one (I called mine "cubemap. vert"). Since cubemaps don't use UV coordinates, and we're only going to be using a cubemap in this shader, the only vertex attribute that we need for this shader is vertex position. We're going to output this object space position unchanged to our fragment shader, so we'll also need to declare an out vec3 parameter to store that. Finally, we'll need to compute our gl_Position the same way we've always done. Put together, this vertex shader should look like Listing 11-3.

Listing 11-3. A Vertex Shader for Working with Cubemaps

```
#version 410

layout (location = 0) in vec3 pos;

uniform mat4 mvp;
out vec3 fragPos;

void main()
{
    fragPos = pos; ❶
    gl_Position =  mvp * vec4(pos, 1.0);
}
```

This is the simplest shader we've written in a long time, so there isn't a whole lot to talk about here except for the fact that we're outputting object space vertex positions (❶), which likely seems a bit odd. However, if you think about it, each vertex position can also be thought of as a vector from the origin point of our mesh's object space. Since the vertices in our cube mesh are centered on that origin point, the vertex positions of our mesh can be used as the direction vectors that each vertex would use to look at a cubemap. Therefore, outputting the object space vectors (and then getting interpolated vectors in our fragment shader) is the cubemap equivalent of outputting our mesh's UVs from the vertex shader.

Our fragment shader is going to be even simpler. All we need to do is use the interpolated object space position that we get from our vertex shader to sample color from our cubemap. Listing 11-4 shows the couple lines of code that we'll need for that, so create a new fragment shader and copy that example code into there.

Listing 11-4. cubemap.frag, Sampling a Cubemap Based on Vertex Positions

```
#version 410

uniform samplerCube cubemap;  ❶

in vec3 fromCam;
out vec4 outCol;

void main()
{
    outCol = texture(cubemap, fromCam);
}
```

The only new thing in this shader is the sampler type that we need to use for cubemaps. All our textures so far have used samplers of type "sampler2D," but since cubemaps aren't 2D textures, they get a special type of sampler called a "samplerCube." Other than the name, the only practical difference is that samplerCubes expect a vec3 to be provided when we're sampling from them, which we've already talked about at length.

That's all we need to do for our first two shaders in the chapter, so it's time to jump into our C++ code and start setting some things up. First off, we need to load our cubemap images into memory. We can do that via the ofxEasyCubemap class that we talked about earlier in this chapter. We also need to load our cube mesh and create a new ofShader object to hold our new cubemap shaders, so let's add those variables to our header file and then add the code shown in Listing 11-5 to our setup() function.

Listing 11-5. Loading Our cubemesh, cubemap shaders, and cubemap Textures

```
cubeMesh.load("cube.ply");
cubemapShader.load("cubemap.vert", "cubemap.frag");
cubemap.load("cube_front.jpg", "cube_back.jpg",
             "cube_right.jpg", "cube_left.jpg",
             "cube_top.jpg", "cube_bottom.jpg");
```

Note that the order in which you specify the cubemap textures matters, so make sure to double-check that you're passing your texture paths to the cubemap.load() function in the correct order.

Once everything is loaded, all that's left is to write a drawCube() function that we can use to set up our cube's matrices and shader uniforms. For this first example, I commented out the drawWater() and drawShield() functions so that we could look at our cube in isolation. I also added some logic to make our cube rotate, so that it was easier to inspect the texture data that we're about to sample from our cubemap. You can see this new drawCube() function in Listing 11-6.

Listing 11-6. The drawCube Function

```
void ofApp::drawCube(glm::mat4& proj, glm::mat4& view)
{
    using namespace glm;

    static float rotAngle = 0.01;
    rotAngle += 0.1f;

    mat4 r = rotate(radians(rotAngle), vec3(0, 1, 0));
    mat4 s = scale(vec3(0.4, 0.4, 0.4));
    mat4 model = translate(vec3(0.0, 0.75, 0.0f)) * r *s;
    mat4 mvp = proj * view * model;

    ofShader& shd = cubemapShader;

    shd.begin();
    shd.setUniformMatrix4f("mvp", mvp);
    shd.setUniformTexture("envMap", cubemap.getTexture(), 0);
    shd.setUniform3f("cameraPos", cam.pos);
    cubeMesh.draw();
    shd.end();
}
```

With all that written, all that's left is to sit back and watch our cube spin! If you've put everything together properly, you should see something like Figure 11-2. Notice that each face of the cube is a different one of our input textures, and that these textures are arranged on the cube so that the seams of the textures exactly match up with their neighbors. This is crucial for using cubemaps; any visible seams will introduce visual problems into the shaders that use them.

Figure 11-2.   *A cubemap rendered on a cube*

The code to render Figure 11-2 is in the "CubemapCube" project in the Chapter 11 example code. Now that we have this working, let's look at a more useful version of this shader, which uses a cubemap as our sky.

Introducing Skyboxes

You've probably noticed that all our 3D example scenes so far have had an area in the background that we aren't drawing to, and as such is colored with a lovely default gray from openFrameworks. Most games don't really want a flat background being shown to their users, and they use different techniques to make sure that these background pixels are filled with color data that helps make the scene look more real. One common way to do this is to use a *skybox*.

A skybox is a large cube that is always positioned in the same place that the camera is. This means that the camera will always be located inside of the cube, and the cube will not appear to move if the camera is translated. A cubemap is applied to the faces of the cube that face inward, so that wherever the camera looks, rather than seeing a background color, it will see a cubemap texture instead. Once we have a cubemap in our scene, rendering the water and shield mesh along with it will look like Figure 11-3, which feels a lot more like something you might see in a game.

Figure 11-3. *Our scene rendered with a skybox*

Creating a skybox is very similar to what we just did with our cube mesh—so much so that we're going to reuse the fragment shader we just wrote for our cube on our skybox. Our vertex shader is a bit of a different story. We always want the faces of our skybox to be the farthest visible thing from the camera, but we don't want to have to continually resize the skybox mesh every time we change how far the camera will draw (remember that we set that in our projection matrix), so our vertex shader has to handle scaling our cube mesh for us based on the matrices we provide. This is a neat trick, but it's going to require some explanation, so let's look at it in Listing 11-7 and then break it down.

Listing 11-7. A Skybox Vertex Shader

```
#version 410

layout (location = 0) in vec3 pos;

out vec3 fromCam;
uniform mat4 mvp;

void main()
{
    fromCam = pos;
    gl_Position =  (mvp * vec4(pos, 1.0)).xyww  ❶

}
```

To understand how this works, we need to dig a little deeper into how the graphics pipeline works with our projection matrix to make things appear 3D, so we're going to take a quick detour to talk about a new graphics concept and then come back to this example.

The Perspective Divide

After a vertex position is output from a vertex shader, the GPU performs what's called the *perspective divide* on that position. This sounds fancy, but all it means is that the XYZ components of our gl_Position vector get divided by the W component. We haven't worried about this until now, because orthographic matrices are set up so that the W component of any position transformed by them is set to 1, meaning that the perspective divide does nothing. Perspective matrices, however, are responsible for setting this W component to something useful. When using a projection matrix, the perspective divide has the effect of moving objects that are far away toward the center of the horizon, like you can see in Figure 11-4. This is how perspective matrices make objects appear to be 3D.

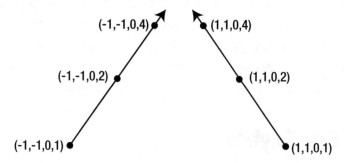

Figure 11-4. *A visualization of the effects of the perspective divide with different W components*

When set up by a perspective projection matrix, the perspective divide has the effect of pulling coordinates with a larger W value toward the center of the screen, like you can see demonstrated in Figure 11-4. Since orthographic projections are explicitly about not providing perspective effects, multiplying a position by an orthographic matrix will leave the W component of the result vector as 1, so that the perspective divide does nothing. Perspective projection matrices want to add perspective to their rendering and are set up so that when we multiply a position by a projection matrix, the farther away that position is, the larger its W component will be. You can see an example of how the perspective divide works with different W components in Figure 11-4.

The actual W value that a position vector is assigned by a projection matrix is dependent on what values we passed to the glm::perspective() function's near and far arguments, so that the perspective effect matches up with our camera frustum's shape. This works great for 99% of objects. But for something like a skybox, which we know we always want to be the farthest possible visible object in the scene, we don't really care about it getting any perspective effects because the user isn't going to be able to see the shape of it anyway (thanks to the seamless textures on it).

Skyboxes and the Perspective Divide

The perspective divide is very handy, but we don't want it applied to our skybox, since we want the box to give the appearance of an infinite sky. This is where line ❶ in Listing 11-7 comes in. Normalized device coordinates go from -1 to 1 in each axis. This means that the maximum Z value that a visible object can have after this transformation is 1.0 (anything larger than that will be outside of the camera frustum). Therefore, we know we want every vertex that gets transformed for our skybox to end up with a Z value of 1.0. We can't simply set Z to 1.0, because the perspective divide is going to divide our Z value after we're done with it. To combat this, we set both our Z and W components of our gl_Position vector to the same number. That way, when the perspective divide is applied, we know for sure that our Z components will always be 1.0.

Finishing Our Skybox

As I mentioned before, we're going to simply reuse the fragment shader from our first cubemap example, so now that we understand our new vertex shader, we're done writing shader code for a moment. Back in C++ land we need to set up a new ofShader object to hold our skybox vertex shader and cubemap fragment shader, and we need to write the function that we'll use to draw our skybox. I have very boringly named this drawSkybox() in the example code, and Listing 11-8 shows what it looks like.

Listing 11-8. drawSkybox()

```
void ofApp::drawSkybox(DirectionalLight& dirLight, glm::mat4& proj,
glm::mat4& view)
{
    using namespace glm;
```

```
mat4 model = translate(cam.pos);
mat4 mvp = proj * view * model;

ofShader& shd = skyboxShader;
glDepthFunc(GL_LEQUAL); ❶
shd.begin();
shd.setUniformMatrix4f("mvp", mvp);
shd.setUniformTexture("envMap", cubemap.getTexture(), 0);
cubeMesh.draw();
shd.end();
glDepthFunc(GL_LESS); ❷
}
```

The drawSkybox() function is remarkable among our draw functions in that it's the first time we've had to use any OpenGL function calls. As it turns out, the default depth comparison function used by openFrameworks (called GL_LESS) will only allow vertices that are *below* 1.0 in normalized device coordinates to be drawn, and openFrameworks doesn't have a way to change this depth comparison function without writing OpenGL function calls.

This is unfortunate for us, because it means that we can't see our skybox at all. We could have gotten around this with hacks in our shader code, but the cleaner fix is to simply change the depth comparison function that we use when we draw our skybox. You can see at ❶ that our function is setting the depth function being used by our program to GL_LEQUAL, which will allow objects that are less than or equal to 1.0 in normalized device coordinates to be drawn. It also has other effects, but they aren't relevant to us right now because immediately after we draw our skybox, we set the depth function back to what it was before (❷).

As a brief aside: way back in Chapter 1, I briefly mentioned the concept of backface culling. This was a rendering optimization technique that saved render time by not rendering the "back" sides of mesh faces. We haven't enabled this in any of our examples, but if we had, we wouldn't be able to see our skybox at all right now. This is because our camera is set inside of the cube mesh, so everywhere we look we see the back side of those mesh faces. In projects that use backface culling, you would either need a different cube mesh (with faces pointed inward), or you would need to disable culling in a similar way to what we just did with our depth function.

Our scene should be looking a lot more convincing right now! However, our two other meshes (the shield and water plane) look a bit out of place now. With a skybox in place, it's obvious that our lighting calculations don't match up with our background image at all. Luckily, we can also use our cubemap to make our lighting a bit more realistic as well.

Creating Cubemap Reflections

We're going to make our meshes feel more grounded in our world by incorporating the same cubemap we used to make our sky into our shield and water lighting calculations. When cubemaps are used to provide lighting information about the environment, this is going to allow us to make the shiny parts of our meshes appear to reflect the world they're in. It's common to hear them referred to as an *environment map*, because they're a texture that will map colors from the environment onto our meshes. The only real trick to this is that our lighting model doesn't support environment lighting, so we'll have to get creative with how we add it in.

Let's start with our water mesh. Since water doesn't have any color of its own, we've been hard coding in a vec3 for the diffuse color so far. To incorporate reflections, all we're going to do is replace this hardcoded color with a sampled color from the environment map. This will only require two lines of shader code but will make a huge difference. The first of these two lines is simply to declare a uniform to hold our cubemap, which the example shader code is going to call "envMap." The second line is our modification to our diffuse color logic. Listing 11-9 shows what this second change looks like.

Listing 11-9. Changing Our Diffuse Calculation to Use a cubemap Reflection

```
//old
vec3 diffCol =  vec3(0.3,0.3,0.4)  *  lightCol * diffAmt;
```

```
//new
vec3 diffCol = texture(envMap, (reflect(-viewDir, nrm))).xyz * lightCol * diffAmt;
```

The difference between this bit of shader logic and the two cube shaders we've already built is that we're not using a vertex position to look up a color in our cubemap anymore. If you think about each fragment as a tiny flat section on our mesh, this makes sense. The color that the environment adds to each fragment is the color of the environment in the direction that the fragment is oriented toward, which is represented by the normal vector. The nice part about this approach is that it works with our water animations by default, since those function by modifying our normal vector.

With that change made, all that's left is to add a line to our drawWater() function to set our cubemap to one of the texture uniforms in our water shader, and to hit play! Figure 11-5 shows off how much of a difference this makes.

Figure 11-5. *Our water without and with cubemap reflections*

This looks a lot more realistic, but our shield mesh is still being rendered without any information from the cubemap. Adding cubemap reflections to objects that have a real diffuse color is a bit trickier than objects like water, which don't have a color of their own. Since we still want the colors of our shield mesh to be visible (at least on any fragments that aren't supposed to be mirror-like), the effect of incorporating our environment map is going to be very subtle.

I mentioned before that our lighting model doesn't support reflections. More modern lighting models incorporate this kind of environment lighting in a way that's accurate to the physical world, but Blinn-Phong lighting does not. This means that how we decide to add cubemap reflections to our shield is more a matter of personal taste than it is anything else. The math we're going to use to do this was chosen because it's simple and looks pretty good without needing to tweak it on a per-cubemap basis. What we're going to do is incorporate the color of our environment into the lightCol variable that we use in all our lighting calculations. To do this, the light color variable that we pass in from our C++ code is going to be replaced by a sceneLight variable that we calculate in our fragment shader. Listing 11-10 shows what this will look like.

Listing 11-10. Adding Environment Reflections to Our Blinn-Phong Shader

```
vec3 envSample = texture(envMap, reflect(-viewDir, nrm)).xyz;
vec3 sceneLight = mix(lightCol, envSample + lightCol * 0.5, 0.5); ❶
```

Notice that in the mix function at ❶, we're adding some amount of our light color to the color we got out of our cubemap. This is because, generally speaking, cubemaps are often a lot darker than the light colors that are set up in a level. This is certainly true for our example code, which uses a white light with an intensity of 1.0. This addition prevents incorporating the cubemap from darkening our meshes by too much. This isn't a perfect solution, since, as you'll see in Figure 11-6—if our cubemap is very bright, like the one we've been using so far—this math will cause our fragments to become brighter than they otherwise would be.

Figure 11-6. *Our scene rendered with and without cubemap lighting applied to the shield (right panel is with cubemap lighting)*

Our current scene has a very white cubemap, a white directional light, and a lot of ambient light, all of which serve to minimize the amount of impact our lighting change will have on our final render. After all, how much visual difference can there be if we're replacing solid white light with mostly white light? In order to showcase what this shader change might look like given different conditions, Figure 11-6 also shows screenshots of how things look if we replace our cubemap with something a bit more colorful, and lower the ambient lighting in our scene. Both cubemaps are included in the example code for you to try out. Figure 11-6 also shows off how well our water shader can adapt to different environment maps, since no changes have been made to that shader to account for the different scene. You can find all the code for generating the screenshots in Figure 11-6 in the "DrawSkybox" project, located in the sample code for this chapter.

There's More to Cubemaps

This is as far as we're going to take cubemap reflections in this book, but it's far from the last word on how to use cubemaps to improve the quality of your lighting. Some games use more complex lighting models that incorporate environment reflections in a more realistic way; others compute cubemaps at runtime so that you can see moving objects in them; and others use specially created cubemaps that allow objects to have glossier or more mirror-like reflections depending on the surface. There are a lot of ways to take what we've done here to the next level, and now that you know the basics of how to work with cubemaps, you have all you need to start tracking down which of these approaches fits your projects best.

Summary

Our scene is looking a lot more realistic now! Here's what we covered in this chapter to make it happen:

- Cubemaps are special textures that allow us to combine six identically sized images into a single texture asset. These six images are sampled from, as though they are the faces of a cube.

- Sampling from a cubemap uses a direction vector instead of UV coordinates. The value you get back assumes that you are located at the center of the cubemap's imaginary cube and are looking in the direction of this sampling vector.

- In shader code, the data type used for accessing a cubemap texture is "samplerCube."

- The perspective divide is when the GPU divides the XYZ coordinates of the gl_Position by its W component after the vertex shader has finished running. Perspective projection matrices use this perspective divide to help create the appearance of a 3D scene.

- Skybox shaders can take advantage of this perspective divide to draw a sky texture that isn't subject to perspective effects.

- Incorporating environment reflections into the shaders used to render regular meshes can take several different forms. In our scene, we replaced the diffuse color entirely for our water mesh, but only changed the light colors used for our shield mesh.

CHAPTER 12

Lighting in Depth

Until now, our scene has been lit only by a single directional light. This has worked for us because we've been trying to light a simple outdoor scene, and a directional light is excellent at simulating light from the sun. Many games get by with lighting that isn't any more complicated than this. However, the drawback for keeping lighting so simple is that it limits the amount of flexibility you have when deciding how your project will look. Since we don't want to always be limited to lighting things with just the sun, this chapter is going to introduce different types of lights commonly used by video games and how to write shaders that work with multiple lights at once. Along the way, we'll change our example project to be a night-time scene, with a number of different sources of light all working together.

Directional Lights

The simplest (and most common) type of light used in game rendering is a directional light. This is the type of light we've been working with so far. As mentioned in earlier chapters, directional lights can be represented by just a color and a direction vector. This is because directional lights are used to simulate light sources that are infinitely far away, and as such, are so far away that their actual position doesn't matter. Therefore, we only worry about the direction that the light from this distance source is coming from. This is great for simulating things like the sun or moon, which has been perfect for our scene so far.

One of the ways we'll be comparing the different types of lights is by the data that's required to render them. Listing 12-1 has a copy of our DirectionalLight struct from the examples we've built so far, so that we have an easy point of reference to use when comparing directional lights to the new light types introduced in this chapter.

© Kyle Halladay 2019
K. Halladay, *Practical Shader Development*, https://doi.org/10.1007/978-1-4842-4457-9_12

Listing 12-1. A Struct That Represents a Directional Light

```
struct DirectionalLight
{
    glm::vec3 direction;
    glm::vec3 color;
    float intensity;
};
```

Light cast by a directional light is unique in that it will hit every mesh in a scene with the exact same intensity and the exact same direction. This is because it's assumed that the light source is so far away that the light rays that are impacting our scene are functionally parallel, as you can see demonstrated in Figure 12-1.

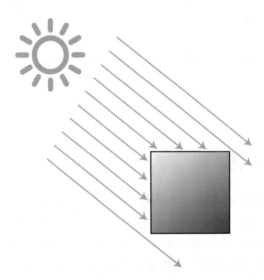

Figure 12-1. *The parallel light rays of a directional light*

Since the lighting math that's required for Blinn-Phong lighting needs the exact data that we store for our directional lights (light color and a direction vector), writing shaders that work with directional lights is very straightforward. This also makes directional lights the cheapest type of light to render in terms of performance, because we don't have to spend GPU cycles figuring out a light direction vector from where the light is located, or how bright a fragment is going to be lit based on how far away it is from a light.

Point Lights

The second commonly used type of light is called a *point light*. This light type is more complicated to set up in code, but it is probably the easiest one to understand conceptually. Point lights are essentially light bulbs. A point light casts light from a single point in 3D space, and the rays cast from that point are directed outward in all directions. You can see this in Figure 12-2, which shows the direction of light rays that get cast by a point light. Notice that, unlike a directional light, the rays from a point light are not all parallel to one another.

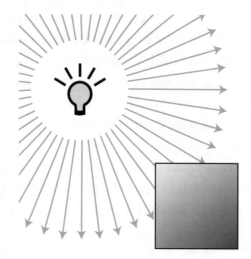

Figure 12-2.   The rays of a point light

The amount of light that a fragment receives from a point light is based on how close that fragment is to that point light's position. This makes sense when you think about how a light bulb works in the real world: objects closer to the light are lit more strongly than objects farther away.

We're going to build a quick shader to demonstrate how to use a point light, so let's start by defining the struct that we'll use to create our point light with in our C++ code. We don't need to store a direction vector for a point light because they emit light in all directions around their position, so there is no single direction to store. Instead, we need to store a position for the light, and the radius of the sphere around that position that will be lit. Listing 12-2 shows the data that we'll be using in our example.

Listing 12-2. A Struct to Represent a Point Light

```
struct PointLight{
    glm::vec3 position;
    glm::vec3 color;
    float intensity;
    float radius;
};
```

One additional piece of data that you often see stored with a point light is information about the light's *falloff*. A point light emits light in a sphere around its position, and fragments that are closer to the center of that sphere will receive more light than objects near the edge. The falloff of a light describes how much light each object that is lit by the light receives, based on its distance from our light's position. Shaders implement a light's falloff as a series of math operations, but it's common to see point light structs store constants that can be used to customize how this math works out. We're going to be using a very simple function for our point light's falloff, so we don't have any data to store today.

Now that we know what our light's data will look like, we can start building a shader to use that data. We'll start by looking at the code for a shader that uses a single point light and only handles diffuse lighting. You can see the code for this in Listing 12-3.

Listing 12-3. PointLight.frag

```
#version 410

uniform vec3 meshCol;
uniform vec3 lightPos;      ❶
uniform float lightRadius;
uniform vec3 lightCol;

in vec3 fragNrm;
in vec3 fragWorldPos;
out vec4 outCol;

void main(){
    vec3 normal = normalize(fragNrm);
    vec3 toLight = lightPos - fragWorldPos;    ❷
    vec3 lightDir = normalize(toLight);
    float distToLight = length(toLight);       ❸
```

```
    float falloff = max(0.0, 1.0 - (distToLight / lightRadius));  ❹
    vec3 adjLightCol = lightCol * falloff;
    float finalBright = max(0, dot(toLight, normal));
    outCol = finalBright * adjLightCol * meshCol, 1.0);
}
```

The first few lines of Listing 12-3 show the new uniforms that we need to declare for our point light: lightPos and lightRadius (❶). These will exactly match up to the data in the struct we just looked at.

The first bit of shader math that's different from working with a directional light starts at ❷. Since point lights emit light in a whole lot of directions, we need to calculate the light direction that is hitting each fragment individually. We also need to know how far from the light source our fragment is. The first step in accomplishing both these goals is to calculate the vector between our current fragment and the position of the point light. To get our light direction vector, we can simply normalize this toLight vector. Calculating the magnitude of a vector can be done with GLSL's length() function (❸).

Once we have our distance and direction, our next step is to calculate the brightness of the light hitting our current fragment. This is where our light's falloff function comes into play. To implement our falloff, we're going to take the radius of the spherical area around our point light that will receive light, and divide our distance value by this radius. The resulting value will express how close to the light our fragment is, as a percentage. As our distance value approaches the maximum effective range of our light, this percentage will increase. Values greater than 1.0 mean that our fragment is too far away to receive any light at all. Subtracting this value from 1.0 gives us the intensity of the light that will hit our fragment, expressed as a percentage of the maximum light intensity. We can then multiply the light color by this value to end up with our final lighting contribution for our fragment. You can see this calculating happening at ❹.

This is known as a *linear falloff* and means that a fragment that is located at our light source gets 100% of the intensity of the light, a fragment located outside the radius will get 0%, and a fragment located halfway between these two values will get exactly 50% of the intensity. There are lots of different functions that people use for light falloffs, each with different trade-offs between physical accuracy and how many GPU cycles they take to compute, but the linear falloff we're using is probably the simplest.

One thing to keep in mind with point lights is that it takes the same time to perform lighting calculations no matter how far away a fragment is from that light. This means that by default, you pay a performance cost for point lights even if a fragment is too far away to be lit at all. This is a problem, because lighting calculations are expensive, and most games don't want to spend GPU cycles handling point lights that aren't contributing a noticeable amount of light. For this reason, most games will do some work on the nonshader side to determine which lights are close enough to matter for a mesh, and only run shaders that deal with those lights. How this is done can vary from engine to engine. The Unreal Engine, for example, can generate versions of each shader that can handle a different number of lights. Meshes that are close to many lights might be rendered with a shader variant that supports four lights at once, while objects far away may use the one light version of the same shader. We aren't going to do anything like that today, but it's something to keep in mind for your projects.

Now that we've walked through Listing 12-3, it's a pretty short jump from there to modifying our Blinn-Phong shader to support point lights instead of directional lights. We aren't going to support multiple light types in our shader yet, so we won't modify the existing Blinn-Phong shader we have. Instead, create a new fragment shader to use for the point light version of our shader; I called mine "pointLight.frag." To drive home the fact that the lighting math that we're using is going to be the same no matter what type of light is shining on our fragment, let's move the lighting code into its own functions. This is going to let us more easily separate the lighting model calculations from the work we need to do to extract information from our light. Listing 12-4 shows off what this function looks like.

Listing 12-4. blinnPhong()

```
float diffuse(vec3 lightDir, vec3 nrm)
{
      float diffAmt = max(0.0, dot(nrm, lightDir));
      return diffAmt;
}

float specular(vec3 lightDir, vec3 viewDir, vec3 nrm, float shininess)
{
      vec3 halfVec = normalize(viewDir + lightDir);
      float specAmt = max(0.0, dot(halfVec, nrm));
      return pow(specAmt, shininess);
}
```

This is the first time we've written a function in GLSL, but they work the same way as any C function would. If we wanted to rewrite the directional light version of this shader to use these new functions, it would look like Listing 12-5.

Listing 12-5. Rewriting main() to Use Our New Lighting Functions

```
void main(){
      vec3 nrm = texture(normTex, fragUV).rgb;
      nrm = normalize(nrm * 2.0 - 1.0);
      nrm = normalize(TBN * nrm);
      vec3 viewDir = normalize( cameraPos - fragWorldPos);

      vec3 envSample = texture(envMap, reflect(-viewDir, nrm)).xyz;
      vec3 sceneLight = mix(lightCol, envSample + lightCol * 0.5, 0.5);

      float diffAmt = diffuse(lightDir, nrm); ❶
      float specAmt = specular(lightDir, viewDir, nrm, 4.0); ❷

      vec3 diffCol = texture(diffuseTex, fragUV).xyz * sceneLight * diffAmt;

      float specMask = texture(specTex, fragUV).x;
      vec3 specCol = specMask * sceneLight * specAmt;
      vec3 envSample = texture(envMap, reflect(-viewDir, nrm)).xyz;

      outCol = vec4(diffCol + specCol + ambientCol, 1.0);
}
```

This is the exact same shader that we wrote in the last chapter, just with some of the lighting math replaced by function calls at ❶ and ❷. It's great that this gives us an example of writing functions in our shader code, but the key point to take away here is that regardless of what type of light we're using, the actual lighting math stays exactly the same. The changes we need to make to this shader code to support point lights should look very familiar after our last example. We just need to calculate our own light direction and multiply a few things by our light's falloff value. Listing 12-6 has all the details.

Listing 12-6. Modifying main() to Work with a Point Light

```
//some new uniforms, we also removed the lightDir uniform
uniform vec3 lightPos;
uniform float lightRadius;

void main()
{
    vec3 nrm = texture(normTex, fragUV).rgb;
    nrm = normalize(nrm * 2.0 - 1.0);
    nrm = normalize(TBN * nrm);
    vec3 viewDir = normalize( cameraPos - fragWorldPos);

    vec3 envSample = texture(envMap, reflect(-viewDir, nrm)).xyz;
    vec3 sceneLight = mix(lightCol, envSample + lightCol * 0.5, 0.5);

    //manual light direction calculation
    vec3 toLight = lightPos - fragWorldPos;
    vec3 lightDir = normalize(toLight);
    float distToLight = length(toLight);
    float falloff = 1.0 - (distToLight / lightRadius);

    float diffAmt = diffuse(lightDir, nrm) * falloff; ❶
    float specAmt = specular(lightDir, viewDir, nrm, 4.0) * falloff; ❷
    //rest of function unchanged
```

Notice that in addition to providing our own lightDir vector, we also need to multiply our diffAmt and specAmt values by the falloff of our light (❶ and ❷). This is because these two variables store how much of each type of light our fragment will receive, and that value needs to be reduced based on the distance that our fragment is from the point light. We also needed to replace the lightDir uniform with two new uniforms, which are also labeled in Listing 12-6, but those are the only changes we need to make! If you make the same modification to our water shader, you'll end up with two completely functional point light shaders. Just like every other example we've built, though, we can't enjoy our shiny new shader without a few changes to our C++ code, so let's jump back there and get things set up.

Listing 12-7. Setting Up a Point Light in Our draw() Function

```
void ofApp::draw() {
        using namespace glm;

        static float t = 0.0f;
        t += ofGetLastFrameTime();

        PointLight pointLight; ❶
        pointLight.color = vec3(1, 1, 1);
        pointLight.radius = 1.0f;
        pointLight.position = vec3(sin(t), 0.5, 0.25); ❷
        pointLight.intensity = 3.0;

        mat4 proj = perspective(cam.fov, 1024.0f / 768.0f, 0.01f, 10.0f);

        cam.pos = glm::vec3(0, 0.75f, 1.0);
        mat4 view = inverse(translate(cam.pos));

        drawShield(pointLight, proj, view);
        drawWater(pointLight, proj, view);
        drawSkybox(pointLight, proj, view);

}
```

Most of setting up our point light is a simple matter of filling out a PointLight struct (❶). In Listing 12-7, the values for the point light have been set up to create a small, intense light, to really show off that we're working with a spherical light instead of a global directional one. To further show this off, the preceding example code has added a bit of additional code to have the light's position oscillate on the X axis, between -1 and +1 over time, using a sin() function (❷). The other change that needs to happen in order to render our light is to modify the drawShield(), drawWater(), and drawSkybox() functions to take a PointLight structure and set up the shader uniforms appropriately. Since this is just a matter of providing some new uniforms, I've omitted providing the code here, but as always, the full code for this is included in the examples for this chapter.

If you run the program as it is now, you should be able to see the lighting on the shield and water meshes move as the light moves left and right. However, everything will look a little bit off, because the skybox that's currently set up in our scene is of a daytime scene but we no longer have a global directional light. This means our meshes are going to appear way too dark for the skybox. To make things a bit more realistic (and really show off our new point light), a night-time skybox is provided in the assets folder for this chapter. With the night-time skybox, the fact that the only source of light in the level is our tiny point light is a lot more believable. You can see what our scene looks like rendered with each skybox in Figure 12-3. You can find all the code used to render Figure 12-3 in the "PointLight" project of this chapter's example code.

Figure 12-3. *Rendering our point light example with two different skyboxes. Note that because our water color is calculated based on the skybox, a darker skybox also means darker water, even in the lit areas.*

Spot Lights

The third type of light that's common to see used in video games is *spot lights*. Spot lights work similarly to point lights, in that they have a definite position in the game world. Unlike point lights, they cast light in a cone instead of a sphere. Figure 12-4 illustrates this in a diagram, but if you've ever used a flashlight, you already know what this will look like.

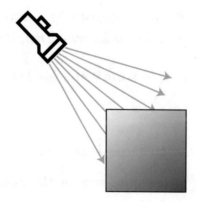

Figure 12-4. *The light rays for a spot light*

Just like we did with our point light, let's start our discussion of spot lights by talking about the data that we'll need to represent one in code. Data-wise, spot lights are a bit of a mashup of directional lights and point lights. We need both a position and a direction vector, and a value to represent the width of our spot light's cone of light. Finally, we'll need the usual suspects: color and intensity. You could also specify a radius or range for spot lights, so that fragments farther away would steadily get less light, but to keep things simple we're going to omit that for now. Listing 12-8 shows what our spot light struct is going to look like.

Listing 12-8. A Struct for a Spot Light

```
struct SpotLight
{
    glm::vec3 position;
    glm::vec3 direction;
    float cutoff;

    glm::vec3 color;
    float intensity;
};
```

Also similar to point lights is that our lighting calculations aren't going to change when we use spot lights, the only thing that will change is the shader code that we use to calculate the inputs to those calculations. To see this in action, let's create a new fragment shader and call it "spotLight.frag." You can copy and paste the point light shader we just made into this file and delete a few lines, or rewrite it yourself, but our starting point for writing our spot light shader should look like Listing 12-9.

Listing 12-9. Modifying main() to Work with a Spot Light

```
uniform vec3 lightConeDir;
uniform vec3 lightPos;
uniform float lightCutoff; //replace light radius

//diffuse() and specular() functions remain the same

void main()
{
      vec3 nrm = texture(normTex, fragUV).rgb;
      nrm = normalize(nrm * 2.0 - 1.0);
      nrm = normalize(TBN * nrm);
      vec3 viewDir = normalize( cameraPos - fragWorldPos);

      vec3 envSample = texture(envMap, reflect(-viewDir, nrm)).xyz;
      vec3 sceneLight = mix(lightCol, envSample + lightCol * 0.5, 0.5);

      //our spot light calculations will go here

      float diffAmt = diffuse(lightDir, nrm) * falloff; ❶
      float specAmt = specular(lightDir, viewDir, nrm, 4.0) * falloff; ❷
      //rest of function unchanged
```

We'll still need to multiply by a falloff value at ❶ and ❷, except now that falloff value will represent whether our fragment is inside the spot light's cone or not. In fact, there's even less difference between our spot light shader and our point light shader than there was between the point light and directional light ones. This is going to come in handy later in this chapter when we start writing shaders that can work with multiple lights at once, but for now it just makes our lives a little bit easier.

Since we deleted a bunch of the shader logic that was calculating inputs to our lighting functions, we need to add in some new code to replace it. The first thing is to get our light direction vector again. It might surprise you to learn that we won't be using the lightConeDir uniform that we're passing into the shader to calculate this. This is because rays that are cast by a spot light still travel in many directions (they aren't parallel like a directional light), so it doesn't make sense to use a uniform light direction vector for our lighting math. The light direction vector will only be used to help us calculate the falloff value that we'll multiply everything by at the end. Calculating the light direction vector is instead going to be identical to how we did this for our point light. Listing 12-10 shows what I mean.

Listing 12-10. Calculating a Light Direction Vector for a Spot Light

```
vec3 toLight = lightPos - fragWorldPos;
vec3 lightDir = normalize(toLight);
```

This is just like what we did for point lights, except that we're leaving out the bit of shader math that calculated the distance from our fragment to the light. This is because, for simplicity's sake, we're creating a spot light that shines infinitely in the direction it's pointed right now.

Our next step is to calculate whether or not our fragment lies within the cone of our spot light at all. This is going to give us a falloff value of either 0 or 1, which we'll multiply the result of our lighting calculations by. In this way, a spot light is just a point light with a different type of falloff calculation. Like most lighting math, this is easier understood with a diagram. Figure 12-5 illustrates the problem that we're faced with.

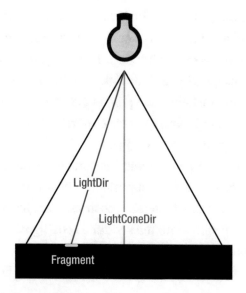

Figure 12-5. *Illustrating spot light math*

We have two direction vectors: the direction of the spot light's cone (LightConeDir) and the direction from our fragment to the light's position (LightDir). If the angle between these two vectors is less than the cutoff angle of the light, then we know that our fragment is within the spot light's cone and should be lit. You may remember from Chapter 8, that the result of a dot product operation is the cosine of the angle between the two vectors. This means that as long as the lightCutoff value that we pass in from C++ is the cosine of our spot light's cone angle, we can use a dot product in our shader code to compare the angle between LightDir and LightConeDir to the cutoff angle. Listing 12-11 shows what this math looks like.

Listing 12-11. Determining if Our Fragment Is Within a Spot Light's Cone

```
vec3 toLight = lightPos - fragWorldPos;
vec3 lightDir = normalize(toLight);
float cosAngle = dot(lightConeDir, -lightDir); ❶
float falloff = 0.0;
if (cosAngle > lightCutoff) ❷
{
      falloff = 1.0;
}
```

There are a couple of things to note about Listing 12-11. First of all, just like the previous times we've used a dot product to compare two vectors, we need to make sure both vectors are pointing in the same direction. The lightDir vector that we calculate for our lighting calculations goes toward the light's position, not away from it like the direction vector we get from the light. This means that in order for us to get meaningful data from our dot product calculation, we have to compare the lightConeDir value from our light against a negated lightDir vector (❶).

The second thing that's important about this code example is the conditional at ❷. At first glance, it might appear like the comparison is backward, which would be the case if we were comparing actual angles instead of cosines of angles. However, since we're going to pass our lightCutoff value into the shader as cos(lightCutoff), it makes sense that we want to know if our cosAngle value is greater than the lightCutoff value, because the closer our cosAngle value is to 1.0, the closer to parallel the lightDir and lightConeDir vectors are.

Listing 12-12 shows the main() function for our shield's shader with all the changes needed to use a spot light. If you're following along with your own code, you'll need to make similar changes to the water shader. The source for all of this can be found in the "SpotLights" example project.

Listing 12-12. Our Shield Shader's main() Modified for Spot Lights

```
void main(){
        vec3 nrm = texture(normTex, fragUV).rgb;
        nrm = normalize(nrm * 2.0 - 1.0);
        nrm = normalize(TBN * nrm);
        vec3 viewDir = normalize( cameraPos - fragWorldPos);

        vec3 envSample = texture(envMap, reflect(-viewDir, nrm)).xyz;
        vec3 sceneLight = mix(lightCol, envSample + lightCol * 0.5, 0.5);

        vec3 toLight = lightPos - fragWorldPos;
        vec3 lightDir = normalize(toLight);
        float angle = dot(lightConeDir, -lightDir);
        float falloff = 0.0;
        if (angle > lightCutoff)
        {
                falloff = 1.0;
        }

        float diffAmt = diffuse(lightDir, nrm) * falloff;
        float specAmt = specular(lightDir, viewDir, nrm, 4.0) * falloff;

        vec3 diffCol = texture(diffuseTex, fragUV).xyz * sceneLight * diffAmt;

        float specMask = texture(specTex, fragUV).x;
        vec3 specCol = specMask * sceneLight * specAmt;
        vec3 envSample = texture(envMap, reflect(-viewDir, nrm)).xyz;

        vec3 envLighting = envSample * specMask * diffAmt;
        specCol = mix(envLighting, specCol, min(1.0,specAmt));
        outCol = vec4(diffCol + specCol + ambientCol, 1.0);

}
```

All that's left to do before we see the fruits of our labors is to make a few quick changes to our C++ code. Just like for point lights, you'll need to modify the drawWater() and drawShield() functions to take a SpotLight struct and pass our light's values to the appropriate uniforms. For the purposes of a really easy to see example screenshot, I set up my spot light to be positioned exactly where the camera is and point in the same direction. You can see this code in Listing 12-13.

Listing 12-13. Setting Up a Spot Light in C++

```cpp
void ofApp::draw() {
        using namespace glm;

        mat4 proj = perspective(cam.fov, 1024.0f / 768.0f, 0.01f, 10.0f);

        cam.pos = glm::vec3(0, 0.75f, 1.0);
        mat4 view = inverse(translate(cam.pos));

        SpotLight spotLight;
        spotLight.color = vec3(1, 1, 1);
        spotLight.position = cam.pos;
        spotLight.intensity = 1.0;
        spotLight.direction = vec3(0, 0, -1);
        spotLight.cutoff = glm::cos(glm::radians(15.0f));

        drawShield(spotLight, proj, view);
        drawWater(spotLight, proj, view);
        drawSkybox(spotLight, proj, view);
}
```

If you run the example scene with all these changes, you should be greeted with something that looks like the leftmost image in Figure 12-6. At first glance this might look like an error, but it's exactly what we're looking for: only the area of the shield that's within our spot light's cone is getting any light. To demonstrate this a different way, the right image in Figure 12-6 shows what it would look like if our cutoff angle was much larger and the spot light was located to the right of the camera. All the code to render Figure 12-6 can be found in the "SpotLight" project of this chapter's sample code.

Figure 12-6. *Rendering our scene with two differently set up spot lights*

Multiple Light Sources

Being able to light our meshes with different types of lights is cool, but it still isn't very useful for building 3D levels. For anything except very simple scenes, we need to be able to have multiple lights shine on our objects at once. Figuring out new ways to handle multiple lights is something that graphics programmers have been working on for decades, and there are lots of different ways that the problem can be approached. We're going to look at two different ways to do it in this chapter. We'll do things the easy way first, which will require that we know how many lights we'll have up front. Then we'll finish with a more flexible approach that can handle as many lights as we want, at the cost of performance.

The easy way is very similar to what we've already done, but requires that we learn some new shader writing techniques. To start with, we're going to define structs in shader code to help manage the types of uniforms needed for different types of lights. Then we're going to create arrays of these structs to store the data for each light in our scene. These arrays will be sized according to how many of each light type we want to support. We'll then use this data to perform our lighting calculations. This is the first time we've worked with arrays or structs in shader code, but it all works pretty much how it does in C++. Listing 12-14 shows what our combined light shader's uniforms will look like, so create a new fragment shader and copy the code below into there.

Listing 12-14. Declaring the Uniforms for Our Light Array Shader

```glsl
struct DirectionalLight {
vec3 direction;
vec3 color;
};

struct PointLight {
vec3 position;
vec3 color;
     float radius;
};

struct SpotLight{
     vec3 position;
     vec3 direction;
     vec3 color;
     float cutoff;
};

#define NUM_DIR_LIGHTS 1
#define NUM_POINT_LIGHTS 2
#define NUM_SPOT_LIGHTS 2

uniform DirectionalLight directionalLights[NUM_DIR_LIGHTS];
uniform PointLight pointLights[NUM_POINT_LIGHTS];
uniform SpotLight spotLights[NUM_SPOT_LIGHTS];
uniform sampler2D diffuseTex;
uniform sampler2D specTex;
uniform sampler2D normTex;
uniform samplerCube envMap;

in vec3 fragNrm;
in vec3 fragWorldPos;
in vec2 fragUV;
in mat3 TBN;

out vec4 outCol;
```

This looks very different from any shaders we've written so far, but there are no tricks about writing this sort of code in GLSL; everything behaves exactly as if we had written it in C. We now have a shader that's expecting a single directional light, two point lights, and two spot lights.

Writing shader code to use all these lights is relatively easy now that we've handled each light in isolation. Lights are always additive, meaning that if we shine more lights on a mesh, it will always result in that mesh appearing brighter. This means that handling more lights is just a matter of calculating the lighting contribution from each of them individually, and then adding up the results. Before we start writing light handling code, though, there are some values that it makes sense to calculate once at the very beginning of our main() function, and reuse for each light. Listing 12-15 shows the beginning of our main() function with these up-front calculations.

Listing 12-15. The Initial Calculations That Our Combined Light Shader Will Make

```
void main(){
    vec3 nrm = texture(normTex, fragUV).rgb;
    nrm = normalize(nrm * 2.0 - 1.0);
    nrm = normalize(TBN * nrm);
    vec3 viewDir = normalize( cameraPos - fragWorldPos);

    vec3 diffuseColor = texture(diffuseTex, fragUV).xyz;
    float specMask = texture(specTex, fragUV).x;
    vec3 envReflections = texture(envMap, reflect(-viewDir, nrm)).xyz;

    vec3 finalColor = vec3(0,0,0); ❶
```

Except for the last line, all of this is code that we've seen before. It just makes sense to move all of it to the beginning of our function, because things like the view direction or sampled colors from our textures are going to stay the same for every light. The last line (❶) is simply declaring the vector that we're going to add to as we calculate the contribution from each light. At the end of the function, this vector will contain the sum of all the lights shining on our fragment, and we'll write that value to our outColor variable.

With the initial calculations out of the way, it's time to handle our lights! Since we're going to be handling one or more lights of each category, it makes sense to encapsulate our lighting calculations inside three different loops (one loop per light type). This is the first time we'll have seen a for loop used in a shader, but it works the exact same way as the C++ equivalent. Listing 12-16 shows what our first loop—the directional light loop—is going to look like.

Listing 12-16. Our Directional Light Handling Loop

```
for (int i = 0; i < NUM_DIR_LIGHTS; ++i)
{
    DirectionalLight light = directionalLights[i]; ❶
    vec3 sceneLight = mix(light.color, envSample + light.color * 0.5, 0.5);

    float diffAmt = diffuse(light.direction, nrm);
    float specAmt = specular(light.direction, viewDir, nrm, 4.0) * specMask;

    vec3 envLighting = envReflections * specMask * diffAmt;

    vec3 specCol = specMask * sceneLight * specAmt;

    finalColor += diffuseColor * diffAmt * light.color; ❷
    finalColor += specCol * sceneLight;
}
```

All the lighting math here is identical to the logic that we wrote when we first made a directional light shader. You can see at ❶ that getting values out of our light arrays is identical to C++, as is accessing member values out of the structs we've defined. The only actually new thing in our lighting calculations is that we're adding our final diffuse and specular values to that finalColor vector that we declared in Listing 12-15 (❷). We've already mentioned that this is going to be the sum of all of our lights, but now you can see it in action.

Our second loop is going to handle our array of point lights. Just like with directional lights, all the actual lighting math that we're doing is the same as it was in the point light shader we wrote earlier in this chapter. The only difference is that it's now in a for loop and adding to finalColor. Listing 12-17 shows what this loop looks like.

Listing 12-17. The Point Light Loop

```
for (int i = 0; i < NUM_POINT_LIGHTS; ++i)
{
    PointLight light = pointLights[i];
    vec3 sceneLight = mix(light.color, envSample + light.color * 0.5, 0.5);
```

```
    vec3 toLight = light.position - fragWorldPos;
    vec3 lightDir = normalize(toLight);
    float distToLight = length(toLight);
    float falloff = 1.0 - (distToLight / light.radius);

    float diffAmt = diffuse(lightDir, nrm) * falloff;
    float specAmt = specular(lightDir, viewDir, nrm, 4.0) * specMask *
    falloff;

    vec3 envLighting = envReflections * specMask * diffAmt;
    vec3 specCol = specMask * sceneLight * specAmt;

    finalColor += diffAmt * sceneLight * diffuseColor;
    finalColor += specCol;
}
```

Finally, we end with our spot light loop, which is shown in Listing 12-18. The only difference between this snippet and the spot light function that we wrote before is that I've collapsed the conditional that compared the lightCutoff angle to our computed angle into a ternary function to save some space (❶). Otherwise, it's business as usual.

Listing 12-18. The Spot Light Loop, and the End of Our main() Function

```
for (int i = 0; i < NUM_SPOT_LIGHTS; ++i)
{
    SpotLight light = spotLights[i];
    vec3 sceneLight = mix(light.color, envSample + light.color * 0.5, 0.5);
    vec3 toLight = light.position - fragWorldPos;
    vec3 lightDir = normalize(toLight);
    float angle = dot(light.direction, -lightDir);
    float falloff = (angle > light.cutoff) ? 1.0 : 0.0; ❶

    float diffAmt = diffuse(lightDir, nrm) * falloff;
    float specAmt = specular(lightDir, viewDir, nrm, 4.0) * specMask *
    falloff;
    vec3 envLighting = envReflections * specMask * diffAmt;

    vec3 specCol = specMask * sceneLight * specAmt;
```

```
        finalColor += diffAmt * sceneLight * diffuseColor;
        finalColor += specCol;
}
```

Our main() function then ends with us adding our scene's ambient color to our finalColor value and writing the sum to outColor. If we condense all the loops and prelighting calculations that have been shown in the previous code examples, our main function in its entirety looks like Listing 12-19.

Listing 12-19. A Bird's Eye View of Our Multi-light main() Function

```
void main(){
        PRELIGHTING CALCULATIONS
        DIRECTIONAL LOOP
        POINT LOOP
        SPOT LOOP

        outCol = vec4(finalColor + ambientCol, 1.0);  ❶
}
```

We now have a completely set up multi-light Blinn-Phong shader. As before, the next step if you're following along at home is to copy over this work to your water shader. This won't be a simple copy and paste job, because the lighting calculations that we use on our water mesh are a little bit different from what we do for our shield (specifically, with how we handle diffuse color). However, the core concepts will stay the same: you'll still be creating arrays of lights and wrapping code you've written before in for loops. Once you're done, I recommend checking your work against the example code, which you can find in the "FixedLightCount" example project.

As with all our examples, the last step is to set up our C++ code. However, this time we're going to do some heavier duty refactoring to our code than usual, since we now need to handle many lights at once. We're going to start off by declaring three arrays of light structures in ofApp.h, one array each of DirectionalLight, PointLight, and SpotLight structs. Make sure the sizes of these arrays are at least as large as the sizes of the arrays in our shader code. We're also going to modify the function signature for our draw() functions, so that they no longer take a light structure as an argument. Listing 12-20 shows the lines in ofApp.h that have been added or changed.

Listing 12-20. Modifications to ofApp.h

```
class ofApp : public ofBaseApp {
    //unchanged code omitted for brevity
    void drawWater(glm::mat4& proj, glm::mat4& view);
    void drawShield(glm::mat4& proj, glm::mat4& view);
    void drawSkybox(glm::mat4& proj, glm::mat4& view);

    DirectionalLight dirLights[1];
    PointLight pointLights[2];
    SpotLight spotLights[2];
};
```

Next, we need to write some code to populate the light structs in each of these arrays with some initial values. I recommend giving each light a different color so that you can see how each one contributes to the final render. Since we've already seen how to set up values for each type of light, I'm going to omit the code here. If you want to use the same values that the example code uses, refer to the example project. If you aren't matching the example code exactly, I recommend still giving every light a unique color so that you can see how each light contributes to the final render.

Our drawWater() and drawShield() functions also need a bit of tweaking, because we need to set the values on our uniform arrays. This is the first time we've done this, but it's very simple. Listing 12-21 shows how to set up the values for one of our point lights. Follow that example and add code to set up the rest of the lights.

Listing 12-21. Setting Up a Light Uniform for Our Multi-light Shader

```
shd.setUniform3f("pointLights[1].position", pointLights[1].position);
shd.setUniform3f("pointLights[1].color", getLightColor(pointLights[1]));
shd.setUniform1f("pointLights[1].radius", pointLights[1].radius);
```

With that set up, running our program should give you something like Figure 12-7. We've covered a lot of new concepts in a very short amount of time to make this example work, so make sure to compare your code to the example project if things don't look quite right initially.

Figure 12-7. *Rendering our scene with five lights. Notice the red and green point lights, blue and cyan spot lights, and the yellow directional light.*

A More Flexible Multi-light Setup

This chapter is already a bit long, but I feel it's important to show you one other way to handle multiple lights in our scene. As we discussed, the previous solution's major downfall was that it didn't scale. We always had to pay the cost of shading five lights, even if we only had one that was contributing to our scene, and we couldn't add more lights than we hard coded up front. This second way of handling multiple lights trades a bit of efficiency for greater flexibility. It also gives us an excuse to revisit alpha blending, which we haven't looked at for a while.

The setup we're going to build will be able to support a single directional light, and any number of point lights. We'll leave out spot lights just to keep our example code a bit shorter. Instead of writing a single shader that combines all our light types together, this second technique works by drawing each mesh multiple times: once for each light that's shining on it. This is sometimes referred to as multi-pass shading, where each "pass" is a draw call that we issue for the same mesh. Each pass will also involve its own shader. The first pass, for our directional light, will render our mesh with a shader virtually identical to our original directional light Blinn-Phong shader. The point light passes (there will be one for each light in our scene) will use a shader like our single point light shader, except modified to not include ambient light, since we don't want each pass adding more ambient light to our mesh.

The secret sauce in all of this is that before we issue the draw calls for our point lights, we enable additive alpha blending, which you may remember lets us simply add color to what's already in the color buffer. We also change our depth test equation to GL_LEQUAL, so that we don't ignore fragments being drawn to the same spot as previous passes of the same mesh. This little bit of set up means that each point light pass simply adds the lighting contribution from the point light to the already drawn mesh underneath, brightening the mesh without clearing out the lighting already done. This lets us draw any number of point lights without needing to know how many we have up front. Instead, we can adjust the number of passes we want on the fly.

Since the shaders we'll use for these passes only need to support a single light at once time, we can reuse the shaders we wrote earlier in this chapter to handle single lights, rather than write entirely new ones. Our base pass is going to be our directional light and ambient light pass, since we only want ambient light added to our mesh once. This means that we can use our single directional light shader as is. Our single point light shader can be used as well, except that you'll need to remove the ambient light code from that shader.

Once that's done, the rest of the work is just C++ code changes. The first of these changes is refactoring our light structs so that we can pass any type of light to our drawShield() and drawWater() functions, and have those lights be able to set themselves up correctly. Listing 12-22 shows what this is going to look like.

Listing 12-22. Refactoring Our Light Structs

```
struct Light
{
    virtual bool isPointLight() { return false; }
    virtual void apply(ofShader& shd) {};
};

struct DirectionalLight : public Light
{
    glm::vec3 direction;
    glm::vec3 color;
    float intensity;

    virtual void apply(ofShader& shd) override
    {
```

```
        shd.setUniform3f("lightDir ", -direction); ❶
        shd.setUniform3f("lightCol ", color * intensity);
    }
};

struct PointLight : public Light
{
    glm::vec3 position;
    glm::vec3 color;
    float intensity;
    float radius;

    virtual bool isPointLight() override { return true; }
    virtual void apply(ofShader& shd) override
    {
        shd.setUniform3f("lightPos ", position);
        shd.setUniform3f("lightCol ", color * intensity);
        shd.setUniform1f("lightRadius ", radius);
    }
};
```

The real meat of this change is to encapsulate the code required to set up shader uniforms in the lights themselves (❶), so that we can use polymorphism to simplify our drawing code later. Admittedly, the isPointLight() function is a hack, but it's a convenient one for our purposes, since we're going to use that to decide which shader our meshes should use.

The drawWater() and drawShield() functions are also going to change. We're going to pass a Light& as the first argument to these functions now. Once we're in the functions, we're going to use that Light& to decide which shader to use, and to set up our uniforms. Listing 12-23 shows what this looks like in our drawShield() function, but identical changes will need to be made to our drawWater() function if you're following along at home.

Listing 12-23. Our New drawShield() Function

```
void ofApp::drawShield(Light& light, glm::mat4& proj, glm::mat4& view)
{
      using namespace glm;

      mat4 model = translate(vec3(0.0, 0.75, 0.0f));
      mat4 mvp = proj * view * model;
      mat3 normalMatrix = mat3(transpose(inverse(model)));

      ofShader shd = light.isPointLight() ? pointLightShieldShader :
      dirLightShieldShader; ❶

      shd.begin();
      light.apply(shd); ❷
      shd.setUniformMatrix4f("mvp", mvp);
      shd.setUniformMatrix4f("model", model);
      shd.setUniformMatrix3f("normal", normalMatrix);
      shd.setUniform3f("meshSpecCol", glm::vec3(1, 1, 1));
      shd.setUniformTexture("diffuseTex", diffuseTex, 0);;
      shd.setUniformTexture("specTex", specTex, 1);
      shd.setUniformTexture("normTex", nrmTex, 2);
      shd.setUniformTexture("envMap", cubemap.getTexture(), 3);

      shd.setUniform3f("ambientCol", glm::vec3(0.0, 0.0, 0.0));
      shd.setUniform3f("cameraPos", cam.pos);
      shieldMesh.draw();
      shd.end();
}
```

You can see why the isPointLight() function is convenient for us at ❶, since it means that we can deduce what shader to use simply based on the type of light that gets passed to our function. Also shown in Listing 12-23 is the apply() function that we added to our lights (❷), which takes the place of the manual uniform setup that we've done in past examples and saves us a lot of code duplication.

With changes made to both drawWater() and drawShield(), it's time to look at our new draw() function. One thing you'll note right away is that the light setup code has been moved out of this function. If you look online in the example code, you'll see the logic for that has been moved to our setup() function now. This is where that code should have been living all along, but keeping everything in the draw() function was convenient for minimizing the number of different code snippets we needed. We've set up lights so many times by now that I think it's safe to move that code where it belongs. The only new thing going on with setting up our lights is that all our point lights are now being stored in a std::vector, which lets us modify the number of point lights we want to use at runtime. The example code sets up three different point lights. For reference's sake, Listing 12-24 shows what setting up the first one looks like in setup().

Listing 12-24. Setting Up a Point Light and Adding It to Our Point Light Array

```
PointLight pl0;
pl0.color = glm::vec3(1, 0, 0);
pl0.radius = 1.0f;
pl0.position = glm::vec3(-0.5, 0.35, 0.25);
pl0.intensity = 3.0;

pointLights.push_back(pl0);
```

Putting our point lights in an array means that our draw() function can simply iterate over this array and call the drawShield() and drawWater() functions once for each of these lights. Remember that we're going to additively blend the result of each point with the color data already written to the back buffer. With that in mind, Listing 12-25 shows off what our new draw() function looks like.

Listing 12-25. The draw() Function for Our New Multi-light Example

```
void ofApp::draw() {
    using namespace glm;
    cam.pos = glm::vec3(0, 0.75f, 1.0);

    mat4 proj = perspective(cam.fov, 1024.0f / 768.0f, 0.01f, 10.0f);
    mat4 view = inverse(translate(cam.pos));

    drawSkybox(proj, view);

    drawWater(dirLight, proj, view);
    drawShield(dirLight, proj, view);

    beginRenderingPointLights();  ❶
```

```
for (int i = 0; i < pointLights.size(); ++i)
{
        drawWater(pointLights[i], proj, view);
        drawShield(pointLights[i], proj, view);
}

endRenderingPointLights(); ❷
}
```

There are two more functions to talk about, shown at ❶ and ❷. These are the functions that handle setting up our blending and depth testing to support our additive lights. Listing 12-26 shows off the few lines of code that make up each of these functions.

Listing 12-26. beginRenderingPointLights and endRenderingPointLights

```
void ofApp::beginRenderingPointLights()
{
    ofEnableAlphaBlending();
    ofEnableBlendMode(ofBlendMode::OF_BLENDMODE_ADD);
    glDepthFunc(GL_LEQUAL);
}

void ofApp::endRenderingPointLights()
{
    ofDisableAlphaBlending();
    ofDisableBlendMode();
    glDepthFunc(GL_LESS);
}
```

Nothing in these two functions is new to us. The alpha blending code is taken from way back in Chapter 4, and the depth function set up is taken straight from our drawSkybox() function, but it's nice to see those concepts applied in a new way.

That's all the code needed to set this up. For fun, I set up a quick test scene with three different point lights—a red, green, and blue one—and a dim yellow directional light. The result looked like Figure 12-8. If you're having trouble recreating the figure, all the code used to render it can be found in the "VariableLightCount" project in the Chapter 12 example code.

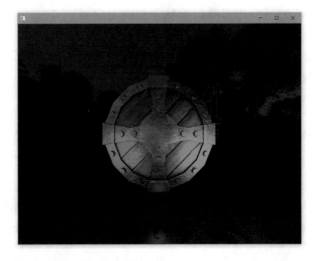

Figure 12-8. *Our multi-light demo scene*

In theory, this multi-light system can support an unlimited number of lights. In practice, however, you'll find that issuing multiple draw calls for every mesh is a relatively slow process, For complex scenes with lots of meshes, you'll run into performance problems. Games that use systems like this go to a lot of trouble to optimize how they issue draw calls, to make sure that every pass that they issue for an object is for a light that's close enough to matter to that specific mesh. Keep that in mind when you want to apply this to a larger project.

Taking Things Farther

Just like the previous two chapters, I want to end this chapter with a quick note about how games take the concepts we learned in this chapter even farther. The type of lighting we've been working with in this book is referred to as *forward rendering*. This means that the lighting for each mesh is computed when the draw call for that mesh is executed. As we talked a bit about earlier, one of the biggest performance concerns when using this style of rendering is managing which lights are used when rendering each mesh. Some games that want to use forward rendering extend it further by using advanced techniques that allow them to decide which lights to consider on a per-fragment basis rather than a per mesh one. If this sounds interesting to you, search online for "Forward+ Rendering" or "Clustered Rendering."

Aside from forward rendering, the other main way that games handle lighting is called *deferred rendering*. In this type of rendering, all objects are rendered to the screen without any lighting calculations done to them. Then, a lighting shader goes through every pixel in the back buffer and computes the lighting for each of those pixels. This has the advantage of not spending time doing light calculations for fragments that don't end up visible to the end user. There's a lot of added complexity involved when using deferred rendering, but the performance gains can be so sizeable that a lot of AAA games shipped in the past few years have used this technique. We're not going to cover how to implement a deferred renderer in this book, but if it sounds interesting to you, learnopengl.com has a great, free article about how it's done.

That's all for this chapter, and for the section of the book that introduces new shading techniques. We've covered more than enough ground so far for you to be able to write all the shaders you need for a simple 3D game, which is pretty awesome! The next few chapters are going to cover common problems that you'll run into while writing shaders, and how to debug and optimize the shaders that you write. So once you're done playing with all the examples we just built, join me in the next chapter and we'll dig into some of the nitty gritty details of how to make all the stuff we've just learned run fast enough to be able to put into a real game.

Summary

Here's a quick rundown of everything we covered in this chapter:

- There are three different types of lights commonly used in video game rendering: directional lights, point lights, and spot lights.

- Directional lights model a light source that is infinitely far away. The rays of light cast by this object are parallel to one another and are the same intensity for every object in the scene. This type of light is good for modeling light sources like the sun or moon.

- Point lights model a spherical light source. They have a 3D position in the game world and cast rays of light in a sphere around this position. Objects closer to a point light's position receive higher intensity lighting from that light. Point lights are excellent for modeling things like light bulbs or lanterns.

- Spot lights model a conical light source. They have a 3D position in the game world and cast rays of light in a cone directed from this position. Some spot lights will cast lower intensity light on farther away meshes, but the ones we built today light everything equally. Spot lights are good for creating things like flash lights or search lights.

- There are lots of ways to make shaders use multiple lights. In this chapter we saw how to create shaders that use a fixed number of different lights, and how to render multiple passes for our objects in order to support a variable number of lights.

CHAPTER 13

Profiling Shaders

We've spent a lot of time learning about new things that we can make our shaders do, but unfortunately simply knowing how to create a visual effect is only half the battle. When you're writing shaders for use in a game or other real-time application, you also need to be able to render that visual effect fast enough that your user's overall experience isn't impacted. Games that fail to present new frames fast enough or do so at an inconsistent speed are said to have a "performance" problem, and shaders that take a long time for the GPU to execute are a major source of performance problems in games. As such, it's important as shader writers for us to be able to measure how each shader we write contributes to the total time it takes to present a frame to our users. This kind of performance analysis is known as *profiling*, and adjusting our program to increase performance is known as *optimization*.

This chapter marks the beginning of Section 2 of this book, which will focus on teaching the basics of profiling and optimization with regard to shaders. We'll start by talking about how to measure the performance of a game as a whole, then dive into how to find where in a project a performance problem is. This will set us up for the next chapter, which is all about how to fix performance problems in shaders once we find them.

How to Measure Performance

The most fundamental part of optimization is measurement. Measurement is important both to identify problems and to verify when those problems are fixed. In games, performance is often talked about in terms of two measurements: frame rate and frame time. Both are ways of expressing how quickly a program can render a frame, and a performance problem can be defined as anything that negatively impacts either of these measurements in an unintended way. Everything that a game renders will take some amount of time, but what we're looking for are cases where something is taking more time than we expect or are comfortable with.

© Kyle Halladay 2019

K. Halladay, *Practical Shader Development*, https://doi.org/10.1007/978-1-4842-4457-9_13

Outside of programming, frame rate is by far the more popular measurement, and you'll often see users and media talking about a game's performance using this metric. Frame rate is measured in frames per second (FPS) and, as you might expect, describes how many frames a program can render per second of operation. The better a game's performance is, the faster it can draw new frames on the screen, increasing this number. Games often try to run at either 30 or 60 FPS, and can be said to have performance problems if they ever go slower than their target frame rate. The bigger the slowdown, the larger the performance problem.

The reason why frame rate is an unsuitable measurement to use when programming is that it's a nonlinear way of measuring performance. If your project is running at 30 FPS, that means it's rendering each frame in 1/30 of a second (or 33 milliseconds). If something causes your game to render one frame slower per second, it means that your rendering has slowed down by ~1.4 ms, which is the difference between 1/30 of a second, and 1/29. However, a one-frame slowdown is not always 1.4ms. Consider the same scenario for a game running at 60 FPS. The difference between 1/60 of a second, and 1/59 is only ~0.3 ms, which is a much smaller slowdown. However, if you just look at the frame rate of an application, it appears that each of these cases is the same magnitude of problem.

To avoid this problem, programmers tend to use frame time when they talk about rendering performance. Frame time simply expresses how fast a game is rendering in terms of how many milliseconds it takes to render a frame. This avoids all the confusing properties of using frame rate, since a 1-ms slowdown is always going to be a 1-ms slowdown, no matter how fast the game is rendering. The easy rule of thumb is to make sure to always use frame time when doing performance work, and frame rate when talking to users about performance.

Measuring frame time can be hard to do well, so let's talk briefly about some of the nuances involved in actually getting this number for our projects.

CPU Time vs. GPU Time

CPUs and GPUs often aren't exactly synchronized, which means that a CPU can be performing calculations for the next frame while the GPU is still trying to render the current one. It's possible to write code such that the CPU must wait for the GPU to finish rendering before starting to process a new frame, but often this isn't how games are structured.

This means that how fast a game renders a frame is dependent on two different times: how fast the CPU can execute all the logic for a frame and dispatch graphics commands to the GPU (called CPU time), and how fast the GPU can execute all those commands (called GPU time). The frame time of a game is dependent on both of these numbers, but more importantly, this frame time is dictated by which of these two measurements is slower.

If we can render a frame in 16.6 ms, but it takes our CPU 33 ms to process all the game logic and issue the rendering commands needed for a frame, our frame time is going to be roughly 33 ms. Even if our GPU could render every frame in 1 ms, we would still have a 33-ms frame time. A program that is performance constrained by its CPU is said to be *CPU bound*; likewise, if our GPU was the slower part of the frame, we would say that our program is *GPU bound*. If you're CPU bound, no amount of optimization on the GPU will improve your rendering speed, and vice versa. For this reason, it's common to measure both CPU and GPU time when tracking performance. Many games will go a step further and break their CPU time down by how much time was spent performing game logic calculations, and how much time was spent issuing commands to the GPU.

Working Around VSync

How fast a game is rendered also depends on the monitor that the user is viewing the game on. Monitors can only display new information at a certain speed, referred to as a *refresh rate*. Virtually all monitors will have a refresh rate of at least 60 Hz, meaning that they can display a new frame to the user 60 times per second. Newer monitors may have a refresh rate even higher than this. What this means for us is that no matter how fast our game can render a frame, the user can only see a new frame when the monitor they're using "refreshes" the data that it's displaying.

You might recall from Chapter 4 that while we're rendering a frame, our application is drawing the results of that render to a buffer that we call the "back buffer." The data that's currently displayed on a monitor is referred to as the "front buffer." When a new frame is presented, these two buffers are swapped. The front buffer becomes the back buffer, and the back buffer becomes the front buffer. This kind of two-buffer setup is known as *double buffering* and is an extremely common way for games to render.

The problem with this setup is that the buffer swap can happen any time, even while our monitor is in the process of reading the front buffer and presenting data on screen. When this happens, part of the screen will have data from the old front buffer, and part of the screen will have data from the newly swapped in buffer. This results in a visual problem known as *tearing*, which you can see an example of in Figure 13-1.

Figure 13-1. *Simulated screen tearing (Credit to Vanessaezekowitz of Wikipedia). Tear points are marked by red lines.*

To solve this problem, many games employ a technique known as vsync (which is short for "vertical synchronization"). Vsync delays a game's buffer swap until the monitor is ready to start a new refresh cycle. This fixes the tearing problem because buffers are never swapped in the middle of a monitor refresh. However, it negatively impacts the frame rate of an application, since by definition, vsync involves adding a delay to when we can start rendering our next frame.

The biggest consequence that this delay has on rendering performance is that it caps our rendering speed at the refresh rate of our monitor. On a 60-Hz monitor, this means that our game will never render a frame faster than 16.6 ms (60 fps). However, it also has consequences for frames that are rendered slower than our screen's refresh rate. To understand why, look at Figure 13-2, which displays our screen's refresh rate as lines on a timeline. In this diagram, the screen will refresh exactly at every numbered vertical line, and the gap between them represents a time period of 16.6 ms.

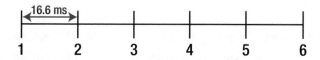

Figure 13-2. *Visualizing screen refresh rate on a timeline*

If our program consistently renders frames faster than the refresh rate of our monitor, vsync introduces a delay that triggers the buffer swap at exactly 60 fps, which you can see in Figure 13-3. In this diagram, every frame will start being rendered at a vertical line, and that frame finishes rendering at the smaller vertical line connected to it. The delay is the lighter line segment that connects the end of a frame to the next refresh point. This diagram shows what this delay looks like if we render each frame in 3.6 ms instead of 16.6. Since the screen will only refresh once every 16.6 ms, this means that the program must wait 13 ms before beginning to render the next frame.

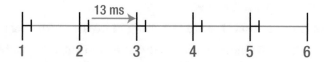

Figure 13-3. *Visualizing the delay that vsync introduces in an application that renders every frame in 3.6 ms*

However, consider what happens if a frame is rendered slightly slower than our refresh rate. Figure 13-4 shows what happens if we render a single frame in 19.6 ms instead of 16.6. Despite being almost as fast as our monitor's refresh rate, that frame is too slow to hit the 60-Hz refresh interval. However, in order to make sure that we never swap a buffer in the middle of a screen refresh, vsync will delay that buffer swap by almost an entire frame, meaning that frame that was only 3.6 ms too slow to render ends up coming out a full 16.6 ms later than the previous frame. It's a bit like a train station—if you miss the train that leaves at 8:00 am, you have to wait for the one that comes at 9, even if you only missed the first one by a few minutes.

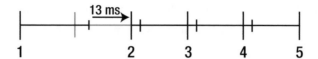

Figure 13-4. *Why vsync results in very low frame rates if an application misses the refresh interval*

Of course, this isn't ideal, so more modern GPU drivers implement what's known as *adaptive vsync*, or *dynamic vsync*, depending on your GPU vendor. This will cap the frame rate of an application to match the monitor's refresh rate but will allow tearing if a frame is rendered too slowly and misses the refresh time. This means that slow frames can still introduce tearing, but the overall frame rate of the application is much more stable. Not all systems have this capability, so it's important to know the hardware that your users will be playing on rather than assume that this functionality will exist.

The reason why all this is important for us right now is that the delay that vsync introduces can impact our ability to measure our performance. If vsync is enabled, an application that may in fact render at a speed much faster than the monitor it displays on may appear in certain measurements to be rendering as slow as the monitor. Therefore, it's important to make sure that you either disable vsync when measuring performance, or you work with tools that can differentiate between your CPU/GPU times and the rate at which your application presents new frames.

Some of the examples in this chapter are going to involve profiling the demo applications that we wrote in Chapter 12. For these scenarios, I've disabled vsync with a bit of openFrameworks-specific code, which you can see in Listing 13-1.

Listing 13-1. Disabling vsync in an openFrameworks Application

```
void ofApp::setup() {
    ofSetVerticalSync(false);
    //rest of function omitted
```

While we're on the topic of things that we need to do to get a decent idea of our program's actual performance, also make sure that any project that you profile has been built in the "Release" configuration, since that's the configuration that your users are going to see.

Working Around Your Computer

Aside from vsync, another common source of problems when debugging your own applications are changes or features added to your programs automatically by other software or drivers installed on your computer. For example, on my laptop, the NVidia drivers were adding a whole host of features to my application that I didn't explicitly turn on. Some of these, like threaded rendering, are meant to improve the performance of applications on your computer. Others, like anti-aliasing, are meant to improve the appearance of these same programs.

Unfortunately, none of this is helpful when trying to measure how fast the code that we wrote is, so in order to get a more accurate benchmark, I needed to use the Nvidia Control Panel to disable a lot of settings for my openFrameworks app. This problem isn't limited to Nvidia cards though; on another test machine with an Intel integrated GPU, the same sorts of things were happening. I don't have an AMD GPU for testing, but it's a safe assumption that all modern drivers are giving the applications your run a little boost. It's important to make sure that you're aware of what these boosts are, and that you turn them off when doing performance testing and optimization work.

In addition to your driver, simply having applications open in the background can influence the results of a profiling session, especially if these applications are doing a lot of background work. Make sure that you're aware of what other work your computer is doing before starting a profiling session. If possible, disable as many background programs as you can in order to have a more controlled test environment.

Practical Profiling

It's about time for us to put all this theory into practice, so let's see how we can get a few useful metrics out of our projects. Let's start by getting an idea of our frame time. This is as simple as finding a function that gets called at the same time each frame and then getting a timestamp from a high precision timer at the same point every frame. The frame time is just the difference between the previous frame's time stamp, and the one for the current frame. This is already handled for us in openFrameworks by the ofGetLastFrameTime() function, which we've been using before. Listing 13-2 shows how we could use this function to draw our CPU time (in milliseconds) to the screen in one of our demo programs.

Listing 13-2. Outputting Frame Time in an openFrameworks Program

```
void ofApp::draw() {
    using namespace glm;

    static char fpsString[128];
    //ofGetLastFrameTime returns a value in seconds,
    //but we want to see that value in milliseconds
    double t = ofGetLastFrameTime() * 1000.0;
    snprintf(fpsString, 128, "%f", t);
    ofDrawBitmapString(fpsString, 100, 400);
```

Depending on how fast the program being profiled runs, outputting the frame time for just the current frame might be too noisy to make much sense of it. For this reason, you may want to opt to store the frame time for a certain number of previous frames and display an average of those times on screen. On my computer, the frame time for the last example project we made clocked in at around 2.4 ms/frame.

The next value we want to get is how long our C++ code is taking to execute. We need to get a timestamp at the beginning of the first function that fires in a frame and compare that to a timestamp that we get after the last CPU side work is done. This is a little bit tricky for us, since openFrameworks is handling a lot of what happens on a per-frame basis. So in order to get an accurate read of our CPU time, we're going to have to learn about the global events that openFrameworks broadcasts.

The per-frame logic in a game is generally referred to as the game loop. The openFrameworks game loop is divided into three phases: update, draw, and swap. The update and draw phases are for handling nonrendering-related logic, and issuing draw calls, respectively. The swap phase is when the front and back buffers are swapped. Additionally, openFrameworks also spends some time each frame polling the operating system for events like mouse clicks or key presses. Swapping and event polling take some amount of CPU time per frame to perform, but we're after how long the code that we write takes, so we're going to just get the time it takes for those first two phases to execute.

openFrameworks uses a system of global events that we can subscribe to, to let us perform actions at different stages of our per-frame loop. We're going to use these events to insert the timing code that we need. The first event that we need to subscribe to is the "update" event. This event fires when the first phase of the game loop is started and calls all registered callback functions in order of their priority. In order to make sure that our callback function is the first one to be called, we need to register it as a 0 priority event listener. Listing 13-3 shows what this looks like. Notice that our callback function is storing the elapsed time in a new uint64_t member variable that has been added to our ofApp class.

Listing 13-3. Registering Our Callback Function as the First Update Event Listener

```
void ofApp::onFrameStart(ofEventArgs& args){
      frameStartMicros = ofGetElapsedTimeMicros();
}

void ofApp::setup() {
      ofAddListener(ofEvents().update, this, &ofApp::onFrameStart, 0);
      //rest of function unchanged
```

The next step is to get the time at the end of the draw phase. This is the phase where we schedule all the work that the GPU needs to perform. Like the update event, this event (and all openFrameworks events) operate on a priority system to determine the order that the event listener functions are called. In the case of the draw event, we want our timing function to be the last event listener called, so that we can properly get the time it takes to schedule all the work for that frame. This means that our draw event listener needs to have INT_MAX priority, to make sure nothing can come after it. Listing 13-4 shows what this looks like in code.

Listing 13-4. Registering Our Draw Event Callback Function

```
void ofApp::onFrameEnd(ofEventArgs& args){
      uint64_t total = ofGetElapsedTimeMicros() - frameStartMicros;
      cpuTime = (total) / (double)1e+6;
}

void ofApp::setup() {
      ofAddListener(ofEvents().update, this, &ofApp::onFrameStart, 0);
      ofAddListener(ofEvents().draw, this, &ofApp::onFrameEnd, INT_MAX);
      //rest of function unchanged
```

Notice that in the onFrameEnd() function, we're getting the difference between the current timestamp and our previously stored frameStartMicros timestamp, and then converting that from microseconds to seconds. This cpuTime value—a new double member variable—is the CPU time for our frame, expressed in seconds. With these changes made, we're finally able to see how long our CPU is taking to handle each frame. On my machine, this ended up being about 1.2 ms per frame.

These two measurements—frame time and CPU time—and tell us a lot about what's going on with our performance. Using my measurements, there's only a 1.2-ms difference between how long our code takes to run and how fast our project is rendering new frames. We know swapping buffers and polling the OS for events is going to take some amount of time, so we can say with confidence that our CPU time is close to (if not exactly) equal to our overall frame time. This means either that our program is CPU bound, or that its CPU and GPU times are roughly equal. This isn't a perfect measurement, but it's a good place for us to start. If this were a real project, we would want to time exactly how long the swap phase and event polling were taking, but that isn't possible without modifying core openFrameworks classes, so we're going to skip that for the purposes of our example.

The next step in our performance investigation is to figure out how long it's taking our GPU to render everything. Getting GPU time is a bit harder than getting CPU time, since there is no per-frame function for us to drop a timer into for the graphics pipeline. Every graphics API has a different way of measuring how long it takes a GPU to do work, and trying to cover how to manually GPU profile our application would require a sharp detour into a lot of OpenGL-specific function calls. Luckily, there are a number of free programs that we can use to calculate this value without having to change our code at all. These programs are called graphics debuggers, and they can provide a whole bunch of information that is incredibly valuable when trying to find and fix rendering issues.

Graphics debuggers are generally created by the companies that build GPUs, and are tailored specifically to the hardware made by that company. So, if you have a Nvidia GPU, you'll need to use a debugging program that is designed to work with Nvidia GPUs; likewise for AMD and Intel. This chapter is going to walk through using the

NSight tool from Nvidia. However, don't despair if you have a GPU made by a different company! The general profiling and optimizing methodology that we're about to use is transferrable to any graphics debugger, and it shouldn't be too hard to see how the tasks we do in NSight translate to whatever debugger matches your hardware.

The rest of this chapter is going to cover how to use Nsight to diagnose performance problems. We'll see examples of how to determine whether we're CPU or GPU bound, and then if we're GPU bound, how to identify what shader (or shaders) are taking up the most rendering time.

Introducing Nsight Graphics

Nvidia's Nsight Graphics tool is available for free on the GameWorks website: `https://developer.nvidia.com/gameworksdownload`. Note that the Internet is a fickle place, so if that link doesn't work by the time you're reading this, you may have better luck just googling for "Nvidia Nsight Graphics."

Nsight Graphics is an immensely feature-rich tool, but for this chapter all we're concerned about is how to use it to measure our rendering performance and help us locate any shaders that might be impacting our frame time. We'll see a case study of a program with a performance issue in a minute, but to get our feet wet, why don't we first use Nsight Graphics to tell us a little bit about the performance of the final program we wrote in Chapter 12 (the multilight demo that rendered our meshes once for every mesh). To get started, launch the Nsight Graphics application and select the continue button under the "Quick Start" section of the startup dialog. You should then see the "Connect to Process" dialog window shown in Figure 13-5.

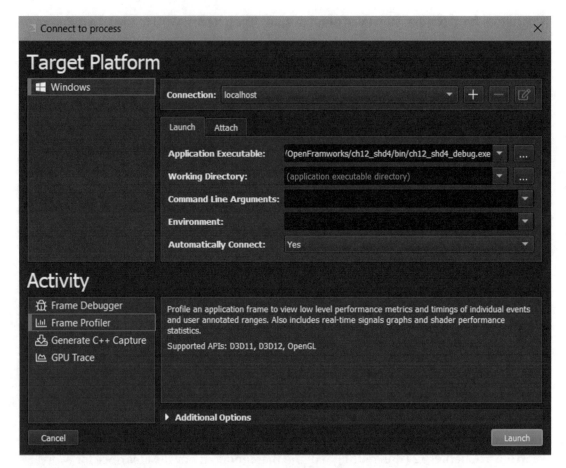

Figure 13-5. *Nsight Graphics' "Connect to Process" dialog*

Press the "…" button next to the Application Executable text box and select the exe file generated for our multilight project (it's located in your project's bin/ directory). Then, just as you see in Figure 13-5, make sure that you have the "Frame Profiler" activity selected in the bottom left section of this window. This is going to start up Nsight Graphics in a mode that provides a lot of high-level performance information about our project while it's running. This is perfect for us, since we don't know anything about how this project performs right now. Once all that is set up, press the blue "Launch" button in the bottom right of the screen. If you've done everything correctly, a lot will happen all at once.

First, the multilight project should start up. Instead of looking like usual, it will now have some onscreen text displaying FPS and frame time, as well as a histogram showing additional statistics about how many triangles are being sent to the GPU with each draw call (since we just want to profile our shaders, we'll ignore this). All of these extra

HUD elements add a small amount of CPU time each frame, so to get a more accurate measure of frame time you can disable the Nsight HUD by pressing ctrl+Z and click the "close" button. Nsight's GPU profiling also adds some overhead, since it's telling your GPU to do a lot of extra time measurements, so don't be surprised if your frame time increases while you have Nsight attached.

Second, Nsight should have transitioned to the frame profiler view and be providing a ton of information about our running project. You can see a screenshot of this in Figure 13-6. There's a lot going on in this view, and it's easy to feel overwhelmed at first, but for right now we're just going to pay attention the three graphs on the left side of the screen. Pretend everything else doesn't exist. The top graph in this view is displaying our running project's FPS over time. The raw FPS value is a little noisy, especially in projects like ours that are rendering so quickly.

On my laptop, the project hovered around 160 fps with Nsight connected, which you can see in Figure 13-6. The middle graph displays a breakdown of the work being done by different parts of your GPU. Since we're focused on just hunting down shader-related performance problems right now, we're going to skip over this graph, but in other situations this graph would provide us with valuable information about where in the graphics pipeline a performance problem might be.

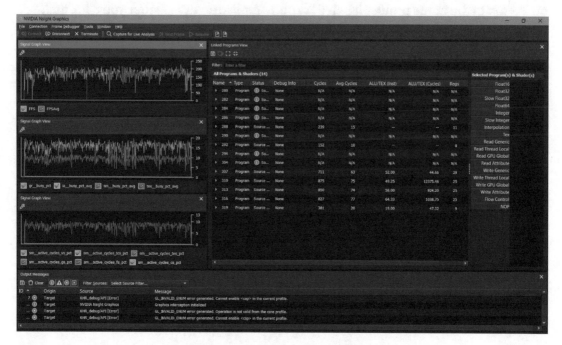

Figure 13-6. *The frame profiler view of Nsight Graphics*

The bottom graph is going to be our bread and butter, since it can tell us how much time we're spending in each type of shader. Since our project consists only of vertex and fragment shaders, we're only interested in two of the options displayed on this graph: sm__active_cycles_vs_pct, which tells us how much of our GPU is being spent processing vertex shaders, and sm__active_cycles_fs_pct, which tells us the same thing about fragment shaders. In Figure 13-6, you can see that most of our GPU time is being spent processing fragment shaders, which makes sense given that our vertex shaders are extremely simple, and our meshes are low poly.

Are We CPU or GPU bound?

We know from looking at our frame profiling view and the frame rate display on our running application that we don't have any performance woes in our demo application. However, if we wanted to speed things up further, our first step would be to determine whether we needed to change a shader or change our C++ code. To do that, we need to compare our CPU time—which we saw how to calculate earlier—against the time being spent on the GPU. To get this second number, we need to switch Nsight from the frame profiling mode to the frame debugging mode, which you can do by pressing the button on the top of the frame profiler labeled "capture for live analysis." After you click that, your application will pause, and you'll be presented with Nsight's frame debugging view, which you can see in Figure 13-7.

Figure 13-7. *Nsight frame debugging view*

There is a lot going on in this view, and most of it isn't going to pertain to us in this book, but the part that we want to look at right now is the timeline view in the top right of the window. This view shows all commands that the GPU performed in the last frame, grouped by the draw call that those commands corresponded to, and arranged on a timeline. Our frame didn't take very long to render, so to get any real information out of this view we need to zoom into the beginning of the timeline. You can zoom in either by adjusting the handles on the horizontal scroll bar or pinching to zoom if you have a track pad. Zooming into the beginning of the timeline in the range profiler view looks like Figure 13-8.

Figure 13-8. *Zooming in to our events in the range profiler view*

Each one of the entries in the "actions" row corresponds to a draw call for a mesh in our scene, so in Figure 13-8 our timeline view is telling us that our frame consists of nine draw calls. If you recall, the last program we wrote for Chapter 12 involved submitting multiple draw calls for each mesh—one for each light that was affecting it—so we end up with four draw calls for our water and shield meshes (three for point lights, one for the directional light), and one draw call for our skybox. To help us figure out which of these actions corresponds to what, Nsight has also helpfully launched a second instance of our program, called the Nsight Graphics Replay, which (if you enable the Nsight GUI) lets you scrub through each of these events and see how they contribute to what ends up on screen. You can see this graphics replay view in Figure 13-9.

Figure 13-9. *the Nsight Graphics Replay view*

However, for right now, all we want to know is whether we're CPU or GPU bound; so what we really want to know is how long all our GPU commands are taking to render. For that, we need to look at the second row in the range profiler view, labeled "All Actions." In that row, you can see a summary of how much time all the actions in our frame are taking the GPU to process, and in Figure 13-8's case, those actions are taking 0.21 ms. We know from earlier that our CPU time per frame is about 1.2 ms, meaning that our application is currently CPU bound, and optimizing any of our shaders won't have any impact on our overall frame time. You can test this by replacing one of the shaders with a simpler one (e.g., one that returns red) and observing what happens to the program's frame time. If an application is truly CPU bound, simplifying a shader will have no impact on the overall frame time.

A Handy Shortcut

While using a graphics debugger to determine whether your CPU or GPU bound is likely the best option when debugging, sometimes you just want a quick way to tell what's going on at runtime without the need for a heavyweight profiling tool. One quick way of determining where your performance lies is to write some code to let you artificially add a fixed amount of time to your per-frame CPU calculations, like you can see in Listing 13-5.

Listing 13-5. Adding 1 ms of CPU Time While the Insert Key is Pressed

```
bool addTime = false;

void ofApp::keyPressed(int key) {
    if (key == ofKey::OF_KEY_INSERT)
    {
        addTime = true;
    }
}

void ofApp::update(){
    if (addTime) ofSleepMillis(1);
}
```

If sleeping for 1 ms increases your frame time by 1 ms, then that's a pretty clear indicator that your performance bottleneck is the CPU. If adding an extra millisecond of CPU work per frame doesn't change how fast your frames are being rendered, then you can be pretty sure that your bottleneck is the GPU. This isn't a 100% bulletproof way to test things, but it's a useful way to get a quick read on your performance for occasions when you don't want to spend too much time looking at things.

Tracking Down A Problem Shader

Now that we know what we're doing, let's look at a case where we are actually GPU bound. In this scenario, I've added a whole bunch of unnecessary (and slow) operations to one of our shaders. If we were to look at our CPU timer, we'd see that our CPU time per frame is still sitting at about 1.2 ms, but our frame time has jumped up to over 9 ms. Since our CPU time hasn't increased, we can be pretty sure that the problem is GPU related. Let's see if we can use Nsight to figure out what shader is causing problems.

Our first step is to hop into the frame profiling view and look at the bottom performance graph, so that we can see whether our problem lies in a vertex or a fragment shader. Figure 13-10 shows what this graph looks like for our new, much slower version of our demo app.

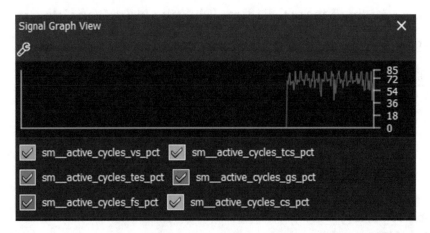

Figure 13-10. *Our fragment shader percentage is so high that we can't even see sm_active_cycles_vs_pct, which is the percentage of GPU time devoted to vertex shaders.*

This graph makes it clear that our problem is how much time we're spending in fragment shaders, which means that we can officially rule out half the shaders in our project as possible suspects. However, we have five fragment shaders in our tiny project, and we need to know which one is causing all of this mess, which means we need more information. As you may have guessed, our next step is to switch over to the frame debugging view, so we need to click the "capture for live analysis" button and take a look at the range profiler view again. This time, it looks like Figure 13-11, which shows that draw 0 is taking up 83% of our GPU time.

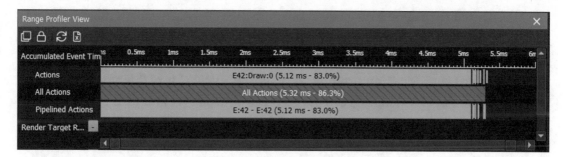

Figure 13-11. *A screenshot of the range profiler view*

Our range profiler view is also giving us another piece of information: that our problem draw call is also the 42nd GPU event that happens in the frame. With this information we can turn to the Events view, which is usually located on the bottom left of the screen (but can also be accessed through the Frame Debugger menu in the menu bar). If we scroll down that view until we get to the 42nd event, we see Figure 13-12.

	Event ▲	Description	Object	CPU ms	GPU ms	Thread
	35	glBindBuffer(GLenum target = GL_ARRAY_BUFFER, GLuint buffer...	0x0002...	0.00	-	17480
	36	glBindBuffer(GLenum target = GL_ARRAY_BUFFER, GLuint buffer...	0x0002...	<0.01	-	17480
	37	glEnableVertexAttribArray(GLuint index = 3)	0x0002...	0.00	-	17480
	38	glVertexAttribPointer(GLuint index = 3, GLint size = 2, GLenu...	0x0002...	0.00	-	17480
	39	glVertexAttribDivisor(GLuint index = 3, GLuint divisor = 0)	0x0002...	0.00	-	17480
	40	glBindBuffer(GLenum target = GL_ARRAY_BUFFER, GLuint buffer...	0x0002...	0.00	-	17480
	41	glBindBuffer(GLenum target = GL_ELEMENT_ARRAY_BUFFER, GL...	0x0002...	<0.01	-	17480
	42	glDrawElements(GLenum mode = GL_TRIANGLES, GLsizei count...	0x0002...	<0.01	5.12	17480
	43	glBindVertexArray(GLuint array = 0)	0x0002...	<0.01	-	17480
	44	glBindBuffer(GLenum target = GL_ARRAY_BUFFER, GLuint buffer...	0x0002...	0.00	-	17480
	45	glBindBuffer(GLenum target = GL_ELEMENT_ARRAY_BUFFER, GL...	0x0002...	0.00	-	17480
	46	glPolygonMode(GLenum face = GL_FRONT_AND_BACK, GLenum...	0x0002...	<0.01	-	17480
	47	glUseProgram(GLuint program = 0)	0x0002...	<0.01	-	17480
	48	glUseProgram(GLuint program = '292')	0x0002...	<0.01	-	17480
	49	glUniformMatrix4fv(GLint location = 1, GLsizei count = 1, GLboo...	0x0002...	<0.01	-	17480
	50	glUniform4f(GLint location = 0, GLfloat v0 = 1.000000, GLfloat v1...	0x0002...	<0.01	-	17480

Figure 13-12. *The events view of Nsight's frame debugger view*

This doesn't tell us much on its own, but if we then click the event number (shown in the red rectangle in Figure 13-12), we hit pay dirt. Clicking this number will bring up the API Inspector view, which provides a ton of different information about what's going on in our selected event. Most importantly for us, the left-hand side of this view lets us filter this information by different stages of the graphics pipeline. We know we're looking for information about the fragment shader, so we can select the "FS" category, which will bring up the screen shown in Figure 13-13.

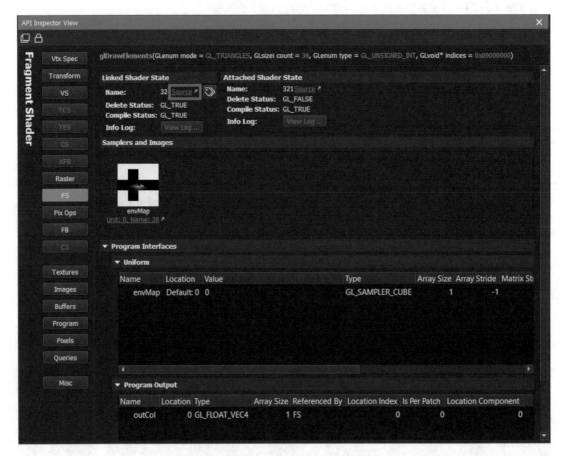

Figure 13-13. *The fragment shader section of the API Inspector View*

This screen tells us a lot of things, but most importantly for us, if we click the "Source" link (shown in the red rectangle of Figure 13-13), this will take us directly to the source code for the fragment shader that we're looking at, which tells us exactly which shader is causing our problems. This shader source view will also let us live edit the shader in question, so we can try out different changes to the shader and see the impact on our performance right away. In this case, the shader that was causing problems was our skybox fragment shader, which is the shader that I had added unnecessary calculations to (shown in Listing 13-6). To fix the problem, all we need to do is delete these calculations.

Listing 13-6. A Comically Bad Skybox Shader

```
#version 410
uniform samplerCube envMap;
in vec3 fromCam;
out vec4 outCol;

void main(){
    //we never actually use f, it's just here to slow things down
    float f = 0.0;
    for (int i = 0; i < 500000; ++i){
        f = sqrt(sqrt(sqrt(sqrt(1))));
    }

    f = mod(f, 1.0);
    outCol = texture(envMap, fromCam);
}
```

That wraps up both our example profiling scenario and this chapter. I know this was a lot of new information, but with enough practice, everything we just did will start to feel like second nature. More importantly, you now have enough knowledge to be able to find slow shaders, and make sure that new shaders that you add to a project aren't causing any problems, which is a big part of being able to write shaders for production grade projects. The next chapter is going to expand on this by diving into how to optimize a shader once you've identified that it's causing a performance problem (sadly, they aren't all as obvious as the one in the example we just worked through).

Summary

Here's a quick rundown of what we covered in this chapter:

- A game's performance is measured in frames per second (FPS), or frame time. When doing profiling or optimization, it's preferable to use frame time because it is a linear measure of performance.

- A game's performance is a combination of the time being spent per frame by both the CPU and the GPU. These times are referred to as "CPU Time" and "GPU Time," respectively.

- VSync is a technique where presenting frames to the user is synchronized with a monitor's refresh rate. When profiling or optimizing an application, it's important to disable vsync, or at least be aware of what impact vsync is having on your measurements.

- Graphics drivers installed on a dev machine may interfere with profiling results. Make sure that you're aware of what your driver is doing, and how to disable those things if necessary.

- A graphics debugger, like Nvidia's Nsight debugger, is a powerful tool for diagnosing and debugging and GPU-related performance problems.

CHAPTER 14

Optimizing Shaders

Now that we know how to figure out how fast our shaders are being computed in a frame, the next step is to learn how we can make them go even faster. Optimizing shaders is probably my favorite part about writing them! It always feels like a puzzle, and I love the feedback loop of making an optimization, measuring how much of an impact that had, and then doing it all again.

Profiling is important, because shader optimization is a very deep subject, and in many cases, the types of optimizations that you make will depend on the hardware that you run on. This makes it very difficult to know how much of a performance impact any one optimization will have on your overall project. That said, there are some general optimization guidelines that are useful no matter what platform you're working on, and we're going look at six of them in this chapter By the end of the chapter you'll have a small toolbox of techniques that you'll be able to apply to any shader that you need to squeeze some extra performance out of.

Writing a chapter of performance tips that apply to everyone is tricky, and I've chosen the tips presented here carefully to try to present the most universal advice I can think of. This means that I haven't spent time presenting advice that's applicable to one platform, or one type of GPU. There are many more things you can do to improve the shaders that you write for your specific projects, so treat this chapter as the starting point for your optimization journey, and not as the final word on how to make your shaders go fast. With that caveat in mind, let's dive in!

Move Calculations to Vertex Shaders

Rendering a frame of game typically involves a lot more fragments than it does vertices. As such, you can save a lot of GPU time by moving as much as possible to your vertex shaders and then sending the results of those calculations to your fragment shader, since the vertex shader will run far fewer times. This is particularly helpful if you can move

© Kyle Halladay 2019
K. Halladay, *Practical Shader Development*, https://doi.org/10.1007/978-1-4842-4457-9_14

calculations that use any sort of trigonometric function (like sin, cos, tan, asin, acos, atan, etc.), since depending on your GPU, these functions can range from a little bit slower than regular math instructions to a lot slower. Listing 14-1 shows an example of a fragment shader with some calculations that can be easily moved to the vertex shader.

Listing 14-1. A Less Than Ideal Fragment Shader

```
#version 410
uniform float time;
uniform sampler myTexture;

in vec2 fragUV;
out vec4 outColor;

void main()
{
    vec2 uv = fragUV + vec2(sin(time), 0); ❶
    outColor = texture(myTexture, uv);
}
```

This shader is offsetting the UVs that it's getting from the vertex shader by a constant value (the same value is applied to each fragment). However, this could easily be done in the vertex shader, since the offset calculation doesn't require and fragment specific (or interpolated) data. To fix this, all that's required is to remove the addition at ❶ from the fragment shader (and as such, the time uniform value as well), and move that logic to the vertex shader, like you can see in Listing 14-2.

Listing 14-2. A Vertex Shader That Handles the Addition from ❶

```
#version 410
layout (location = 0) in vec3 pos;
layout (location = 2) in vec2 uv;

uniform mat4 mvp;
uniform float time;

out vec2 fragUV;
```

```
void main()
{
    fragUV = uv + vec2(sin(time), 0.0);
    gl_Position = mvp * vec4(pos, 1.0);
}
```

Sometimes it may even be worth it to add some vertices to a mesh in order to allow a calculation to be moved from the fragment shader to the vertex shader. I can recall one project I worked on that had to render a lot of lights moving over top of a floor mesh. Rather than calculate these lights per pixel, it ended up being far cheaper to add enough vertices to the floor to make the lights look "good enough" when the lighting calculations were only done on a per-vertex basis. Many problems won't be able to be solved like this, but it's always a good option to have in your tool box.

It's important to note that there are some things that cannot be moved to a vertex shader. A common error is to try to save some performance by normalizing a vertex's normal vector in the vertex shader and then removing the normalize() function from the fragment shader. Unfortunately, normalized vectors are not guaranteed to remain that way after the per-fragment interpolation process runs, meaning that this optimization will introduce rendering problems into your game. Before moving any logic to a vertex shader, it's important to double-check that your calculation's result isn't changed when the interpolation step runs.

Avoid Dynamic Branching

A commonly repeated bit of shader optimization advice is to avoid any sort of conditional branching. This advice is unlikely to be harmful, but the truth of whether it's OK to use an if statement in a shader is a bit more complicated.

When a GPU processes a draw call, it needs to perform shader calculations on every vertex, and every fragment, that will be written by that call. GPUs have specialized hardware that is designed to run these calculations concurrently, to make this process as fast as possible. In practice, this means assigning each vertex or fragment its own thread and running many threads at once. These threads are organized into groups (sometimes referred to as *warps* or *wavefronts* by various GPU vendors), and are grouped at least partially by location on screen. For example, fragments that are closer together spatially are more likely to be processed in the same thread group. This thread group architecture is at its most efficient when a shader performs the same calculations on every vertex or fragment that it touches. If a shader has no sort of branching or control flow, then every vertex or fragment it processes will perform the same work, and the GPU can schedule the work that these thread groups do as efficiently as possible. However, once we start to introduce control flow, like an if statement or a while loop, things get a lot trickier, and in general, get more expensive in terms of performance.

This is a simplified (and rather hand-wavy) explanation of things, of course, but it's enough background for us to talk about why not all branching in a shader is considered equally. For example, if a shader has an if statement, but every thread in a thread group is going to take the same path through the code (all of them executing or skipping over the conditional branch), then there is no extra performance cost for that branch. For this reason, there are two different types of branching that we need to talk about to get a clear picture of when it's OK for a shader to use any sort of conditional branching: uniform branching and dynamic branching.

Uniform branching is the easier of the two types of branching to think about. It occurs when a shader has a branch that depends only on a uniform value that has been passed into the shader, like you can see in Listing 14-3.

Listing 14-3. A Uniform Conditional Branch

```
uniform float controlVal;

void main(){
      if (controlVal > 0.5)
      {
            //do some work
      }

      //rest of code omitted
```

Notice that in Listing 14-3, all the fragments that are processed by this shader will take the same route through the code, since the "controlVal" uniform value will be the same for every run of the shader. This type of branching is generally safe to use throughout shader code, since it doesn't cause threads within a thread group to perform different calculations.

Dynamic branching is the opposite of the example we just saw. It occurs when a conditional branch depends on calculations that vary on a per-fragment basis, like the result of a texture sample, or are based on a fragment's world position. This kind of branching is what causes a thread group to diverge. Deciding whether a dynamic branch is the right call in shader code is a much more nuanced discussion than it is for uniform branching. To help provide some context for this discussion, let's look at an example of a shader that uses dynamic branching in Listing 14-4.

Listing 14-4. A Dynamic Branching in a Shader

```
void main()
{
    vec3 nrm = texture(normTex, fragUV).rgb;
    vec3 viewDir = normalize( cameraPos - fragWorldPos);

    vec3 toLight = lightPos - fragWorldPos;
    vec3 lightDir = normalize(toLight);
    float distToLight = length(toLight);
    float falloff = 1.0 - (distToLight / lightRadius);

    vec3 diffCol = vec3(0,0,0);
    vec3 specCol = vec3(0,0,0);

    if (falloff > 0.01)
    {
        float diffAmt = diffuse(lightDir, nrm) * falloff;
        float specAmt = specular(lightDir, viewDir, nrm, 4.0) * falloff;

        diffCol = texture(diffuseTex, fragUV).xyz * lightCol * diffAmt;

        float specMask = texture(specTex, fragUV).x;

        specCol = specMask * lightCol * specAmt;
        vec3 envSample = texture(envMap, reflect(-viewDir, nrm)).xyz;

        vec3 envLighting = envSample * specMask * diffAmt;

        specCol = mix(envLighting, specCol, min(1.0,specAmt));
    }
    outCol = vec4(diffCol + specCol, 1.0);
}
```

You may recognize Listing 14-4 as a slight variation of our point light shader from Chapter 12. The difference here is that rather than always executing the lighting calculations for a point light, we're instead using a conditional to make sure that we don't perform calculations for lights that our fragment is far away from. If this was CPU code, this would be an obvious improvement, but as we've been talking about, on a GPU things aren't as straightforward. As a simple rule of thumb, evaluating whether a dynamic branch is the right call in shader code is a combination of two factors: branch size and coherency. The higher a dynamic branch scores in each of these categories, the better the chances are that it's the right decision for your code.

The first criterion, "Branch size," refers to how much work is encapsulated in our conditional block. In general, the more work that is encapsulated in a dynamic branch, the better. We're going to incur a performance penalty for our branch regardless of how much work is saved by not taking the branch, so the more work that we're going to skip, the better the chances are that our dynamic branch is a performance win. In the case of Listing 14-4 all our lighting calculations, including three texture samples, are skipped if our falloff value is too low; however, this is still a very simple shader in the grand scheme of things. This branch would score high on the "Branch Size" criteria when compared with the shaders we've written in this book, but is likely still too small for the branch to provide a performance win.

The second criterion, "Coherency," refers to how likely it is that all the threads in a thread group will take the same path through the branch. This is a difficult thing to know for sure, but a good rule of thumb (at least for fragment shaders) is that the greater the chance that fragments that are close to one another will take the same path through the shader code, the better the odds are that the branch is going to be the right choice in terms of performance. For Listing 14-4, it's very likely that neighboring fragments will take the same path through the shader most of the time, since our branch depends on a world space distance calculation, and neighboring fragments will have very similar locations. Thus, this branch would score high on the "coherency" criteria as well.

Combining these two criteria together, we end up with two very simple questions to help us estimate the performance impact of a dynamic branch:

1. Will fragments that are close together usually take the same code path?

2. Is there enough work in the body of the conditional statement to justify the performance cost of the branch?

These are just an estimation tool of course, and how much work a branch needs to encapsulate for it to be worth your while is going to depend heavily on the hardware that you're running on. But it should help you decide the right time to use a dynamic branch, and when you should refactor your shader logic to avoid needing the branch at all.

Get MAD

We briefly talked about MAD operations way back in Chapter 3, but now we're going to look at them a bit more closely. A "MAD" operation is when the GPU can perform a calculation as a combination of a multiply and then an add (in that order). MAD operations are extremely fast on GPU hardware, and are generally the best possible scenario for any calculations you need to write in terms of optimization. If you can express your logic in a MAD operation (or a couple of them), you should opt to do so. The tricky thing when trying to optimize using MAD operations is, as we just mentioned, that order matters, which means the placement of parentheses in your code matters as well. Consider Listing 14-5, which shows two very similar calculations.

Listing 14-5. One MAD Calculation, and One Slightly Less Angry One

```
float X = 0.0;
float Y = 1.0;
float Z = 2.0;

float mad = (X * Y) + Z; ❶.
float not_mad = X * (Y + Z); ❷
```

You may have guessed from the names of the variables that only one of these two calculations is a MAD operation (❶ Is the MAD). Note that the only difference between these two lines is that the parentheses have been moved around, shifting the order of operations from a multiply-then-add to an add-then-multiply, which is not nearly as efficient to compute. Despite the mnemonic, MAD operations can also involve subtraction, as you can see in Listing 14-6, which also shows off that MAD operations can be applied to vector types in addition to single float variables.

Listing 14-6. More Examples of MAD Operations

```
vec3 val = (value * 2.0) - 1.0;
vec3 val2 = (value * -2.0) - 1.0;
```

It's important to note that while MAD operations are excellent for performance, doing an add and then a multiply is likely not the end of the world in terms of your graphics performance, so apply this tip where it makes sense (or when you really need to squeeze some more speed out of your app), but don't get too dogmatic about it. It's unlikely that a single MAD operation is going to make a shader go from too slow to blazing fast.

Prefer GLSL Functions over Your Own

Speaking of not getting too wrapped up with micro-optimizations to shader logic: if you can express a bit of logic using a built in GLSL function, you should almost always opt to use that instead of your own handwritten code. Built in GLSL functions can use fast paths in your hardware that aren't available for our own client code to use, and have been tested and documented far more than any code that you write will be. Listing 14-7 shows a few examples of code that can be refactored to use a single GLSL function (including one that we haven't seen yet in this book!), but once you've understood these examples, google for a "GLSL Quick Reference" to find a short list of GLSL functions and look up what each of them do. Your GPU—and users—will thank you.

Listing 14-7. Two Examples Replacing Custom Code with Built-in GLSL Functions

```
//Example 1:  calculating squared length of a vector

//bad idea
float lengthSquared = vec.x*vec.x + vec.y*vec.y + vec.z*vec.z;

//good idea
float lengthSquared = dot(vec,vec);

//Example 2: constraining a value between a minimum and a maximum
float x = 1.2;
```

```
//bad idea
x = x < 0.5 ? 0.5 : x;
x = x > 1.0 ? 1.0 : x;

//better
x = min(1.0, max(0.5, x));

//best
x = clamp(x, 0.5, 1.0);
```

Use Write Masks

Often when working with vectors or textures in shader code, you can find yourself in a position where you only care about some of the channels of the vector that you're working with. For example, you could be sampling a texture (and getting an rgba vec4 from it), but your shader only needs the red and green channels of that texture sample. In these cases you can specify a write mask, which looks like a swizzle being applied to the left side of the equals sign in an assignment, to tell the GPU to only use some components of the calculation being done. Listing 14-8 shows two examples of this.

Listing 14-8. Examples of Write Masks

```
vec4 myVal = vec4(1,2,3,4);

myVal.zw = vec4(5,0,0,5); ❶
//output is (5,2,3,5)

//only use the red channel of a texture sample
myVal.x = texture(myTexture, fragUV);
```

While a write mask may look like a swizzle, there's one important difference: you can't repeat or rearrange channels in a write mask. This means that while a swizzle of .xxzy is completely valid GLSL, it is not a valid write mask, both because the x channel is being duplicated and because the z channel is being specified before the y channel. You can still skip over channels in a write mask though, which is shown at ❶ in Listing 14-8, as long as you make sure to maintain the order of the channels that your write mask uses.

Avoid Unnecessary Overdraw

One common way that games can end up using too many GPU resources is to have a high degree of *overdraw*. Overdraw is what it's called when a scene renders to a pixel which has already been written to, drawing over top of it. This can happen with both opaque and translucent geometry, but it's easier to visualize what's going on with translucent meshes, so we'll start with them first. Consider the scene being rendered in Figure 14-1. The right side of this screen shot shows a set of translucent cubes being rendered in front of one another, and you can clearly see which pixels have been written to by more than one cube.

Figure 14-1. *Opaque vs. translucent objects*

Of course, blending colors with the values already stored in the back buffer is how translucent rendering works, so there isn't a whole lot that can be done to avoid overdraw when you're rendering translucent geometry. However, it's still important to be aware of how much overdraw you have. A large puffy cloud floating across a screen can very quickly cause a frame to require double the amount of pixel writes, fragments processed, and blending operations required. This can add up to a lot of frame time, so it's important to always have one eye on your frame time as you add translucent elements to a scene.

If you have any translucent materials at all, there will be some amount of overdraw, and that's not a bad thing. However, just like most things, overdraw is best in moderation. If you notice that your performance is fluctuating depending on what's happening on screen, check to see if the performance drops match up to areas or times where your screen has a lot of translucent geometry onscreen. If so, speeding things up may be as simple as not rendering as many of those types of objects.

This same problem crops up with opaque geometry, even though it's harder to see. In Figure 14-1, there might be just as much overdraw going on with our solid cubes as we saw with our translucent ones. However, this isn't a guarantee. This is because opaque geometry will occlude objects rendered behind them, preventing them from being rendered. If we have already drawn a solid brick wall in a scene, for example, that wall will have stored information about its position in the depth buffer. Any time we try to draw an object behind the wall, the fragments for that object will see the wall's depth buffer information and won't be drawn. However, if we draw the wall last, then we pay the cost of rendering everything behind the wall before covering it all up.

To help mitigate this problem, opaque objects are usually drawn in front to back order, so that the depth buffer can be populated by the objects most likely to be seen by the user first. Many engines will also opt to perform what's known as a depth prepass, which involves rendering objects to the depth buffer (using a very simple fragment shader) before then rendering the objects a second time using its real fragment shader. If you're using any of the major engines on the market today, this is likely already being handled for you, but it never hurts to inspect a frame with a tool like Nsight to make sure of that.

Final Thoughts

That wraps up our small chapter on shader optimization. As mentioned before, there are many optimization tips that are specific to a single platform or GPU vendor that have been left out of this chapter, but which can make a huge difference for projects that they apply to. Many GPU vendors publish "performance recommendation" or "best practices" documents that give you easy to follow optimization advice for their specific platform. You should absolutely seek out these documents and follow as many of their guidelines as possible if they apply to your project. There are also many excellent resources online that provide more specific optimization advice for shader development—just make sure to verify that the advice you're getting works for your project by profiling before and after you make changes.

Summary

Here's a quick list of all the optimization tips we covered in this chapter:

- Move calculations to vertex shaders

- Avoid dynamic branching

- Use MAD operations wherever possible

- Prefer existing GLSL functions over ones you write yourself

- Use write masks

- Avoid unnecessary overdraw

CHAPTER 15

Precision

To wrap up our section on shader debugging and optimization, I want to spend some time digging into a topic that's one of the most common sources of shader problems that I've encountered in my career: precision problems. These sorts of problems can manifest as visual glitches on any platform, but if you're writing shaders for platforms like mobile phones, or for web-based applications, precision problems can also be a huge source of performance issues. Luckily, once you understand what's going on, these sorts of issues are relatively easy to track down and fix.

To start this chapter, I'm going to briefly cover what floating-point precision is, and then dive into how that applies to writing shaders. Once we have the theory out of the way, we're going to look at a few case studies of shaders that have precision problems and see how to fix them.

What Is Floating-Point Precision

Floating-point numbers, or "floats", are the most common data type that programs use for storing decimal numbers. The term "floating point" refers to the fact that, depending on the value of the number, a floating-point variable will store a different number of digits on either side of the decimal point. This lets us use the same data type to store values like 0.000000000001 and 100000000.0 without worrying too much about how floating-point numbers actually store data. The same is true for most shader development—if you can store a value in a full 32-bit float (like we've done a lot in this book), you usually don't have to worry too much about how that data type works.

Unfortunately for us, it's a lot faster for some GPUs to work with data types that are smaller than a standard 32-bit float. As we'll see in this chapter, it's very common to work with 16-bit or smaller variables to speed things up in shader code, and once we start shrinking the sizes of our floating-point numbers, it becomes very important to understand how things are working under the hood. If you've programmed for any length

© Kyle Halladay 2019
K. Halladay, *Practical Shader Development*, https://doi.org/10.1007/978-1-4842-4457-9_15

of time, you've probably encountered the IEEE 754 standard, which defines in detail how floating-point numbers work, and may even have come across the math notation for how a floating-point number works, which looks like this:

$$-1^s * 1.M * 2^{(e - 127)}$$

I don't know about you, but the standard explanation of how floats work never really clicked for me, so we aren't going to spend much time unpacking the equation above. Instead, I want to share a different way to understand how floats work, which I believe originated with Fabien Sanglard, the author of the excellent "Game Engine Black Book" series.

A regular float is 32 bits, and that memory is divided up into three sections. The first bit is the "sign" bit, which decides whether our value is positive or negative. The next 8 bits are commonly referred to as the "exponent" bits, but for our explanation I'm going to call them the "range" bits, for reasons I'll explain in a second. The final 23 bits are commonly called the "mantissa," but that term never really made sense to me, so we're going to refer to these numbers as our "offset" bits. Figure 15-1 shows this memory layout visually.

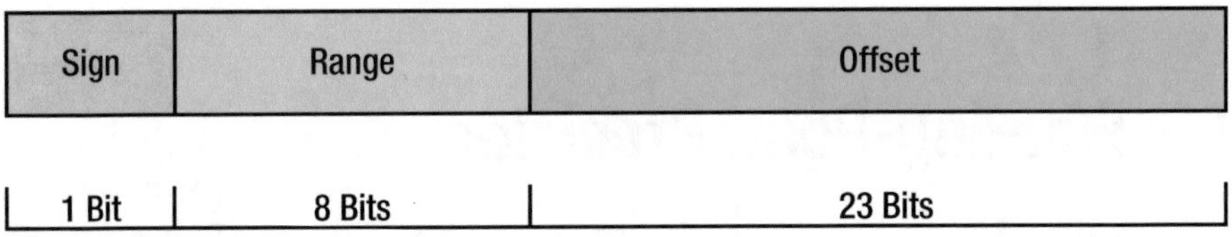

Sign	Range	Offset
1 Bit	8 Bits	23 Bits

Figure 15-1. *The layout of a 32 bit float*

Using these 32 bits to represent a decimal value can be thought of as a three-step process, and each step is handled by the sign bit, range bits, and offset bits, respectively. These steps are as follows:

1. Determine whether our value is positive or negative

2. Define a range which encapsulates the value we want to represent

3. Choose a value within that defined range

Step one is very simple. If our sign bit is 1, our floating-point value will be negative, and vice versa.

Step two is a bit more complicated, but not by much. The 8 "range" bits are used to define an integer. Since we have 8 bits to work with, this integer can be any whole number between 0 and 255. However, we want to be able to get negative values as well, so after we define our integer, we subtract 127 from the number we end up with. This way the range of values we can represent is -127 to +127, and not 0 to 255. To that end, if we want to end up with a value of 0, our range bits need to be set to 0111 1111, which is binary for the number 127.

Now, I said that I prefer to refer to these bits as "range" bits, and that's because this integer that we end up with is used to define a range of values that our float can represent. To do this, our integer is going to be treated as an exponent that we'll raise the number 2 by. For example, if our range bits are set to 0000 0001—or 1 for those of us who don't speak binary—the lowest possible value that our float can represent will be $+/- 2^1$. The highest possible value that our float can represent is simply the next largest power of two, so if 2^1 is our lower bound, then 2^2 must be our upper bound.

Finally, step three is to select a single value from the range provided by step two, which is what the final bits of a float are used for. To make things a bit simpler to start off, let's pretend that a float only uses 2 bits of data for this step, instead of the 23 bits that a real float has. The only values representable by 2 bits are 00, 01, 10, and 11, which are the numbers 0 to 3, respectively. This means that our float can represent one of four possible values within the range that we defined in step two. To see this visually, imagine the upper and lower bound of our range placed on either end of a number line, like Figure 15-2.

Figure 15-2. *Our float's range displayed on a number line*

The four possible values that our 2 bits of "offset" data can represent can be visualized on the number line as evenly spaced steps between our lower and upper bound, like Figure 15-3. Notices that 4.0 is not a possible value for our number; if we want to represent 4.0, we need to increase the value in our range bits rather than our offset bits.

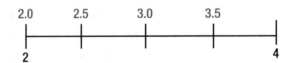

Figure 15-3. *The possible values that our 2 "offset" bits can represent, displayed above the number line from Figure 15-2*

To put what's being shown in Figure 15-3 a different way, the values that our offset bits can represent are fractions of the difference between our upper bound and our lower bound, added to the lower bound. In Figure 15-3, the difference between 2^1 and 2^2 is 2, so our offset bits can be used to choose the numbers 2.0, 2.5, 3.0, or 3.5. To understand how we got those numbers, it might be helpful to see how they were calculated, which is shown in the table in Figure 15-4.

The value…	Is calculated like this:
2	$2^1 + \left(\frac{0}{4} * 2\right)$
2.5	$2^1 + \left(\frac{1}{4} * 2\right)$
3.0	$2^1 + \left(\frac{2}{4} * 2\right)$
3.5	$2^1 + \left(\frac{3}{4} * 2\right)$

Figure 15-4. *How we calculated our four possible values*

The four values in the left column in Figure 15-4 are the only values that our imaginary floating-point number can represent. If our code attempts to store a value like 2.4 in this float, the value will be "snapped" to the closest possible value, which is 2.5. When our bounds are 2^1 and 2^2, this looks inconvenient, but at least we still get every whole number and a useful decimal value to work with. However, consider what this means for us if our range is between two larger numbers, like 2^{10} and 2^{11}. You can see this in Figure 15-5.

1024	$2^{10} + (\frac{0}{4} * 1024)$
1280	$2^{10} + (\frac{1}{4} * 1024)$
1536	$2^{10} + (\frac{2}{4} * 1024)$
1792	$2^{10} + (\frac{3}{4} * 1024)$

Figure 15-5. *The values we can represent if our exponent bit is set to 10*

Now the system has really broken down. With only four possible values to work with, as the range of our number gets higher, the less accurate we can be about representing values between our bounds. This means that as the value we're storing in our float increases, the more inaccurate our representation of it will be.

Now, a real float has a much larger number of bits available for its "offset" data, 23 of them in fact. This doesn't change how the math works, it just changes the denominator of the fraction that we use to calculate possible values. Twenty-three bits of offset data means that we can represent 2^{23} possible different numbers. 2^{23} is equal to 8,388,608, which means the first four values between 2^1 and 2^2 that a full 32-bit float can represent are shown in Figure 15-6. To make this figure a bit easier to read, I've rounded the values in the left-hand column to only display their first 12 digits.

2	$2^1 + (\frac{0}{8388608} * 2)$
2.00000023842	$2^1 + (\frac{1}{8388608} * 2)$
2.00000047684	$2^1 + (\frac{2}{8388608} * 2)$
2.00000071526	$2^1 + (\frac{3}{8388608} * 2)$

Figure 15-6. *The first four possible values we can represent using 23 "offset" bits*

Obviously having 23 bits to work with instead of 2 means that we can represent numbers with a much larger degree of accuracy, but it's important to note that even in a full precision float, this accuracy is not perfect. You can see in Figure 15.6 that we still are unable to represent a value of 2.0000003 accurately. Instead, our value will be snapped to the second row of the table, and just like with our 2-bit example, as our range increases, our accuracy decreases. The only difference is that our range needs to be a lot larger before a full 32-bit float's precision breaks down so much that it's noticeable in most game scenarios.

You can test this out yourself in code. In a simple C or C++ project, create a float and assign it the value of 2.0000003. Then either examine that value at runtime with the debugger or print out the value of that float using printf(). In both cases, you'll see that the value assigned to your float has been snapped to the value shown in the second row of Figure 15-6.

Case Study: Animation over Time

All of this is very interesting on its own, but as mentioned at the start of the chapter, it's much more applicable to shader writing than it is to many other kinds of programming. This is both because we often deal with smaller floating-point values (16 bits or less), and also because even when we deal with full precision floats, any loss of precision can manifest as very visible problems in our rendering. To understand what I mean, consider the vertex shader shown in Listing 15-1.

Listing 15-1. A Vertex Shader That Animates over Time

```
#version 410

layout (location = 0) in vec3 position;
uniform mat4 mvp;
uniform float time;

void main()
{
    vec3 finalPos = position + vec3(0,sin(time),0); ❶
    gl_Position = mvp * vec4(finalPos, 1.0);
}
```

This vertex shader will make a mesh oscillate up and down over time, using the sin() function at ❶. This is the first time we've seen the sin() function used in a shader, but it works exactly how the sin() function in C++ does: no matter what value is passed to the function, it will return a value between -1 and 1. The output of the sin() function is a sine curve, so you can visualize what numbers will produce what output from the function with a graph like Figure 15-7.

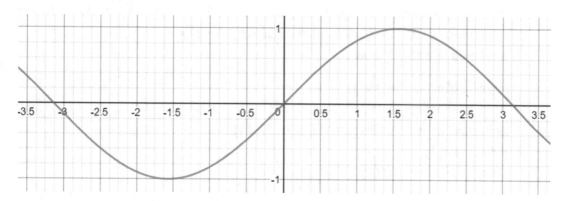

Figure 15-7. *A graph of a sine curve, the output of a sin() function. This curve repeats infinitely along the X axis.*

If you set up a quick example to test out this function (or run the example provided online), you'll see that it works exactly as we intended: whatever object is being rendered will bob up and down over time. The problems start as our time value gets larger. If our time value starts at 0 and increases as the demo runs, we don't see any problems, but if we start our time value at a large number like 131,072 (which is 2^{17}), our formerly smooth animation starts becoming more erratic. This is because as our time value gets larger, the amount of precision it has decreases, and with a sufficiently large number, it decreases so much that we can't accurate represent the difference between the time in one frame to the next. It's important to note that our shader is still working correctly through all of this, but it appears to have problems because of the input we're feeding it. Listing 15-2 shows a draw() function that's set up to immediately cause problems. Note the large starting value for our time variable.

Listing 15-2. A Terrible draw() Function

```
void ofApp::draw(){
    using namespace glm;

    static float t = 1310729999;
    t += ofGetLastFrameTime();

    mat4 proj = perspective(radians(90.0f), 1024.0f / 768.0f, 0.01f, 10.0f);
    mat4 view = inverse(translate(vec3(0,0,10.0f)));
    mat4 mvp = proj * view;

    moveCubeShader.begin();
    moveCubeShader.setUniformMatrix4f("mvp", mvp);
    moveCubeShader.setUniform1f("time", t);
    cube.draw();
    moveCubeShader.end();
}
```

This example is a bit contrived, but these kinds of animation glitches are very common, even when working on large projects. In my career, these kinds of problems have cropped up on water shaders, shaders for buttons that make them pulse with a color, and even shaders that animate the leaves of trees to make them appear to sway in the wind. Any time you write a shader that does work based on a steadily increasing uniform value, you need to worry about the precision of that uniform. The sneaky part of precision issues like this is you won't see them if you test your game by playing in small bursts. Instead, you have to either force your shader inputs to large numbers for testing or leave your game running in an idle state for long enough that your input variables increase to a large enough value, like a player might see if they left their game idling overnight and then woke up to play in the morning.

Fixing these kinds of issues is sometimes a bit tricky. If you're lucky enough to have an animation that repeats itself over time (like our sin() function), then you need to figure out exactly how long it takes for that animation to fully complete one iteration. This is sometimes referred to as the "period" of a function, and if you google for the period of sin(), you'll find out that it's equal to 2 * PI. Once you know what the period is of your animation, you can use the fmod() function to adjust your input accordingly. Here's our draw() function from Listing 15-2, modified to properly account for the period of our shader animation.

Listing 15-3. A Less Terrible Draw Function

```cpp
void ofApp::draw(){
    using namespace glm;

    const double two_pi = 2.0 * 3.14159;

    static double t = 1310729999; ❶
    t += ofGetLastFrameTime();

    mat4 proj = perspective(radians(90.0f), 1024.0f / 768.0f, 0.01f, 10.0f);
    mat4 view = inverse(translate(vec3(0,0,10.0f)));
    mat4 mvp = proj * view;

    moveCubeShader.begin();
    moveCubeShader.setUniformMatrix4f("mvp", mvp);
    moveCubeShader.setUniform1f("time", fmod(t, two_pi)); ❷
    cube.draw();
    moveCubeShader.end();
}
```

The most important thing to note in this updated example is that the core of the fix is to increase the precision of our time variable (❶). Since we can't subtract or otherwise reset the value of time in our program without completely defeating the purpose of that variable, the only option we have is to increase the number of bits we use to store it. A double is just a 64 bit float, which has more than enough precision for our purposes. We could pass this double value to our shader as is. GLSL actually does have a double data type, but many GLSL functions don't support double precision values, which makes them awkward to work with and not very common to see in practice.

Instead, we can use the period of our animation to adjust the value that gets passed to our shaders, using the fmod() function (❷). If you're unfamiliar with fmod(): all it does is divide the first argument by the second, and return the remainder, exactly like the modulus operator (%) does, except for float values. This will keep the input to our shader low enough to maintain precision, while not introducing any hitches in our visuals, since our value will reset every time the animation does.

We'll see some more complicated examples of this sort of problem in the next section, but the solution to any kind of precision problem is always very similar: either reduce the size of the values you're working with (like we just did with fmod) or increase the precision of the problem value.

Working with Lower Precision Variables

Although this book has focused on writing shaders for games that run on desktop PCs, mobile gaming is only getting more popular, and precision is a much greater concern when writing shaders for these devices. Given that this chapter is all about how precision relates to shader writing, I want to take a brief detour from the world of desktop shaders and talk a bit about how precision works on these devices.

The mobile phone landscape is a bit of a jungle when it comes to how each different mobile GPU implements lower precision floating-point numbers. GPU makers for these devices have to worry about power consumption, heat output, and how big the physical hardware is, in addition to how well the hardware performs. One of the factors that they can change to affect these things is how much floating-point precision their GPUs support. In addition to playing with the number of bits given to a regular float, mobile GPUs also define two new kinds of floating-point data types that can be used in shaders: half precision and low (or "fixed") precision values. These have even fewer bits than the "full" precision regular floats, but are much, much faster for mobile GPUs to work with. In GLSL you can choose which of the three types of float types you want by adding "highp," "medium," or "lowp" in front of your variable declaration, like you can see in Listing 15-4. Note that you can also specify a precision qualifier for vectors and matrices, which will dictate the precision of each float that makes up that data type.

Listing 15-4. How to Declare Float Values with Different Precision

```
highp float fullPrecision;
mediump vec3 halfPrecision;
lowp mat4 lowPrecision;
```

These new prefixes for our float variables are known as *precision qualifiers*, and it's important to note that if you try to use them when writing shaders for a desktop GPU, they'll almost always be ignored (the only notable exception is if you're writing shaders for WebGL, which is a version of OpenGL that runs in a web browser). On platforms that do support them (like mobile phones), however, these qualifiers let you choose between three very different float data types. The minimum guaranteed range and precision of these types depends on the version of OpenGL that your program is running. Generally, platforms that support these qualifiers use a subset of OpenGL called OpenGL ES. The values shown in Figure 15-8 are taken from the OpenGL ES 3.0 specification and will be different if you're targeting a different API version.

Data Type	Range Bits	Offset Bits	Range
"highp" or "full precision"	8	23	-2^{126}, 2^{127}
"mediump" or "half precision"	5	10	-2^{14}, 2^{14}
"lowp" or "fixed precision"	1	8	-2^{1}, 2^{1}

Figure 15-8. *The three different types of float variables*

It's important to note that the number of range and offset bits in Figure 15-8 are the "guaranteed" number of bits that each data type has, and the range listed in the last column is the minimum range that a GPU must give that datatype to conform to the standard. Phones are free to implement more than this minimum required amount of precision for each data type, and many do. GPUs in newer iPhones, for instance, treat all low precision values as though they were half precision, since those GPUs are optimized for working with half precision numbers. This is why you will sometimes encounter a shader that works fine on some phones but has precision issues on others; each mobile GPU implements their floats a little differently.

It's also worth calling out that the "lowp" data type is a little bit weird, because it only has 1 range bit. This is because the spec only requires that lowp values be able to represent numbers between -2 and +2, with a constant 8 bits of precision (no precision loss as you approach 2). This means that lowp floats aren't really floats at all, since the amount of precision they have within their range is fixed (hence the term "fixed precision").

All of this makes being able to spot and deal with precision issues even more important, and more complicated, so let's take a look at another case study to see how lower precision variables can cause problems in a game's visuals.

Case Study: Point Light Problem

The first shader we're going to look at comes from a program that uses a shader that supports a single directional light, and a single point light. In our level, the point light's position is set to (0, 5, 0). If we position our geometry near the point light, our scene renders correctly. However, if we position our geometry very far away from where the level's light is placed, say at positions around 300 units away from it, our scene looks very wrong. You can see both scenarios in Figure 15-9.

Figure 15-9. *Our scene rendered near the point light compared witho when our geometry is located very far away from the point light*

This shader works completely correctly when run in the editor of our game engine (which uses our desktop GPU), but when deployed to a phone it looks very wrong. Whenever you encounter a shader that only has problems when deployed to a mobile device, precision problems should be one of the first things you start looking for. In this case, the fragment shader that's causing the problem uses half precision variables exclusively and is shown in Listing 15-5. To save on space, I've left out the struct definitions for point and directional lights, and the function body for the diffuse() function, since it's the same one we used earlier.

Listing 15-5. Our Problem Shader

```glsl
#version 410

precision mediump float; ❶

uniform DirectionalLight dirLight;
uniform PointLight pointLight;
uniform vec3 cameraPos;
uniform vec3 ambientCol;
uniform vec3 meshCol;

in vec3 fragWorldPos;
in vec3 fragNrm;

out vec4 outCol;

void main()
{
     vec3 nrm = normalize(fragNrm);
     vec3 viewDir = normalize( cameraPos - fragWorldPos);

     vec3 finalColor = vec3(0,0,0);

     float dirDiffAmt = diffuse(dirLight.direction, nrm);
     finalColor += dirDiffAmt * dirLight.color * meshCol;

     vec3 toLight = pointLight.position - fragWorldPos;
     vec3 lightDir = normalize(toLight);
     float distToLight = dot(toLight, toLight); ❷
     float falloff = max(0.0,1.0 - (distToLight / pointLight.radius));
     float pointDiffAmt = diffuse(lightDir, nrm) * falloff;
     finalColor += pointDiffAmt * pointLight.color * meshCol;

     outCol = vec4(finalColor + ambientCol, 1.0);
}
```

The only new thing in this shader is the line at ❶. This is a shorthand way of saying "unless I say otherwise, make every float in this shader a half precision (or medium precision) float." Without this line, we would have to add "mediump" to every variable we declared in order to have our shader only deal with half precision values. After that line, this is essentially a stripped-down version of the shaders that we wrote back in Chapter 12, except that it only handles diffuse lighting, which means that we don't have to spend too long understanding what's going on, so we can jump straight to figuring out what's going on with our precision issue.

Looking at the shader in Listing 15-5, the most obvious way for things to go wrong is if our fragment's world position or our light's position is set to a value that exceeds the possible range of a half precision variable. This is dangerous because exceeding the range of a float can result in that value being set to infinity (or -infinity), which can cause all sorts of problems in your math later on. Unfortunately for us, even in our problem case, everything is well within the range that we should be able to represent. This means that if our problems are precision related (and we know they are in this case because this is the precision chapter), then the problem must be that some of the math our shader is doing is ending up with values that are either too small or too large.

The real clue as to what's going on in this scene comes from the fact that it only happens when the geometry is located far away from the location of the point light, which means that we should be looking at wherever we're calculating how far away our fragment is. Since this is a point light shader, we need to get that distance value to calculate our falloff (you can see this at ❷). Just like we saw in the chapter on improving shader performance, to avoid doing a costly length() operation, this shader is using the squared distance between the point light and the current fragment, rather than the actual distance, to calculate the falloff valuec. This is great for performance but means that our distance value can exceed the bounds of even a full precision floating-point number well before any object in our scene is that far away from the origin. If you look back at the table in Figure 15-8, you can see that the minimum guaranteed value that can be stored in a half precision number is 2^{14}, or 16,384. The square root of 2^{14} is 2^7, which means that as soon as our fragment is >128 units away from the world origin, the squared distance from there to our fragment exceeds the guaranteed bounds of our half precision number, and we can end up with a problem value in our shader when we get the dot product at ❷.

This doesn't necessarily mean that a value of exactly 256 will cause a visual problem. Due to differences between GPUs and drivers on different phones, you may not see a problem until your distance value is much larger, and on some phones you may not see an issue until your value is large enough to exceed a full precision variable. How mobile GPUs handle precision can vary wildly between models, which is why it's important to test on as wide a range of hardware as possible when making a mobile game: just because everything looks OK on one phone does not mean it will look the same on others.

For our case study shader, we're going to fix the problem by increasing the precision of our distance value to a highp float, as you can see in Listing 15-6.

Listing 15-6. Specifying the Precision of Our Distance Variable

```
highp float distToLight = dot(toLight, toLight);
```

However, this isn't the whole story, because now we have a bunch of math that's going to try to use this high precision variable to generate new half precision values, and if this highp float causes that math to wind up with values too large for the rest of the mediump shader, things could still go wrong. In our case, we only use this distToLight variable when calculating the falloff of our light, which should keep things in the range of 0 to 1 (although that can break if we try to use a value of infinity in that math.), so we're in the clear, but in many cases things aren't so straightforward. Whenever you start changing the precision of a single value, it's always important to think through how that value will be used later on, to ensure that you haven't just moved your precision problem deeper into your shader code.

I'm going to end our discussion of reduced precision variables here, because this book isn't all about mobile shader development. The short takeaway from all of this (and in fact, the whole chapter), is that it's important to understand the data that you are sending to your shaders and ensure that the data types that you're using to store and manipulate that data have enough precision for the job.

With those final words of advice, it's time for us to leave our discussion of precision behind and start looking at how to use all the stuff we've learned so far in a few different game engines. Each engine handles shaders a bit differently, but now that we have a good grounding in the basics of game graphics, and understand how to work with shader code, it shouldn't be too hard for you to jump into your engine of choice and start getting your hands dirty. The next three chapters (the last ones in the book!) will provide a short guide to help you get started with three of the most popular game engines out there right now: Unity, UE4, and Godot, in that order. If you're only interested in one of these engines, it's OK to skip straight to the one you want, but each of these engines handles things in their own way, and it might come in handy to have a bit of exposure to each of them as well. So don't feel like these chapters are useless to you if you only ever use one engine, or your engine of choice isn't talked about specifically.

Summary

Here's a summary of what we covered in this chapter:

- Decimal numbers are stored in shaders as "floats" (aka "floating-point numbers").

- Floating-point numbers use a fixed number of bits to represent a large range of values. Due to the nature of how this is implemented, they can't represent every number exactly. This precision loss gets more pronounced as the values being stored increase.

- When working with very large values, it's possible that this precision loss can manifest itself as visual artifacts in your renderings. We walked through an example of a shader that exhibited animation problems as a time value increased.

- Some platforms allow shaders to specify how much precision a floating-point value needs, for the purposes of optimization. Less precision means fewer bits needed to store a value, and faster computation.

- When working with smaller floating-point data types, it's important to make sure that you're aware of the possible range of values that your calculations result in, to avoid precision-related bugs.

CHAPTER 16

Writing Shaders in Unity

The first engine that we're going to dive into is Unity. Unity is an amazingly flexible platform to build a game with, and is my personal favorite environment to prototype new shaders or graphics techniques in. However, Unity is a very complex engine to wrap your head around, and this chapter is not going to provide a ground-up tutorial in how to work with Unity, just how to write shaders for it. If you'd like to learn to use Unity, but haven't before, I recommend jumping into some tutorials online before trying to tackle the content in this chapter; otherwise you'll likely be a bit lost. You don't need to be a Unity expert to start writing shaders for the engine, but you do need to at least be able to navigate the editor and get an object onto your screen.

With that foreword out of the way, let's get right to it. Our Unity chapter is going to be divided up into three sections. First, we're going to look at how Unity treats shader assets. After that we'll take a quick look at the standard shader that Unity gives you out of the box, and then finally we'll dive into the nuts and bolts of writing shaders that work with the engine.

Shaders and Materials in Unity

One of the most important things that a game engine does for you is provide you with an asset management system for your game's content. Every engine does this slightly differently, so it's important to know how your engine of choice is deciding to store the data that your game will use. For our purposes, we're interested in two types of Unity assets: Shaders and Materials.

Shaders, unsurprisingly, are the asset type that stores the actual shader code that a project will use to render objects on screen. However, Unity's shader assets also contain information about how to set up the graphics pipeline to render an object, and meta information about the inputs that the shader expects. If you think back to the demo programs we were writing in Chapter 12, you may recall that each of our different

© Kyle Halladay 2019
K. Halladay, *Practical Shader Development*, https://doi.org/10.1007/978-1-4842-4457-9_16

meshes required their own function to set up the graphics pipeline for that mesh. These functions included things like setting up the depth comparison functions and specifying blend equations. In Unity, those types of tasks are handled in the shader asset itself. We'll see how this is done in this chapter.

Unity doesn't apply shaders directly to meshes. Instead, it uses a second asset type, called a Material, which contains a shader and all the inputs to that shader. Unity's materials save a lot of time because they allow you to specify all the inputs that a shader will use without needing to write code to render each specific type of object in your game. These assets are what are actually applied to objects to define their visual appearance.

Creating materials in Unity is very simple, all you need to do is hit the "Create" button in the project panel and choose "Material" from the drop-down menu. Even if you haven't written any shader code, Unity ships with a number of built-in shaders for you to use, and you can select any one of these for your material assets to use. By default, materials that you create will be assigned Unity's "Standard" shader, but there are a lot of different shaders to choose from without ever having to open a shader editor. The code for these built-in shaders is available for download from Unity's website.

Using a built-in shader isn't what we're here to do though. We want to write our own, totally handmade shaders! To do that, select the "Create" button again, and this time navigate to the "Shader" submenu. This menu has four options, and which one you choose depends on what type of shader you want to start writing. We're going to start from as blank a slate as possible, so we're going to select the "Unlit Shader" option. This will create a new shader asset for us in our project panel. If you open up this file, you'll see that Unity has already added a lot of code to it for us. We're going to be deleting most of this so that we can start from scratch, but before we do so, we can use this default code to talk about the structure of a Unity shader.

Introducing ShaderLab

All shaders in Unity are written in what's called "ShaderLab" syntax. ShaderLab is Unity's custom data format, which encapsulates pipeline settings, shader code, and information about the uniforms that a shader expects. If we remove all the actual shader code from our new Unlit shader file, the text we're left with is all the ShaderLab data needed to make a simple shader work. This looks like Listing 16-1. There's a lot of new stuff going on in just these few lines of code, so before we start writing a shader, let's take a look at what all of this boilerplate means.

Listing 16-1. A Simple Unity Shader with the Shader Logic Removed

```
Shader "Unlit/SolidColor" ❶{
    Properties ❷{
        _MainTex ("Texture", 2D) = "white" {}
    }
    SubShader ❸{
        Tags { "RenderType"="Opaque" }
        LOD 100

        Pass{ ❹
            CGPROGRAM

            //actual shader code goes here

            ENDCG
        }
    }
}
```

To start with, all shaders in Unity need to be assigned a name so that they can show up in the drop-down menus that let you choose what shader a material uses. You set this at the first line of any shader file (❶). The rest of the data in a shader file is contained within a set of curly braces underneath the name declaration of the shader. Usually, the next thing that you'll see in a Unity shader is the "Properties" block (❷). This section lets you define shader uniforms, which can be set using the Unity material GUI back in the actual Unity editor (an example of this is shown in Figure 16-1). The "Properties" block also allows you to assign default values for these uniforms, which is very handy. It's important to note that the properties block doesn't actually declare your shader uniforms; you still have to do that in shader code. It just provides information about those uniforms to the Unity editor.

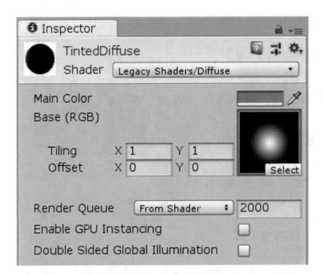

Figure 16-1. *A material with a number of properties available to modify*

After the Properties block, shaders in Unity will contain one or more "SubShader" blocks (❸). Each SubShader block will contain the code for one or more complete shaders and some information about them. When Unity tries to render an object, it will use the first SubShader block that contains a shader that the user's machine can run. Our shaders will all contain a single SubShader block, but if you were writing a game that could run on multiple platforms, you could write custom shaders that were specially tailored to each of your platforms. Supporting multiple SubShader blocks is how Unity provides that flexibility.

Finally, within every SubShader block, there will be a few lines of information about that shader, like whether it is an opaque or translucent shader and what LOD level that shader should be used with; then there will be one of more "Pass" blocks (❹). Each Pass block will contain the source for a single complete shader, and when a SubShader is used, the object being rendered will be rendered once for each Pass in that SubShader that matches the current usage flags set by the engine, executed in order. This is very handy for doing multi-pass rendering, like we did in Chapter 12, where each type of light needed a different shader to light our object. In Unity, you could write each different type of light as a different pass in a single shader. We're going to see an example of how to do this later in this chapter.

You may have noticed that Listing 16-1 has a comment that says the shader code for a pass has to be located between the tags CGPROGRAM/ENDCG. This is because Unity shaders generally are written in the CG shader language, as opposed to GLSL.

Cg is a high-level shader language that can be transpiled into any of the platform- or API-specific shader languages that a Unity application might use (HLSL, GLSL, Metal, etc.). It is technically possible to write GLSL shaders in Unity, but you lose out on all the cross-platform portability offered by Cg, so it's relatively uncommon to see plain GLSL in a Unity project. If you really want to, you can replace the CGPROGRAM/ENDCG tags with GLSLPROGRAM/ENDGLSL, but there's still a lot of Unity-specific stuff to keep in mind, so I recommend reading through the Unity documentation before trying to use GLSL in a Unity project.

We're going to follow convention and write our shaders in Cg. Luckily for us, the Cg programming language is very similar to GLSL, so it doesn't take too much work to switch to using it.

A Solid Color Shader

Now that we have a general idea of how ShaderLab works, let's see what a very simple shader would look like in Unity. We're going write a shader that takes a single vec4 uniform and set every fragment to the color stored in that vec4. To start with, let's look at what the ShaderLab code would look like without the actual Cg shader code present. This is shown in Listing 16-2.

Listing 16-2. The ShaderLab for our SolidColor Shader

```
Shader "Unlit/SolidColor"{
    Properties{
        _Color ("Color", Color) = (1,1,1,1)
    }
    SubShader{
        Tags { "RenderType"="Opaque" }
        LOD 100

        Pass{
            CGPROGRAM
            //shader code goes here
            ENDCG
        }
    }
}
```

This is almost identical to the ShaderLab code that we started with, with the exception of the Properties block, which now has information about the _Color uniform that our shader is going to use. In our case, we've told Unity that this uniform's name is "Color," that we want it to represent a color instead of a regular vector, and that the default value of this uniform should be white (1, 1, 1, 1). When our shader is finished, this property block is going to generate a material GUI that looks like Figure 16-2. Note that there are a couple properties ("Render Queue" and "Double Sided Global Illumination") that are automatically added to every shader. We're going to ignore them for now, but we'll talk about the "Render Queue" property later in this chapter.

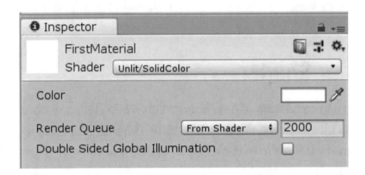

Figure 16-2. *The Unity editor GUI for our material. Notice that we have a color picker for our uniform, because we specified it was going to store color data.*

With that out of the way, let's now move to looking at what we're going to put between the CGPROGRAM/ENDCG tags in our subshader's pass. This is the first time that we've looked at Cg shader code, so we'll walk through it slowly. To start with, let's look at the structure of a Cg shader, which you can see in Listing 16-3.

Listing 16-3. The Skeleton of a Cg Shader

```
CGPROGRAM
#pragma vertex vert    ❶
#pragma fragment frag

v2f vert (appdata v) ❷ {
        //vertex logic goes here
}

float4 frag (v2f i) : SV_Target ❸{
        //fragment logic goes here
}
```

One of the big differences between GLSL and Cg is that Cg combines the code for the vertex and fragment programs into a single file. This saves on redundant typing, since you only need to define uniforms in one place, but it means that we need to add a couple lines to our program to specify which function is the main function of our vertex program and which is the main of our fragment program. You can see in Listing 16-3 that the first lines of our shader (❶) do exactly that. The pragmas at ❶ declare that the function called "vert" will be the main() for our vertex program and "frag" will be for our fragment program. You'll often hear the term "vertex function" and "fragment function" when talking about a Cg shader, since the vertex and fragment shaders are in the same program and are represented as functions. Don't get confused by the naming differences, though; under the hood you still end up with two separate shaders.

Combining both shaders into a single file means that we can share code and uniforms, but it also means that GLSL style "in" and "out" variables don't make much sense. Instead, Cg shaders define structs to represent the data the data sent between different pipeline stages. In Listing 16-3, our vertex function is going to receive it's input in the form of a struct of type "appdata," and send data to the fragment function by returning a struct of type "v2f" (vertex to fragment). This also means that shader functions in Cg will actually have return statements, instead of writing to out variables like we've been doing in GLSL. Don't get confused by the new syntax; this is just a cosmetic change. The type of data each shader function is using is going to stay pretty much the same as GLSL. Our vertex function's inputs will be things like vertex position, normals, and UVs, and our fragment's inputs will be whatever we decide to the vertex shader should send it. Listing 16-4 shows the two structs that our shader is going to use.

Listing 16-4. The I/O Data Types for Our Shader Functions

```
struct appdata
{
      float4 vertex : POSITION;    ❶
};

struct v2f
{
      float4 vertex : SV_POSITION;  ❷
};
```

Since our shader is just going to output a solid color from the fragment function, we actually don't have very much data to pass around. In the case of the vertex function input, the only data we need is vertex position, which you can see at ❶. Notice that in Cg, some variables are declared with "semantics" at the end of them to denote what they're used for, or where they come from. In ❶, the POSITION semantic flags that the vertex variable should receive vertex position. We're storing this position data in a "float4" variable, rather than using a vec4. Unlike GLSL, which used precision qualifiers like highp and medium to specify the precision of any vec datatype, Cg's types contain their precision right in the name. So instead of writing "highp vec4", the Cg equivalent is "float4." Likewise, "mediump vec3" would end up as "half3," and "lowp vec2" would be "fixed2." We're going to keep all our values as high-precision variables for simplicity, but since Unity is used a lot for mobile games, it's very common to see half and fixed datatypes on shaders you find online or purchase on the asset store.

Our vertex shader output struct, "v2f," also needs a bit of explaining. Unlike GLSL, where we wrote our vertex position to gl_Position and then never thought about it again, in Cg, we need to explicitly pass the vertex position to the fragment shader. We do this by creating a member variable (almost always a float4) and flagging it specifically as the vertex position variable with the semantic "SV_Position." The "SV_" stands for "system value," and in Unity's Cg shaders they generally are only used to flag data which is going to be read by a non shader part of the graphics pipeline. In the case of vertex position, that data is going to end up being read by the "shape assembly" and "rasterizer" stages of the pipeline, which occur before our fragment shader even starts running. I've included our graphics pipeline diagram in Figure 16-3 as reference. As we'll see later, other data that we include in the vertex output struct, which we want to be read by the fragment shader, will not need an SV_ semantic.

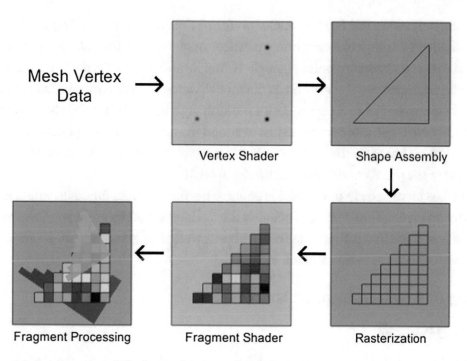

Figure 16-3. *Our simplified graphics pipeline diagram*

Moving on from our structs, let's take a look at the body of our vertex function, which is shown in Listing 16-5.

Listing 16-5. The Body of Our Cg Vertex Function

```
v2f vert (appdata v)
{
    v2f o;
    o.vertex = mul(UNITY_MATRIX_MVP, v.vertex);   ❶
    return o;
}
```

Aside from returning a value instead of writing to gl_Position, the body of this function is should look a lot like vertex shaders we wrote in GLSL. The only bit of logic that our shader needs to perform here is to transform our mesh vertex position into clip space, and just like before, we're going to do that by multiplying our vertex position by the model-view-projection matrix of our mesh (at ❶). Unity automatically provides the MVP matrix for every object as the uniform UNITY_MATRIX_MVP, so there's no need for us to declare it in shader code or set it up manually in our project.

Unity defines several built-in shader uniforms that are automatically provided to every shader, for things like commonly matrices or global data (like game time). A list of all of them can be found online (google "Unity Built-In Shader Variables"), but the most common one you'll see, by far, is the model-view-projection matrix that we just saw. You'll also notice that the syntax for multiplying a vector by a matrix has changed slightly: where GLSL was content to just overload the multiplication operator, Cg uses the mul() function to do the same. This is just a syntax difference; functionally, mul() is identical to the matrix multiplication we did in GLSL.

The last bit of code in our shader is going to be our fragment function, which is included in Listing 16-6. I've also included the declaration of the uniform _Color value that we described in our Properties block here as well, simply because this seemed like the most logical time to talk about it too.

Listing 16-6. Our Cg Fragment Function

```
float4 _Color; ❶

float4 frag (v2f i) : SV_Target   ❷
{
      return _Color;
}
```

Declaring uniform variables in a Cg shader is very simple—you don't even need the uniform keyword! All you need to do is declare the variable outside of the scope of a struct or shader function, and then that uniform value will be accessible to both your vertex and fragment shaders. You can see this at ❶.

Our fragment function, frag(), is shown at ❷. You'll notice that the function signature for frag() also has a system-value semantic, "SV_Target." Fragment shaders in Cg can optionally write to SV_Target, which means that they'll write a color to the buffer that the shader is rendering to, or SV_Depth, which means they will write directly to the depth buffer. It's much less common to see a shader in Unity write to SV_Depth than it is to write to SV_Target, so unless you're sure of what you're doing, you can just blindly add SV_Target and not worry too much about it. Finally, just like our vertex function, fragment shaders in Unity actually return the color value that they want to write, instead of writing it to an output variable. This means that the return type of the fragment function is always a color type (although it's common to see fixed4 and half4 used as well), and the last line of any Cg fragment shader returns a value of this type.

Now that our shader is written, it's time to use it in a Unity project. Create a new material and select the shader "Unlit/SolidColor" from the shader selection drop-down list. Since the default value we provided for our _Color uniform was white, putting this material on an object will render that object with a solid white color. Since we set up this uniform in our properties block, you can use the editor GUI to change which color the material is going to use. For example, I set my material to output a light green color and added it to a cube mesh. The results are shown in Figure 16-4. The source for this shader can be found in the example code for this chapter, in the file "SolidColor.shader."

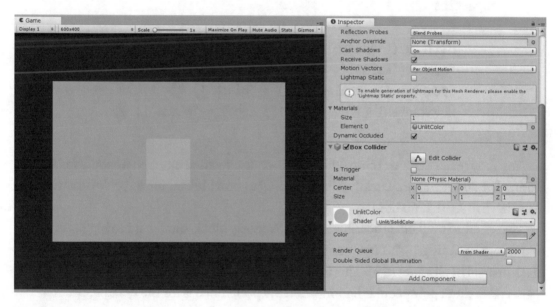

Figure 16-4. *A screenshot of my editor with our Unlit/Color material added to a mesh*

Porting Our Blinn-Phong Shader

We're going to port our Blinn-Phong shader to Unity next. This is going to involve learning a lot of Unity-specific info, so we're going to start by just implementing support for a single directional light and then build from there. To get started, create a new shader file in Unity, open it up, and delete all the text that has been added for us. We're going to write everything completely from scratch.

First, we need to name our shader (I chose "BlinnPhong") and set up the properties block for our uniforms. If you recall, our Blinn-Phong shader used four textures as inputs: a diffuse map, a normal map, a spec map, and a cube map. Put together, our shader name and properties block is going to look like Listing 16-7.

Listing 16-7. First Few Lines of Our Blinn-Phong Shader

```
Shader "BlinnPhong"
{
    Properties
    {
        _Diffuse ("Texture", 2D) = "white" {}
        _Normal ("Normal", 2D) = "blue"{}
        _Specular ("Specular", 2D) = "black"{} ❶
        _Environment ("Environment", Cube) = "white"{} ❷
    }
```

You may recall that our Blinn-Phong shader also needed a bunch of uniforms for storing light information. Luckily, Unity is going to provide that for us by default, so we don't have to set that up here.

We've already talked about ShaderLab's Property block, but I want to highlight two new things in Listing 16-7. First, our specular map's default texture is being set to all black instead of all white (❶). This is because black in a specular map corresponds to regions that don't get specular lighting, and my preference is for the default specular map to make an object complete matte, rather than perfectly shiny. Second, notice that when specifying that a property is a cubemap, rather than call the texture type "3D", we use "Cube" (shown at ❷). 3D textures are very different from cubemaps, so it's important to not get them confused.

Our Property block is complete, so now we need to set up our SubShader block. We're going to start with one SubShader, with a single Pass. Both of these need a little bit of extra information specified to make sure Unity knows how we want our shader to be used. You can see the code for this in Listing 16-8.

Listing 16-8. Setting Up Our SubShader and Pass

```
SubShader{
      Tags { "RenderType"="Opaque" "Queue"="Geometry" } ❶

      Pass{
            Tags {"LightMode" = "ForwardBase"} ❷

            CGPROGRAM
            ENDCG

      }
}
```

The first thing you'll notice is that we've added some information to our SubShader's "Tags" block (❶). This block is used to provide metadata about how the engine should use our shader. In Listing 16-8 we added the "Queue" tag and specified a value for it. The order that Unity draws meshes in depends partly on the queue that they are assigned to. This is necessary because translucent objects need to be drawn after all opaque objects are done drawing in order to work correctly, and there are a number of shader techniques that can take advantage of explicitly specifying the draw order of some meshes. If you don't specify a queue in a Unity shader, it is assumed to be the "Geometry" queue; I've simply made this more explicit in our shader.

Our "Pass" block now has tags of its own as well, specifically, the "LightMode" tag (❷). This tag is important because it tells Unity how this pass interacts with the lighting system. Just like when we wrote our multishader lighting in Chapter 12, you can set up shaders in Unity to use different shader passes for different types of lights. The "ForwardBase" light mode means that our Pass is going to be used as the base pass in forward rendering. The base pass is the opaque pass of the multishader lighting setup, which, just like when we built this system ourselves, is the directional and ambient lighting pass.

With our tags set up, it's time to start writing Cg code. We're going to start by setting up our pragmas to specify which functions are which in our CG code, and defining the vertex shader input and output structs. We have a lot more data to pass between our shaders now, and you can see that reflected in Listing 16-9.

Listing 16-9. Pragmas and Data Structure for Our Blinn-Phong Shader.

```
CGPROGRAM
#pragma vertex vert
#pragma fragment frag
#include "UnityCG.cginc"
#pragma multi_compile_fwdbase  ❶

struct vIN{
      float4 vertex : POSITION;
      float3 normal : NORMAL;
      float3 tangent : TANGENT;
      float2 uv : TEXCOORD0;  ❷
};

struct vOUT{
      float4 pos : SV_POSITION;
      float3x3 tbn : TEXCOORD0;
      float2 uv : TEXCOORD3;  ❸
      float3 worldPos : TEXCOORD4;
};
```

There are a few new things going on in Listing 16-9. First off, we have a new pragma, shown at ❶. This pragma is the Cg code equivalent of the ForwardBase tag that we specified for our pass, and simply tells the Unity shader compiler to do some extra work to make sure this shader code can be used as the ForwardBase pass. Immediately above this new pragma we have an #include statement, which includes "UnityCG.cginc," a helper file that contains several Unity-specific shader functions that we're going to use to make our lives a bit easier.

Below all of this, we have our vertex shader I/O structs: vIN for data that is being input to the vertex shader, and vOUT for data being sent from the vertex shader to the rest of the pipeline. We'll talk about vIN first. You'll notice that we have a number of new semantics being used to specify which vertex data each variable in our struct should be assigned. Functionally, these semantics are the same as us manually assigning vertex attributes to variables in GLSL, just in a different wrapper. One thing that may be a bit different, however, is the TEXCOORD0 semantic (❷). Unity's shaders use the semantic

TEXCOORD to refer to UV coordinates. The zero at the end of the semantic is because a vertex can have a number of different UV coordinates at the same time, so we need to specify which ones we want.

Let's talk about the vertex output struct next. We have our SV_POSITION value just like before, but Listing 16-9 has also added TBN matrix and the UV coordinates for our fragment. Both of these chunks of data are being assigned TEXCOORD semantics, which probably doesn't make much sense at first glance. In practice, Unity shaders use the TEXCOORD semantic to specify generic high-precision data in the vertex output struct. Each TEXCOORD is a float4 under the hood, which is why our float3x3 matrix takes up three slots, and why our "uv" variable needs to be assigned the third TEXCOORD, instead of TEXCOORD1. Just like "out" variables in GLSL, these values will be interpolated before they are read by the fragment shader.

Now that we have a handle on the data types that it will deal with, it's time to talk about our vertex function. This is going to look very similar to when we were doing normal mapping in previous chapters—most of the work that our vertex function is going to do is package up a matrix to properly transform the normal that we get out of the normal map. The only differences are going to be minor syntax differences and some Unity-specific variable names. Listing 16-10 has all the goodness.

Listing 16-10. The Vertex Function for Our Blinn-Phong Shader

```
vOUT vert(vIN v)
{
    vOUT o;
    o.pos = UnityObjectToClipPos(v.vertex); ❶
    o.uv = v.uv;

    float3 worldNormal = UnityObjectToWorldNormal(v.normal); ❷
    float3 worldTangent = UnityObjectToWorldDir(v.tangent.xyz);
    float3 worldBitan = cross(worldNormal, worldTangent);

    o.worldPos = mul(unity_ObjectToWorld, v.vertex).xyz; ❸
    o.tbn = float3x3( worldTangent, worldBitan, worldNormal);

    return o;
}
```

While the math is identical to when we added normal mapping to our GLSL shaders, the syntax that we're using is very Unity-centric. To start with, I've replaced the line of code we used before to multiply our vertex position by the MVP matrix with the Unity-provided function, UnityObjectToClipPos(), at ❶. This function does the same thing, while making sure to handle any platform-specific idiosyncrasies that you may encounter while building a cross platform game. You'll notice that we also have Unity-specific functions at ❷, which handle the matrix multiplication that we would otherwise have to do here. Interestingly, there is currently no function to transform a position from object space to world space, so we have to do the matrix multiplication ourselves for the worldPos variable (❸). Finally, we combine our T, B, and N vectors into the TBN matrix that we know and love, and return our newly filled out vOUT structure from the vertex function.

Listing 16-11 shows what our fragment function is going to look like. Remember, we're only implementing the directional light handling of our Blinn-Phong shader right now. Just like before, our code snippet for our fragment function will also contain the Cg declaration of the uniforms defined in our property block, mostly because there isn't a better place to put them in our example snippets.

Listing 16-11. The Fragment Function for Our Blinn-Phong Shader

```
sampler2D _Normal;
sampler2D _Diffuse;
sampler2D _Specular;
samplerCUBE _Environment;
float4 _LightColor0;

float4 frag(vOUT i) : SV_TARGET
{
    //common vectors
    float3 unpackNormal = UnpackNormal(tex2D(_Normal, i.uv)); ❶
    float3 nrm = normalize(mul(transpose(i.tbn), unpackNormal));
    float3 viewDir = normalize(_WorldSpaceCameraPos - i.worldPos); ❷
    float3 halfVec = normalize(viewDir + _WorldSpaceLightPos0.xyz);
    float3 env = texCUBE(_Environment, reflect(-viewDir, nrm)).rgb;
    float3 sceneLight = lerp(_LightColor0, env + _LightColor0 *
    0.5, 0.5); ❸
```

```
    //light amounts
    float diffAmt = max(dot(nrm, _WorldSpaceLightPos0.xyz), 0.0);
    float specAmt = max(0.0, dot(halfVec, nrm));
    specAmt = pow(specAmt, 4.0);

    //sample maps
    float4 tex = tex2D(_Diffuse, i.uv);
    float4 specMask = tex2D(_Specular, i.uv);

    //compute specular color
    float3 specCol = specMask.rgb * specAmt;

    //incorporate data aboout light color and ambient
    float3 finalDiffuse = sceneLight * diffAmt * tex.rgb;
    float3 finalSpec = specCol * _ sceneLight;
    float3 finalAmbient = UNITY_LIGHTMODEL_AMBIENT.rgb * tex.rgb;    ❹

    return float4( finalDiffuse + finalSpec + finalAmbient, 1.0);
}
```

Obvious syntax differences aside, there's quite a bit of Unity-specific stuff going on in this function. To start, just like when we wrote our GLSL Blinn-Phong shader, we need to unpack the normal vector from our normal map. We did this manually in our GLSL code, but Unity provides the function UnpackNormal() (shown at ❶) to handle this for us. This is important, because it means that we don't have to change our shader code if Unity decides to encode normal vectors differently in normal maps on certain platforms. Another very important difference with handling our normal vector is that matrix data types in Cg store their data row by row, which is the reverse of GLSL, which stored data column by column. To correct for this, we need to multiply our normal vector by transpose(i.tbn) rather than the regular TBN matrix. The transpose() function simply returns a new matrix whose columns are the rows of the original matrix. Figure 16-5 shows a quick example of what the transpose() function does.

$$transpose\left(\begin{bmatrix} 0 & 1 & 2 \\ 3 & 4 & 5 \\ 6 & 7 & 8 \end{bmatrix}\right) = \begin{bmatrix} 0 & 3 & 6 \\ 1 & 4 & 7 \\ 2 & 5 & 8 \end{bmatrix}$$

Figure 16-5. *What the transpose() function does*

The rest of the "common vectors" section in Listing 16-11 should look very similar to our old shader, except for the use of some new variables: _WorldSpaceLightPos0 and _WorldSpaceCameraPos (❷). These two variables are automatically provided for us by Unity, so we don't have to pass them into the shader manually. It's worth noting that when dealing with a directional light, like we are in our current shader, _WorldSpaceLightPos0 refers to the direction of the light.

The meat of this function is almost identical to our GLSL Blinn-Phong shader, both because Cg and GLSL aren't that different in terms of syntax, and because the math for Blinn-Phong lighting is the same regardless of shader language being used. One notable syntax difference is that Cg's version of the mix() function is called lerp(), which you can see used at ❸. Other than the name, however, the function is identical to mix(). Additionally, some of the lighting calculations make use of two more Unity provided variables: _LightColor0, and UNITY_LIGHTMODEL_AMBIENT (❹). These variables store the color of the current light, and the ambient lighting for the current scene, respectively. The function ends with us returning the color of the fragment, rather than writing to an out variable, just like we saw earlier in the chapter.

With all that out of the way, you should be able to use this shader to recreate the shield mesh that we used in our openFrameworks applications, inside Unity. If you import the textures and mesh from our previous demo programs, and set things up in a Unity scene, using the new shader, you should end up with something like Figure 16-6. The example code for this chapter contains a full Unity project that should exactly replicate Figure 16-6, so if you get stuck, check out the "BlinnPhong" project in the Chapter 16 examples.

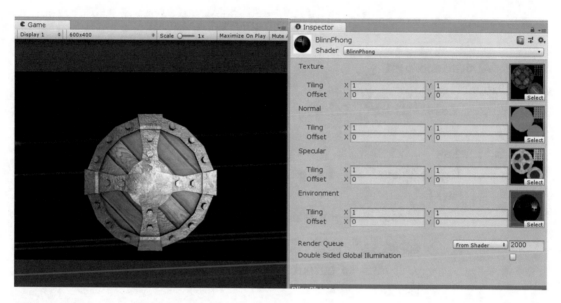

Figure 16-6. *Our shield mesh being rendered in Unity with our Blinn-Phong shader*

We're going to finish this chapter by adding support for multiple point and spot lights to this shader, but first I want to take a quick detour and talk about writing translucent materials in Unity, since knowing that will make it easier to understand the multilight code we need to write later.

Translucent Shaders in Unity

In openFrameworks, when we wanted to render a translucent object, we had to set the blend mode that that object used in our C++ code before we issued a draw call. In Unity, as you might expect by now, the blend mode that a shader needs can be specified immediately in that shader's code. All we have to do to make this work is to set our subshader's queue tag to "Transparent" and specify a blend function inside each of our passes. The ShaderLab code for this is shown in Listing 16-12, which shows how to create a translucent shader that renders objects as a solid color.

Listing 16-12. The ShaderLab Code for a translucent Shader

```
Shader "AlphaBlendColor"{
     Properties{
          _Color("Color", Color) = (1.0,1.0,1.0,1.0)
     }
     SubShader{
          Tags {"Queue" = "Transparent"}
          Pass{
               Blend SrcAlpha OneMinusSrcAlpha ❶

               CGPROGRAM
               //shader to output _Color
               ENDCG
          }
     }
}
```

Other than simply showing off the ShaderLab syntax for setting all this up, Listing 16-12 is also the first time we've seen a blend mode expressed as a blend equation (❶). In openFrameworks, the two blend equations we wanted to use were set up as presets for us: OF_BLENDMODE_ALPHA and OF_BLENDMODE_ADD. Unity doesn't provide similar presets, and instead requires us to fill in the actual blend equation we want to use. We talked about how to read a blend equation way back in Chapter 4, so if you're a bit rusty on what "SrcAlpha OneMinusSrcAlpha" is referring to, take a moment to jump back and reread that part of the chapter.

I'm not going to bother filling in the Cg code here, since it will be identical to the first shader we wrote in this chapter, which returned a solid color. The only difference is that now the alpha channel of that color will make a real difference, because we've set up our queue and blend equation to take advantage of it. That's all there is to making a translucent shader in Unity, which means that we're ready to jump back to our Blinn-Phong shader and finish things off by adding support for multiple lights.

Handling Multiple Lights

Just like we did in Chapter 12, we're going to add support for any number of additional lights to our Blinn-Phong shader by issuing a draw call for each light that is shining on our object and blending the result of each of these calls on top each other. We already have our base pass, which handles a single directional light, and we're going to build on that shader now.

Rather than write a whole new shader, we're going to instead add a new pass to our Blinn-Phong shader's SubShader. Our first pass used the "ForwardBase" tag to specify that it should be used to render our object with a directional light. Our new pass will use the "ForwardAdd" tag, which declares that this pass will be an additive light pass. Listing 16-13 shows how to set up this new pass in our shader.

Listing 16-13. Setting Up a ForwardAdd Pass in a Shader

```
//old pass
Pass{
      Tags { "RenderType"="Opaque" "Queue"="Geometry" }
      CGPROGRAM
      ENDCG
}
//new pass
Pass{
      Tags {"LightMode" = "ForwardAdd"   "Queue"="Geometry" }
      Blend One One  ❶

      CGPROGRAM
      ENDCG
}
```

If you recall from Chapter 12, the additional draw calls that we issue for each light need to use the additive blend mode, because we want these passes to only be able to brighten what has already been rendered by any previous draw calls. To equation for additive blending is "One One" (❶), meaning that we take 100% of the color that is output from our fragment shader and simply add it to whatever is already in the back buffer. With that set up, we're ready to move on to filling in our CGPROGRAM tags and having a fully functioning Blinn-Phong shader.

The first part of our new pass is going to be our set of #pragmas and #includes. This time we're going to include an additional file, AutoLight.cginc, which is going to save us an awful lot of headache when it comes to working with different types of lights. We'll also need to change our mutli_compile pragma to use fwdadd instead of fwdbase. Listing 16-14 shows what all of this looks like in our code.

Listing 16-14. The Pragmas and Includes for Our Forward Add Pass

```
#pragma vertex vert
#pragma fragment frag
#include "UnityCG.cginc"
#include "AutoLight.cginc"
#pragma multi_compile_fwdadd
```

The structs that we use for our vertex function are going to be almost identical to the ones our base pass used, with one notable exception: we need to add a Unity-specific macro to the end of our vOUT struct. This macro is going to define two variables that Unity's lighting code will use to calculate our light falloff for us. It looks a bit like magic when you see it in code, but unless you want to dive deep into Unity's lighting system, that bit of magic is the best way to calculate the light falloff for whatever light is currently being processed. Listing 16-15 has both data structures that our forward add pass will use.

Listing 16-15. The vIN and vOUT Structs for Our Forward Add Pass

```
struct vIN{
    float4 vertex  : POSITION;
    float3 normal  : NORMAL;
    float3 tangent : TANGENT;
    float2 uv   : TEXCOORD0;
};

struct vOUT{
    float4 pos : SV_POSITION;
    float3x3 tbn : TEXCOORD0;
    float2 uv : TEXCOORD3;
    float3 worldPos : TEXCOORD4;
    LIGHTING_COORDS(5,6)   ❶
};
```

In order for the LIGHTING_COORDS macro to function, we need to give it the numbers of two unused TEXCOORD slots for it to use for the variables it defines. In Listing 16-15, our code is allowing the macro to define variables in the slots TEXCOORD5 and TEXCOORD6 (❶).

Our vertex function is also going to be identical to the one we wrote for our base pass, except for a single lighting macro that we'll add near the end of the function. This macro, "TRANSFER_VERTEX_TO_FRAGMENT" handles calculating and writing the correct values for our current light into the variables defined by the LIGHTING_COORDS macro. Listing 16-16 shows what this is going to look like in code.

Listing 16-16. The One Line We Need to Add to Our Vertex Function

```
vOUT vert(vIN v){
    vOUT o;
    //this section is identical to the vert function in the base pass

    //below here is new for our forward add pass
    TRANSFER_VERTEX_TO_FRAGMENT(o);   ❶
    return o;
}
```

The single argument passed to the TRANSFER_VERTEX_TO_FRAGMENT macro is the name of the struct that you are going to return from the function. In 16-15, this struct is simply called "o" (for output), so that is the argument that we are passing to the lighting macro. Bear with me: I know these macros are weird, but they're going to pay off.

The final part of our forward add pass is the fragment function, and this is where it all comes together. The payoff of using these macros is that we can use the exact same code to handle point lights and spot lights, rather than needing to write an individual pass for each. This means that the shader we're about to end up with will actually be more fully featured than the ones we wrote in Chapter 12, since we omitted writing a spot light shader in Chapter 12 to save time. Listing 16-17 shows how this is going to look in our fragment function. To save some space, I'm going to omit the lines that declare the uniforms used by the fragment function, since they're identical to the ones needed in our forward base pass.

Listing 16-17. The Fragment Function for Our Forward Add Pass

```
float4 frag(vOUT i) : SV_TARGET{
    //common vectors
    float3 unpackNormal = UnpackNormal(tex2D(_Normal, i.uv));
    float3 nrm = normalize(mul(unpackNormal, i.tbn));
    float3 viewDir = normalize(_WorldSpaceCameraPos - i.worldPos);
    float3 toLight = (_WorldSpaceLightPos0.xyz - i.worldPos.xyz);
    float3 halfVec = normalize(viewDir + toLight);

    float falloff =  LIGHT_ATTENUATION(i);   ❶

    //light amounts
    float diffAmt = max(dot(nrm, toLight), 0.0) * falloff;
    float specAmt = max(0.0, dot(halfVec, nrm));
    specAmt = pow(specAmt, 4.0) * falloff;

    //from here to the final line is identical to the forward base pass

    //don't add ambient lighting in forward add passes.
    return float4( finalDiffuse + finalSpec, 1.0);
}
```

As shown in Listing 16-17, our lighting falloff calculation is now handled by the LIGHT_ATTENUATION macro (❶). This makes our life incredibly easy, at the cost of introducing some black box macros into our code. Luckily, if you're really curious about what these macros are doing, you can download the source code for all of Unity's built-in cginc files, and shaders, from the Unity website (try googling "Unity built-in shaders" to get to the right page) and see exactly what's going on. However, a deep dive into Unity's built-in shaders is beyond the scope of this chapter, so we're going to move on.

Writing multilight shaders by hand in Unity can get a bit hairy, especially when you're first starting out. If you've gotten stuck while reading through the last chapter, check out the "MultiLightBlinnPhong" project included in this chapter's example code to see how everything works in practice.

Passing Data from C# to Shader Code

The last thing that I want to talk about is how to set a shader variable from C# code in a Unity project. We've just seen numerous examples of how Unity's built-in variables save us from having to set a lot of uniforms ourselves, but there will always be instances where a specific visual effect needs some custom data passed to it. There are two ways to accomplish this: we can either set a uniform on a specific material object, or we can set a global uniform value that can be seen by all shaders in a project. Each of these use cases can come in handy, so Listing 16-18 shows what both look like.

Listing 16-18. Setting Shader Uniforms from C# in a Unity Project

```
public class SettingUniforms : MonoBehaviour {

    public Material mat;
    public Texture2D myTexture;

    void Start() {
        mat.SetFloat("_FloatName", 1.0f); ❶
        mat.SetVector("_VectorName", Vector4.zero);
        mat.SetTexture("_TextureName", myTexture);

        Shader.SetGlobalFloat("_GlobalFloat", 1.0f); ❷
        Shader.SetGlobalVector("_GlobalVector", Vector4.one);
        Shader.SetGlobalTexture("_GlobalTexture", myTexture);
    }
}
```

Unity's Material class has several functions for setting uniform values, and three of these are shown in Listing 16-18 (❶). You can find the full list in the API documentation for Unity's material class. One important thing to note is that you don't need to declare a uniform that is set through code inside the Properties block of a shader; that section of the shader code is reserved for uniforms that you want to be able to set through the GUI shown for the material in the Unity editor. For uniforms that will only be set through code, you can get away with just declaring them inside the Cg file itself.

The Shader class in Unity also has a set of static functions, shown in the preceding code at ❷, for setting uniform values that can be seen by all the shaders in a project. These functions are incredibly useful for setting things like a color value that needs to be applied to every mesh in a scene, or a cube map texture that all shiny objects need to be able to read from. Just be careful to choose names for these variables that aren't in use by any of the shaders in your project already.

Next Steps, ShaderGraph, and the Future

Even with a firm understanding of how shaders work, we needed to cover a lot of topics in this chapter to be able to apply that knowledge to Unity, and what we've covered in this chapter only scratches the surface of all the different shader techniques you can use in the engine. One of the major strengths of the Unity is how flexible it is. If you want to dive more into the nuts and bolts of shaders and graphics development, you might find yourself learning about Unity's deferred renderer, or the Scriptable Render Pipeline system. However, if all of this seems like a lot of work for some simple shaders, the Unity team is developing a tool called ShaderGraph, which aims to eliminate the need to write shader code at all.

ShaderGraph will let users create shaders using a visual, node-based editor, without ever having to write shader code at all. We'll see a system like this in the next chapter when we talk about UE4. At the time of writing this chapter, the ShaderGraph feature was still in preview, and as such, is likely a bit too rough around the edges for use in a commercial project. However, it's very possible that by the time you're reading this book, ShaderGraph will be fully rolled out and likely the most popular way for users to create shaders for Unity projects. The important thing to keep in mind with visual tools like this is that under the hood, it's still just shader code. Whether you're writing GLSL, Cg, or dragging nodes around a visual editor, the core principles are the same.

All that said, the Unreal Engine is almost entirely driven by a visual style shader editor, so if you want to see an example of how one of these visual shader editors works in a major engine, all you have to do is turn the page and join me in the next chapter!

Summary

Here's what we covered in this chapter:

- Unity stores shader code in "Shader" asset files. To use these shaders to render a mesh, you need to create a "Material" asset, which contains shader inputs as well as which shader to use.

- Unity's "Shader" assets are written in the "ShaderLab" format, which is a custom Unity format that combines shader code with information about how to set up the graphics pipeline to properly use that code.

- Shader code in Unity is most commonly written using the Cg shader language, which we saw several examples of.

- Unity requires that you manually specify the blend equation you want to use when writing shaders for translucent geometry. We saw an example of how to write a simple alpha blending shader.

- Unity provides support for writing multi-pass lighting shaders using the "ForwardBase" and "ForwardAdd" tags. We walked through how to port our shaders from Chapter 12 to Unity.

- To pass data from code to a material, you can either set a uniform value directly on a material, or globally for all materials. We looked at an example of how to do this in C#.

CHAPTER 17

Writing Shaders in UE4

We're going to look at how to apply what we've learned to projects built with the Unreal Engine (UE4). One of the hallmarks of UE4 is the quality of the tools it provides for authoring in-engine content. Nowhere is this more evident than UE4's material editor, which is one of the best visual material creation tools on the market today. This chapter is going to dive head first into using this tool. Like the previous chapter, it assumes that you already know enough about UE4 to get an object on screen and apply a material to it. If you haven't gotten that far, there are lots of excellent resources online, and I recommend checking out a few to get your feet wet before returning to this chapter.

Just like our Unity chapter, this chapter will be divided up into three sections. We'll first talk about how Unreal handles shader and material assets. Unlike Unity, however, the main way to create shaders in UE4 is through the Material Editor, which involves using a visual programming language to define shader logic, rather than writing code as text. So rather than cover writing shader code in UE4, this chapter is going to cover how to use the Material Editor to create shaders, and then talk about how the work that we do in the Material Editor is translated into shader code by the engine behind the scenes.

One final note: at the time of writing this chapter, the latest version of UE4 was 4.20. It's likely that by the time you're reading this there will be a new version of the engine out, so don't be surprised if a few things have been moved around. The core concepts will stay the same.

Shaders, Materials, and Instances (Oh My!)

UE4 handles shaders differently than anything we've seen so far. The actual shader code that's used to render any given mesh is a combination of code written in the HLSL shader language, and shader logic defined in a visual programming language. The idea behind this is that while a game may use many shaders to render all the different objects

© Kyle Halladay 2019
K. Halladay, *Practical Shader Development*, https://doi.org/10.1007/978-1-4842-4457-9_17

in a scene, the lighting calculations that these objects use largely stay the same. We saw this with our shield and water shaders, which only differed in how we calculated inputs to our lighting functions. The actual lighting math used in both was identical.

UE4 takes this idea one step farther and creates a physical separation between the logic used to provide values to the lighting code, and the lighting code itself. UE4's lighting code is written in the HLSL shading language and stored in ".usf" files located with the engine source code. These files don't contain complete shaders. Instead, they define what UE4 calls "Shading Models," which are skeleton shaders that contain all the lighting functions needed to render an object, but with the inputs to these functions stubbed out. The code to fill in these functions comes from UE4's "Material" assets. UE4 materials consist of a reference to which shading model to use, a node graph containing the logic that's used to fill in the stub functions located in that shading model. You can see an example of one of these node graphs in Figure 17-1. Additionally, materials can define "parameters," which are uniform values that can be modified by material instances.

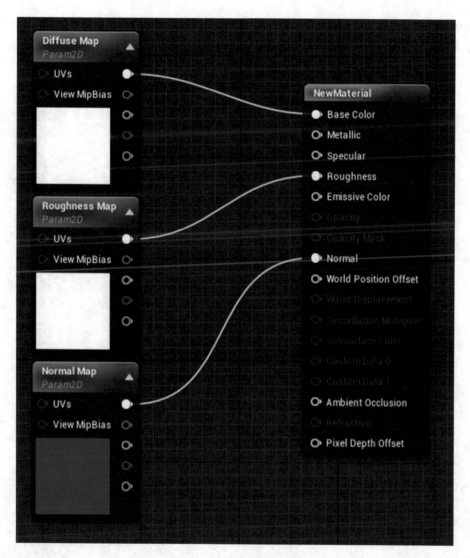

Figure 17-1. A node graph in UE4's material editor

Material Instances are assets that reference a material but can provide new values to any uniforms exposed as a "parameter" by their parent material. Importantly, a material instance cannot provide any new shader logic (they don't even have a node graph). Generally speaking, a UE4 project will have many more material instances than they do materials, since many objects can usually reuse the same material logic but will have different textures and uniform inputs. For example, the material in Figure 17-1 implements some bare bones logic for rendering an object using three different textures, but all of these textures have been set to neutral placeholder values. If we wanted to use our shield mesh's textures with this material, we could create an instance of this material and override these defaults with the textures for our object. You can see an example of what this looks like in Figure 17-2.

Figure 17-2. *A material instance that uses our shield's textures*

In summary, material assets in UE4 choose what shader code they want to use by specifying a "Shading Model." These materials can then add their own shader logic to this shading model using the material editor's node graph. Finally, material instances can reference a material to reuse its logic, while providing their own uniform inputs to replace those found in the material. Don't worry if all this is making your head spin, the UE4 material model is very different from how we've been interacting with shaders up until now, but it will make more sense in a moment when we create our first material.

In practice, UE4 projects end up with many material instances, fewer materials, and few, if any, custom lighting models. Creating your own lighting model in UE4 isn't something that I'd recommend to beginners and is totally unnecessary for many projects. For this reason, this chapter is going to focus on how to we can use the UE4-provided shading models and the Material editor to create a wide variety of materials.

Making Things Red

Working with the UE4 material editor is unlike anything we've done in this book so far, since rather than writing code, we'll be connecting nodes together. This is probably going to feel very alien at first. For this first example material, don't worry about understanding everything right away. We'll talk through the fundamentals of how the material editor works in the next section, but I want to quickly walk through making a simple material first, so that you have some context for when we dive into the nuts and bolts of how the UE4 material node graph works. Treat this first example more as a way to get broadly familiar with how the material editor works, rather than getting hung up on any small details.

Let's start off by creating a material that outputs red for every fragment of an object. Unlike when we did this in Unity, our first red material in UE4 is also going to support all the light types in the engine, because it's easier to do that in UE4 than it is to create an unlit material (although not by much). To begin, click the "Add New" button on the Content Browser panel, and select "Material" from the list of asset types to create. Give this material whatever name you'd like, and then double-click it in the Content Browser. This should open the Material Editor window, which looks like Figure 17-3.

Figure 17-3. *The UE4 Material Editor Window*

You can see that all materials in UE4 start off with a set of material inputs waiting for us to provide data for. These inputs are dictated by the shading model that you've selected for your material. In the case of Figure 17-3, we can see the inputs associated with the "Default Lit" lighting model, which is what you'll usually use to create opaque objects. As mentioned earlier, this lighting math is entirely contained in the shading model that our material is using. All we have to do is fill in how we'd like our object's surface to look, and behind the scenes the shading model's math is applied for us. You can see in the preview window that without us doing anything, our material is already creating a perfectly lit, relatively shiny, black sphere. This is only possible because the Default Lit lighting model is handling the lighting for us automatically.

For our first material, we're simply going to change this sphere to be red, which means we need to provide the color red to the "Base Color" input of our material. To do that, right-click in the material editor's node graph (where there are grid lines in the background). This should open a context menu that shows you all the different kinds of nodes you can create. Type in the word "constant" and select the option "Constant3Vector." This will create a new node in your material editor view that looks like Figure 17-4.

Figure 17-4. *A Constant3Vector material node*

The first thing we're going to do with our new node is change its value from a black color to a red color. If you click the node, you'll notice that the details panel of the Material Editor window changes to show the details of the node you've highlighted, rather than the material. For our node, we want to worry about is the "constant" value, which is the value that our node has. If you click the small arrow next to the color picker, the details panel will reveal a set of three text boxes, which we can use to set the value of our node. Set this to (1,0,0) to give us a solid red. If you're a bit lost, look at Figure 17-5, which shows what the details panel for our node looks like.

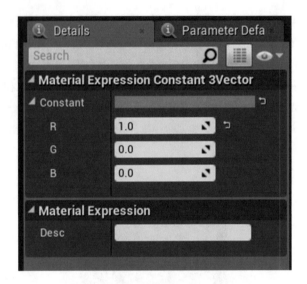

Figure 17-5. *The details panel for our node*

Once our node's value is set, all that's left is to connect this node to the material input that we want to set to red. To do this, click the circle located at the top right of our node, and drag it to the circle that's next to the "Base Color" material input. This should make a line between the two, and immediately change the sphere in your preview window to a solid red sphere. Once you see that, click the save button on the top right of the editor window to save your work and you've successfully created your first UE4 material!

UE4 Material Node Graph Fundamentals

Now that we've had a bit of a whirlwind introduction to the material editor, let's take a minute to catch our breath and go over some basics, starting with a closer look at how nodes are structured. Figure 17-6 shows two nodes that we just worked with: the Dot and Multiply nodes.

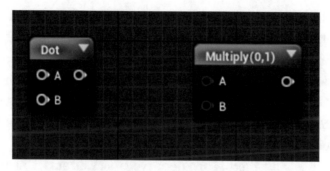

Figure 17-6. *The dot and multiply material nodes*

The circles that you can see are the nodes and input and output slots. Input slots are located along the left side of a node, and outputs are along the right side. For example, if you wanted to multiply the dot product of two vectors by something else, you could connect the output node of the dot note to one of the input nodes of the multiply node. To connect these slots, you would simply click one and drag your cursor to the other one. This will create a line in the material editor to show the connection.

You'll notice that the top of the Multiply node has a number in the header. This is because some nodes—usually ones that can contain scalar inputs—will let you specify constant values for inputs without needing to connect a constant node to an input slot. This is purely a time-saving thing. You can adjust these values by clicking a node and modifying the default values shown in the Details panel for that node, or by using a Constant node to provide the input. You can see both approaches in Figure 17-7.

Figure 17-7. *Two examples of using the multiply node. On the left, the second value is provided by a constant node; on the right, that value has been set on the node itself.*

Some nodes, like the multiply node, can accept different types of data as input, like scalars and vector types. In these cases, the node graph is smart enough to figure out what you want simply based on the types of input, and won't let you set up a node with input types that don't make sense together. There are a lot of different nodes to work with in a UE4 material, and we won't be able to cover them all here, but in many cases these nodes will match math operations that we've used throughout the book, like Dot, Cross, and Multiply.

To finish off this section, there is one node type that warrants a bit of extra attention: the "Texture Sample" node. As you can see in Figure 17-8, this node has a lot of different inputs and outputs and is one of the most complicated nodes that you'll work with day to day in UE4, so it makes sense to spend a bit of time with it.

Figure 17-8. The texture sample node

Let's start by talking about the input slots for this node. The UVs slot is the slot used to provide the UV coordinates that will be used to sample the texture. This accepts a float2 as input or can be left blank if you want the node to use the first set of UV coordinates for that mesh. If you want to get access to a mesh's UV coordinates, so that you can manipulate them—like you'd need to for a scrolling material—you can access these via the Texture Coordinate node. Figure 17-9 shows how you'd grab the second set of UVs on a mesh and scroll them over time to the right.

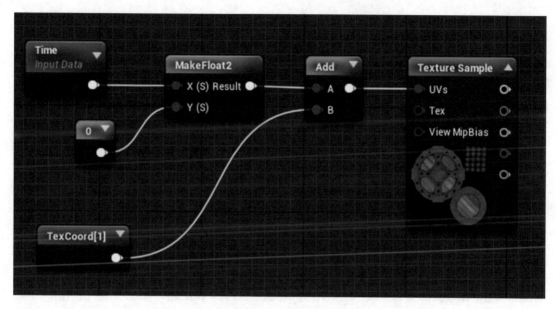

Figure 17-9. *A node graph to scroll UV coordinates to the right*

The next input is the "Tex" input. This is where you provide the texture object that the Texture Sample node will use. You can specify this with a "Texture Object" node, or you can simply click the Texture Sample node and provide a texture value in the details panel of the Sample node itself; either is valid. Finally, the last input is the "View MipBias" input, which has to do with mip maps, which is a concept we haven't covered in this book. It's safe to ignore this input for now; many materials will have no need for it.

The outputs of the Texture Sample node are easier to understand, although there are a lot of them. The top output slot (which is colored gray) is what you'll use if you want to grab the full vec4 of color values for your texture sample. Each output slot below that corresponds to a single channel of the texture. If you only want the red value of the texture sample, you can simply connect the red output slot to wherever you want that value to go.

Making a Rim Light Material

We've gotten our bearings, and understand how to connect nodes and modify node values, so let's take this a step further and make a material that has a red rim light effect. If you forget what rim light is, you can always jump back to Chapter 8 to refresh your memory. What we're going to do is get the dot product between each fragment's normal vector, and the camera's look direction vector, and use that to determine how much red we need to add to our object. If we do it right, our sphere should have a red ring around the edges of it, no matter what direction we look at the sphere from. This means that instead of connecting to the "Base Color" input, we're going to connect to the "Emissive" material input, to specify that we want this red color to emit its own light.

In the UE4 node graph, start by disconnecting our red color from the "Base Color" input. You can disconnect a node by right clicking at a connection point (the circles we dragged between) and selecting the "Break" option. The line between your node and the material input should disappear, and the sphere in the preview window should return to being black.

Now we need to get our hands on the two direction vectors that we need. These values are provided by two special nodes, the PixelNormalWS node and the CameraVector node. Add those two nodes to your material, along with the "Dot" node, which is the node to for performing a dot product. Once you have all of that in your material, connect the two vector nodes to the dot product node, and drag the result of that to the "Emissive" material input. What you should see once that's connected is a white sphere with black around the edges. This is because what we want is to subtract the dot product of these two vectors from one and use that for our emissive input. Luckily, this is such a common operation that a node exists called the "OneMinus" node. Create one of those, connect your dot product to it, and connect that to your emissive output. When that's set up correctly, it should look like Figure 17-10.

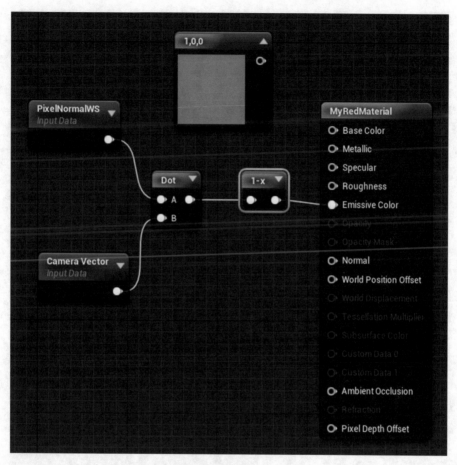

Figure 17-10. *Our rim light material so far*

Notice that our red node isn't connected to anything yet, and our object currently has a white rim light applied to it. Our stated goal was a red rim light, so we need to multiply the value we're currently feeding into the Emissive input by the value of our red node. As you might expect, there's a "Multiply" node for just this purpose. Create one of those and connect the nodes so that the output of the OneMinus node is multiplied by the red node before being passed to the Emissive input. The completed material should look like Figure 17-11. This node graph is roughly equivalent to the shader code in Listing 17-1.

Listing 17-1. An Approximation, in GLSL, of the Node Graph Connected to Emissive Color

```
emissiveColor = vec3(1,0,0) * (1.0 - dot(PixelNormalWS, CameraVector));
```

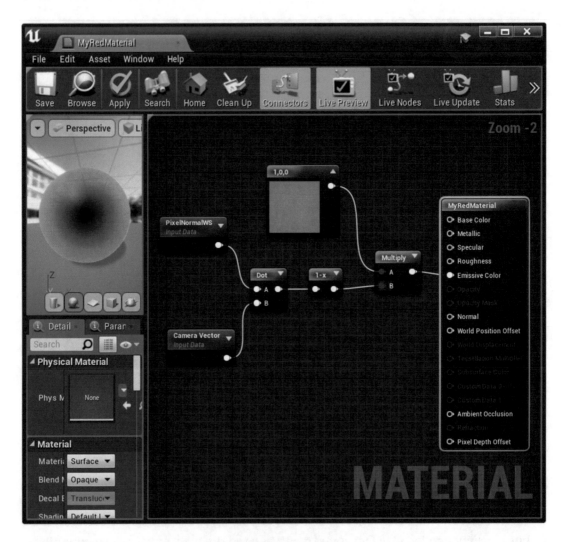

Figure 17-11. Our completed rim light material

The Default Lit Material Inputs

You should have a basic understanding of how shader logic is authored in UE4 materials now, but the material inputs that we've been connecting nodes to are likely still a bit of a mystery. This is both because until now we've been writing shader code and haven't needed to think about parts of our shader code as different inputs to a material, and also because we've been working with Blinn-Phong lighting up until now, and the inputs that we have in UE4 are for a physically based shader. Understanding the nuances of physically based shading is beyond the scope of this chapter, but unless you write your own shading model, you'll need to work with these material inputs, so it seems worthwhile to briefly describe the inputs we've seen so far.

- **Base Color (RGB)**: This roughly maps to what we might call our "Diffuse Color" in a Blinn-Phong shader. Since this is a physically based shader, however, this input is more accurately called "albedo." The main difference between a diffuse and an albedo texture is that an albedo texture should not have any lighting information in the texture itself.

- **Metallic (float)**: This describes whether or not a fragment is a metal. In physically based shading, metals are treated differently from nonmetals. In most cases, this input should be either a 0 (nonmetal) or a 1 (fully metallic).

- **Specular (float)**: For nonmetallic objects, this input adjusts how much light a surface reflects.

- **Roughness (float)**: This describes how rough the surface of an object is. A low roughness means a fragment will reflect more of the environment and have a tighter specular highlight.

- **Emissive Color (RGB)**: The color of the light given off by a surface. Any color plugged in here will be visible even if no light is illuminating the fragment. You can also use this to make parts of a surface glow, by using colors with values greater than 1.0 (e.g., 5.0, 5.0, 5.0)

- **Normal (RGB)**: The normal vector for our fragment. If you have a normal map, this is where you will plug that in. If nothing is plugged in, the object will default to using vertex normals.

- **World Position Offset (XYZ)**: This node allows you to use custom logic to animate the vertex positions of an object. You could use this to make all the vertices wobble with a sine function, for instance.

- **Ambient Occlusion (float)**: This is used to simulate the self-shadowing that occurs at crevices on an object. You'll often see a grayscale texture used to provide data for this input.

- **Pixel Depth Offset (float)**: This is used to adjust the value written to the depth buffer for a given fragment.

There are lots of guides available online to help you make sense of how to best use these inputs, but as we're more interested in the nuts and bolts of how what we've learned in the rest of the chapter maps to UE4, we're going to stop here and move on.

Vertex Shader or Fragment Shader?

The Material Editor does its best to abstract away all the nuts and bolts of how shaders work behind the scenes, so that it's as easy as possible for content creators to make the materials they need without needing to really understand how shader code works. Unfortunately, this abstraction also means that if you do understand how shaders work, it can sometimes be a bit frustrating to figure out how to end up with the shader code you want. One place where this is especially true is when trying to put logic into the vertex shader rather than the fragment shader.

The Material Editor has no concept of vertex or fragment shaders, but if you examine the shader code it generates, you'll see that in most cases, all the logic that you create with the material editor ends up in the fragment shader. In order to move logic to the vertex shader, you need to tell your material to use "Custom UVs." You can set this in the details panel for the material, but it's hidden by default. To get to this option, find the "Material" section of the details panel, which you can see in Figure 17-12. At the bottom of this section, there is a small button with a downward arrow on it. If you click this button, the section will expand to reveal more advanced material options, and the number of custom UVs that your material uses is one of these.

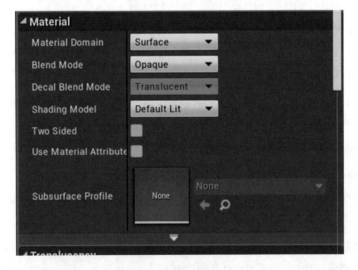

Figure 17-12. *The Material section of the details panel*

If you set the number of custom UVs to a value other than zero, you'll see some additional material inputs get created in your node graph. These inputs allow you to provide two-component vectors that can be used in place of the standard texture coordinates for the material, but one thing that isn't advertised is that any logic connected to a Custom UV input is handled in the vertex shader. If you want to move some work to the vertex shader, all you have to do is create a Custom UV input and connect some logic to it. Just because it says the input is for UV coordinates, doesn't mean that you can't put any other kind of data (that you can pack into a vec2) into that input slot.

To see how this works, consider the material graph in Figure 17-13. I've gone ahead and added three Custom UV inputs to this material, as well as three texture sample nodes. Since we're going to be using the Custom UV material inputs, it's important that we know how the Material Editor interprets those inputs in the rest of the material graph. Notice that the Texture Sample nodes have an optional input for the UV coordinates used to sample the texture that they reference. If you don't provide any data to this input, Texture Sample nodes default to using the first set of UV coordinates, referred to as "texcoord[0]" in the Material editor. This means that in Figure 17-13, both the BaseColorMap and SpecMap nodes are using the UV coordinate "texcoord0" to sample their texture, although BaseColorMap is also doing a bit of math to manipulate those coordinates.

All this is important to know, because if you provide data to the material input "Customized UV0", whatever data you provide is going to override the default value in texcoord0. In Figure 17-13's material, we also have a texture that's using texcoord1 to look up a texture. So if we want to move arbitrary math to our fragment shader, the first safe input to use is going to be "Customized UV2", since it's the first texture coordinate not being used in our node graph. It's important to note that if you leave a Customized UV input blank, the material will default to using the mesh's UV coordinates, so it's perfectly fine for us to create the "Customized UV0" input and not connected anything to it, to keep the rest of our node graph working correctly.

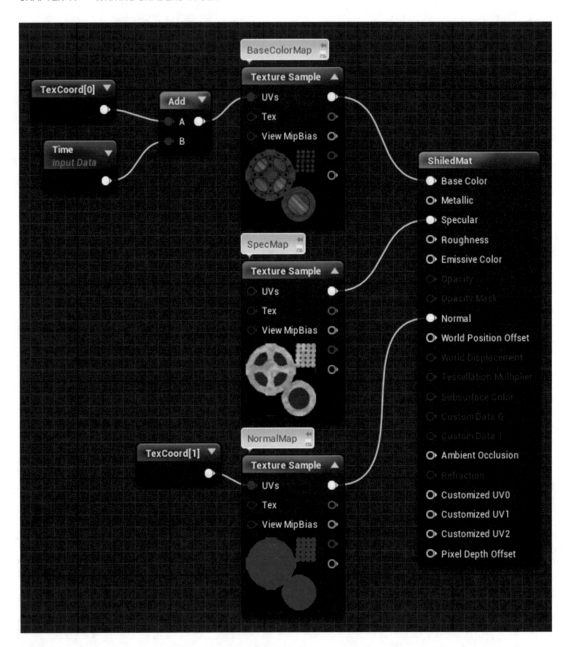

Figure 17-13. *An example of a material using multiple texture coordinates to sample textures*

Let's say that we want to do some math to determine what our Metallic material input's value will be, and we want to have that math take place in the vertex shader. Now that we know which Customized UV we can use without messing up the rest

344

of the material, all we have to do is connect the nodes for the math we want to that material input, and then reference that data elsewhere using a "texture coordinate' node, set to use coordinate index 2, since we'll be connecting our logic to Customized UV2. This will look like Figure 17-14. For this figure, I removed the normal map texture sample node to save space.

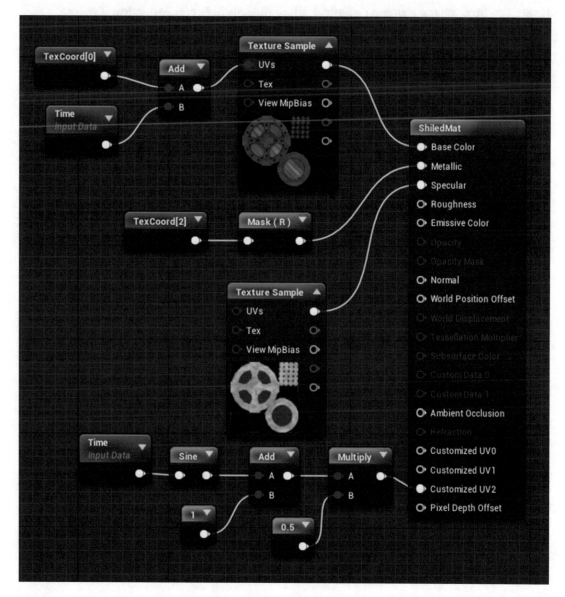

Figure 17-14. *Using a custom UV input to move logic to the vertex shader*

Working with Different Shading Models

As I've mentioned a few times already, the shader code responsible for turning material inputs into a final, fully lit, fragment color is represented in UE4 as a "Shading model." So far, we've only worked with the default UE4 shading model, helpfully called the "Default Lit" model, but that's far from the only model that the engine provides. We don't have time to go through each of the default shading models in this chapter, but if you're working with Unreal, it's worth the time to read the documentation about each of them and experiment on your own. One shading model that's especially useful is the "Unlit" shading model, which only gives you a single material input, and completely disables any lighting math that would be applied by a shading model after your material logic executes. You can see the details panel with the shading model drop-down expanded in Figure 17-15. Changing a shading model will also enable or disable different material inputs, which we'll talk about in the next section when we want to create an unlit translucent material.

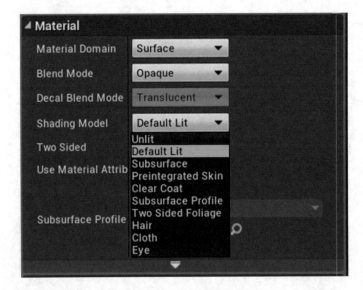

Figure 17-15. *The different shading models available out of the box in UE4*

Blend Modes and Texture Sample Nodes

In addition to what shading model a material uses, you can also specify a material's "blend mode." Just like in openFrameworks, which had several preset blend equations we could use by calling ofEnableBlendMode(), UE4 comes with several preset blend modes that materials can use without having to write out a blend equation by hand. You can choose the blend mode for a material in the "Blend Mode" drop down found in the material's details panel—an example of this is shown in Figure 17-16.

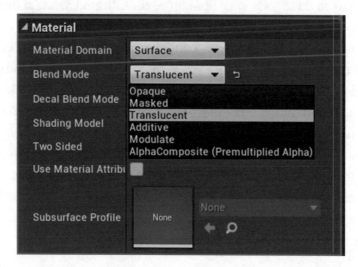

Figure 17-16. *The Blend Mode drop-down menu in a material's Details Panel*

We've worked with three different blend modes so far in this book: alpha testing, alpha blending, and additive blending. In UE4, these blend modes are provided by the "Masked," "Translucent," and "Additive" blend modes. As you can see in 17-16, there are other blend modes provided out of the box too. While explaining what each of them does is beyond the scope of this chapter, I highly recommend giving each of them a try so that you know what options are available to you in a UE4 project.

Whenever you change blend modes, or shading models, you can expect some or all of your material inputs to change as well. For example, changing the blend mode to Translucent also enables two new material inputs that we didn't have before: Opacity, and Refraction. Opacity is the input we're going to use to provide our surface's alpha channel. We aren't going to work with refraction today, but this input is used to provide information about how light bends as it moves through a translucent surface and interacts with a post process effect provided by the engine. For our blinking material, we only need to be concerned with the Emissive and Opacity material inputs, and we're going to use a single texture sample to drive both.

Passing Data from Code to Materials

One of the downsides of things like the Material Editor is that trying to turn shader writing into something that can be done without writing any code means that some things that are easy to do in code get a little more complicated. One example of this is trying to pass uniform data to a UE4 material.

In UE4, if you want a material to have configurable parameters, you have to first create your material with the values you want to be configurable, set up using "parameter nodes." These nodes—usually scalar, vector, or texture sample nodes—work identically to their nonparameter counterparts, with the added benefit of exposing the values of those nodes so that they can be modified.

Once you have parameter nodes set up, you'll need to create a material instance of your material. As mentioned earlier, a material instance is an asset that uses the node graph of a material but can provide its own values to parameters. Material instances provide logic for changing the textures or values used as inputs to these parameters that can be accessed either by C++ or by UE4's blueprint system.

How Does All This Relate to Shader Code?

After spending a whole book talking about writing, debugging, and optimizing shader code, it might feel a bit odd to jump into a visual tool like this. Rest assured that behind the scenes the engine is turning your material node graphs into shader code, just like we were doing by hand in the rest of the book. Behind the scenes, UE4 has a shader compiler that combines the shader code written for each light model, with the logic that you create in the node graph, and packages it up into complete shader files. This allows developers who don't know how to write shader code to create the visual effects that their projects need, without needing to find a shader programmer.

That's not to say that you can't write shader code for UE4, it's just more complicated. The shaders written for the engine have been created by professional programmers, and have been written for efficiency and interoperability with the material editor, not for readability. In addition, the UE4 renderer is very complex, and has not been designed to be easy to write shader code for, so in many cases it's best to simply use the material editor.

If you want to peek under the hood and see what these shaders look like, you'll need to get the engine source code from github (available for free for anyone using UE4) and open the Engine/Shaders directory. There's a lot of shader code to parse through, but the best place to start is the file "BasePassPixelShaders.usf," which contains the pixel (or fragment) shader code provided by any of the shading models that you can select in the Material Editor; and "MaterialTemplate.usf," which is where code that is generated by the material editor gets inserted when a shader is being compiled.

There is a lot to learn with UE4, and unfortunately, we only have time to scratch the surface. If you want to dive deeper into building materials with UE4, there are lots of tutorials available online, as well as a lot of excellent documentation provided by Epic on the Unreal Engine website.

Summary

Here's what we covered in this chapter:

- UE4 shaders are a combination of HLSL shader code and logic, defined using a visual material editor.

- The engine comes with a collection of predefined "Shading Models," which provide flexible lighting functions that can cover a wide variety of project needs.

- Customizing the inputs to these lighting functions is done through the Material Editor's node graph system. We walked through several examples of how to use this system to build different types of materials without needing to create a new lighting model.

- The Material Editor also has controls for customizing the blend equation used to render translucent geometry. We build a simple alpha blending shader using these controls.

- Setting a uniform from code involves creating a material parameter and a material instance, and then using the API provided by UE4's Material Instances to pass data to these parameters.

CHAPTER 18

Writing Shaders in Godot

The final engine that we're going to look at is the Godot engine. Godot is a relative newcomer to the game engine scene, having been released to the public for the first time in 2014.

Writing shaders in Godot is a bit of a mix between Unity, where we had to write all our shader code out by hand, and UE4, which gave us our lighting code and only required us to provide logic to fill in material inputs. We'll be working with code files instead of a visual editor, but the code that we write is going to get a lot of help from the Godot engine, including getting a lot of different lighting math provided for us. This makes Godot an excellent choice for applying everything that we've learned in this book.

Just like the past two chapters, this chapter assumes that you have a basic amount of familiarity with the Godot engine. Before proceeding, you should at least know how to add a mesh to a scene and apply a material to that mesh. The Godot documentation is very good, so if you're picking up the engine for the first time, I recommend reading through the first few of their tutorials before proceeding with this chapter.

This chapter is going to be divided up into two sections. First, we'll talk about how the Godot engine handles shader and material assets, and then we'll move into writing shaders of our own. Unlike the previous two chapters, we aren't going to spend time talking about the default shader that Godot provides for rendering meshes, because the Godot engine documentation already does a great job of providing that information. If you want to learn more about how to work with this material, check out the "Spatial Material" tutorial available on the Godot engine website.

One final note: because the shader files that we're going to be creating in Godot are going to all be set up the same way, rather than break each shader into individual example projects, all the example code for this chapter is available in the "ExampleShaders" Godot project included in this chapter's example code.

© Kyle Halladay 2019

K. Halladay, *Practical Shader Development*, https://doi.org/10.1007/978-1-4842-4457-9_18

Shaders and Materials

Like most engines, Godot treats shader code and the data to fill that shader's uniforms as two separate assets. In the Godot engine, these assets are called Shaders and Materials. Shaders are the assets on disk that contain the shader code used to render objects in the engine. To apply a shader to an object in the scene, you need a Material asset, which specifies both what Shader asset to use and what data to provide as that shader's uniforms.

Godot is unique among the engines talked about in this book in that if provides four different types of material assets for us to work with. All these material types provide controls for configuring the inputs to a shader (or shaders) that will be used to render an object on screen. However, in most cases, the shaders that these materials reference are hidden from view by default. The Particle Material, Spatial Material, and CanvasItem Material all reference shaders specified in engine code, rather than shaders that we write ourselves. As you might guess, the Spatial Material is the engine-provided material type for rendering meshes in a Godot project, and works with the engine's default physically-based shader.

To use a custom shader, you need to work with a ShaderMaterial. Luckily, the other materials can be converted to a shader material with a single button press, so that if you want to keep most of the default shader logic intact, but make a small adjustment or two, you can do that without having to reimplement everything. To make this conversion, all you need to do is go to the inspector panel for the object that's using one of these materials and select the "Convert to ShaderMaterial" option from the material properties dropdown menu. You can see a screenshot of this in Figure 18-1

Figure 18-1. *Creating a new ShaderMaterial in Godot*

If you want to write a shader from scratch (which is what we're about to do), you can also create a ShaderMaterial directly. You'll also need to create the shader asset that the material is going to use. Creating both Shader and Material assets in Godot is very easy. All you need to do is find your Inspector panel in the editor GUI and click the "Create" button, which is the button located in the top left of that panel. You can see a screenshot of what this button looks like in Figure 18-2.

Figure 18-2. *The top of the inspector panel. The create button is the leftmost button immediately under the word "Inspector."*

Once you click that, you'll be presented with the type of asset that you wish to create. Create a shader asset first and save that to your project. Next, create a ShaderMaterial and point it to the shader asset that you just created in the material's Inspector panel. Once you specify the shader you want to use, you can double-click on the name of the shader file to open Godot's shader editing window. This window is handy for working with shader assets, both because you don't need to open your file in a secondary editor like visual studio, and because it will automatically check for errors while you work, so you'll know immediately if you've made a mistake. If you'd prefer to work with a different editor, you can of course open the shader assets in whatever text editor you prefer to work in.

The Godot Shading Language

Now that we've covered how to create a new shader file for us to work in, we need to talk about the shader language used by the Godot engine. Shaders in Godot projects are written in a simplified shading language, which is based on a subset of GLSL. This is good news for us, because it means that once you wrap your head around how Godot shaders are structured, the rest of the syntax will look almost identical to what we did in openFrameworks.

The big difference between regular GLSL and the Godot shader language is that all the lighting code for a Godot shader is provided by the engine. All we need to do is specify which lighting model we would like to use and write shader code to output some key bits of information in "out" variables, which are then used by the lighting code. This makes it more difficult to implement your own lighting model, but if you're OK with using one of the numerous options provided by the engine, you don't need to write nearly as much code. To see this in practice, consider the following shader, shown in Listing 18-1, which is a fully lit Blinn-Phong shader that makes any object a shiny red color.

Listing 18-1. A Fully Functional Blinn-Phong Shader in Godot

```
shader_type spatial; ❶
render_mode specular_blinn; ❷

void fragment() ❸
{
      ALBEDO = vec3(1,0,0); ❹
      ROUGHNESS = 0.5;
}
```

In fact, if all you want is to render an object with some lighting, and a texture or two for things like the albedo (the color of the surface), what regions are metal, normal map, etc, then you don't need to write any code at all. Godot's SpatialMaterial is set up to allow you to do exactly that just by clicking a few buttons in an inspector panel. What this means is that it's only necessary to write your own shader code in Godot if you want to do something unique. If you wanted to, you could set up exactly the shader we just made with this material editor; however, we're here to learn how to write shader code, so let's break down exactly what's happening in our shiny red shader.

First off, all shaders in Godot start with a declaration of what type of shader the file is going to be. In our case, we want to write a shader to apply to a mesh, which means we're going to write a "spatial" shader, which we specify at ❶. The other possible shader_types are "particle" and "canvas_item," which match up exactly with the types of material that these shaders can be used with. We're going to stick with spatial shaders for the duration of this chapter.

The next line of our shader defines what lighting math we want to use when rendering our object. This is only necessary to specify if you want to use a nondefault lighting model for either your diffuse or specular calculations. In our case, we're using the Blinn-Phong specular model, instead of the engine default one, so we specify it ourselves ❷. This render_mode declaration is also where you'll define things like what blend equation to use and how your object should interact with the depth buffer. We'll see a couple of examples of different render_mode values in this chapter, but we won't cover anything close to all the possible inputs. The Godot documentation has a complete list in their tutorials, which would be a great place to head after finishing up with this chapter.

After our render_mode declaration, we get to the meat of our shader code. In Godot shaders, the vertex and fragment shaders are combined into a single file, with a function called vertex() for the vertex shader and one called fragment() for the fragment shader. If you don't write one of these functions, the engine will fill in a default one for you. Our shiny red shader doesn't need to do anything fancy in the vertex shader, which is why the shader in Listing 18-1 only has a fragment() function. Rather than outputting a single color, fragment shaders in Godot write to a set of output variables, which are then used with the lighting math in the engine to create a complete shader. If you don't specify a value for one of these variables, a default value is used. In Listing 18-1, the only values we want to override are the color of our surface and how smooth our surface will be (❹).

These values—albedo and roughness—are a bit different from when we wrote our own Blinn-Phong shader earlier. In our shader, the color of our surface was referred to as our diffuse color and our shininess was referred to as our specular color. Godot's renderer uses physically based calculations, which means its inputs are slightly different. For our purposes, it's enough for us to know that rather than specify how shiny a fragment is, in Godot, we specify how rough it is. Smoother fragments will reflect more light and appear shinier. We can also gloss over the nuances of physically based rendering and treat albedo like our diffuse color value. The reality is a bit more complicated than that, but the nuances of physically based rendering are beyond the scope of this book. We're going to focus just on the nuts and bolts of how Godot shaders are put together in this chapter, and an imperfect understanding of how these inputs work behind the scenes will suit us just fine.

Fragment Shader Output Variables

Our first Godot shader wrote values to two engine-provided output variables: ALBEDO and ROUGHNESS. Fragment shaders in Godot can write to a variety of these sorts of variables to control the appearance of the objects that they're being used to render. Following is a list of some of the most common of these variables, and what they do. The full list is available on the Godot website, but these will be the only ones we need to know for this chapter.

- **ALBEDO (RGB)**: This roughly maps to what we might call our "Diffuse Color" in a Blinn-Phong shader. Since this is a physically based shader, however, this input is more accurately called "Albedo." The main difference between a diffuse and an albedo texture is that an albedo texture should not have any lighting information in the texture itself. This defaults to white.

- **METALLIC (float)**: This describes whether a fragment is a metal. In most cases, this input should be either a 0 (nonmetal) or a 1 (fully metallic). Default is 0.

- **ROUGHNESS (float)**: This describes how rough the surface of an object is. A low roughness means a fragment will reflect more of the environment and have a tighter specular highlight. Default is 0.

- **EMISSIVE (RGB)**: The color of the light given off by a surface. Any color plugged in here will be visible even if no light is illuminating the fragment, which is useful if you want to make something appear to glow. This defaults to black.

- **NORMALMAP (RGB)**: This value should contain the RGB color from our mesh's normal map for the current fragment. If you don't write to this value, Godot will use the normal provided by a mesh's geometry.

- **RIM (float)**: This allows you to specify a value between 0 and 1 that represents how much rim light a fragment should get. By default, this rim light will be white, but you can control that using the RIM_TINT variable described below. The appearance of the rim light effect is dependent on the roughness of the fragment, so if you aren't seeing the results you expect, try adjusting ROUGHNESS. The default value of this variable is 0.

- **RIM_TINT (float)**: This value lerps the color of the rim light provided by the RIM variable between pure white and the ALBEDO color for a fragment. 0 is pure white (which is the default value); 1 is pure ALBEDO.

- **ALPHA_SCISSOR (float)**: If written to, allows you to specify a minimum alpha for your fragment. If the alpha value of a fragment goes below the ALPHA_SCISSOR value, the fragment will be discarded. This is like the alpha test shader we wrote back in Chapter 4.

- **ALPHA (float)**: The alpha value for a fragment. It defaults to 1.0, so you only need to write to this value if you're trying to render a translucent object.

Now that we have a better idea of some of the option available to us, let's see how to use these outputs to create something a bit more interesting than our shiny red shader.

Making a Custom Rim Light Shader

Although we just saw that we could use the RIM variable to add some engine-provided rim light to our shaders, that functionality is a bit limited. We don't have complete control over the color of the light (for example, we can't create a blue rim light on a red object), and the rim light effect is dependent on roughness, which is great when you need your effect to be physically based, but not so great if you just want a quick rim light effect on an object. So we're going to write our own simple rim light shader instead.

You may recall from previous chapters that to calculate rim light, all you need to do is get the vector that goes from the current fragment to the camera, dot that against the normal vector for the fragment, and then subtract that dot product value from 1.0. This will give you something like Figure 18-3, which shows what the default rim light in Godot looks like when applied to an object.

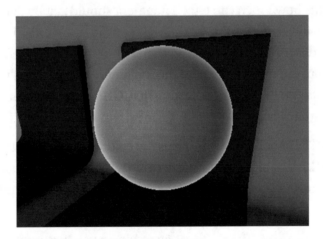

Figure 18-3. *The default rim light effect*

Since we're not going to be using the RIM output variable to make our rim light shader, we're going to need a few vectors: the world position of our fragment, the normal vector for our fragment (in world space), and the position of the camera (also in world space). Getting these values is going to require us to do some matrix math, and the matrices that we want to use are only accessible from the vertex shader, which means that to start our rim light shader off, we have to write our first vertex shader in Godot to calculate and pass these values to our fragment shader. This is shown in Listing 18-2.

Listing 18-2. Our First Custom Vertex Function in a Godot Shader

```
shader_type spatial;

varying vec3 world_position;  ❶
varying vec3 world_normal;
varying vec3 world_camera;

void vertex()
{
    world_position = (WORLD_MATRIX * vec4(VERTEX, 1.0)).xyz;
    world_normal = (WORLD_MATRIX * vec4(NORMAL, 0.0)).xyz;
    world_camera = (CAMERA_MATRIX * vec4(0,0,0,1)).xyz;  ❷
}
```

There's a lot of new stuff going on here, but hopefully it doesn't look too alien, given that we did a lot of similar stuff in our openFrameworks projects. To start with, we need to declare the variables that we're going to be passing to the fragment shader. In Godot shaders, these variables are called "varyings," rather than "out" variables, because they are interpolated values that "vary" per fragment. The concept is the same as in/out variables though, and they're created in the exact same way as our output variables in openFrameworks (which you can see at ❶). Once they've been declared, we need to fill them with data, which means creating our vertex function. This is as simple as creating a function called vertex().

Our vertex shader might be a bit confusing, not because of what it does but because of what it leaves out. In Godot, there's no need to manually transform your mesh's vertices into clip space, even when you're writing a vertex shader, unless you want to do something custom. Since we don't want to change the shape of our mesh in the vertex shader, we can simply omit modifying the VERTEX variable at all, and Godot will take care of it for us.

What's more confusing about working with Godot shaders is that, even though they are specified in the same file, both vertex and fragment shaders have multiple uniforms that only one type of shader can see, and an equal number of output variables that only one can write to, like the WORLD_MATRIX and CAMERA_MATRIX uniforms earlier. This makes logical sense, given that behind the scenes our one shader file is being turned into multiple shaders, but when you're just starting out, it can be a bit frustrating to try to remember which variables belong to which function. My recommendation is to keep a browser window open to the Godot documentation's "Shading Language" page, which lists all the inputs and outputs specific to each kind of shader, and keep referring to that as you go until you've memorized things by osmosis.

The last thing we need to talk about before continuing is how we're calculating the camera position. Godot doesn't give us the camera position directly, but it does give us the transformation matrix that represents the camera's current position and rotation—essentially the camera's model matrix. Since this matrix is used to position the camera in the world, we can multiply a zero vector by that matrix to put a point at (0,0,0) and then apply the same translations and rotations as the camera has had applied to it to that point instead. This will give us the position, in world space, of the camera. You can see this at ❷.

With all that said, it's time to move on to the fragment shader that we'll need to write in order to make our own rim light shader. To make our shader configurable, we're also going to declare a few uniforms to store some input data. Godot will automatically adjust the inspector panel for any material that uses our shader, to let us set the values for these uniforms directly in the editor. To start with, let's simply define a uniform to hold the color we'd like our rim light to be, and a second value to control how wide our rim light effect is. Listing 18-3 shows what this fragment shader will look like.

Listing 18-3. The Beginning of Our Rim Light Fragment Shader

```
uniform vec3 rim_color;
uniform float rim_tightness;

void fragment()
{
    vec3 toCam = normalize(world_camera - world_position);
    float rim = 1.0-dot(normalize(world_normal), toCam);
    EMISSION = rim_color * pow(rim, rim_tightness);
}
```

Notice that we're using the EMISSION output variable to store our rim light's final color. This is so that no matter what sort of lighting is applied to a mesh, our rim light is always visible. In a dark scene, this will give the appearance of an object glowing with our rim light, which you can see in Figure 18-4. This figure shows a screenshot of what our shader looks like right now, as well as what the material editor panel looks like with slots available for our two uniforms. I've set the color of our rim light to solid red in the screenshot, simply to demonstrate that, unlike the default RIM effect, our shader will let us set our rim light to whatever color we want.

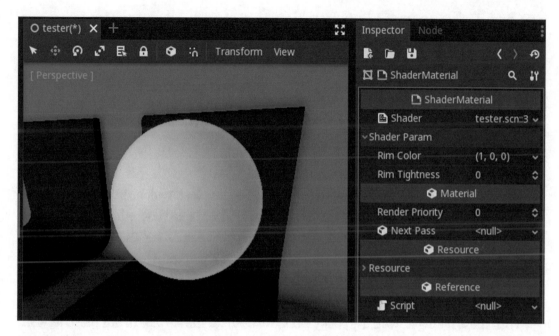

Figure 18-4. Our custom rim light shader creating a red rim on a white sphere

The last thing I want to do before moving on to a different shader example is to add support for a diffuse (or ALBEDO) texture to our shader, so that we can specify a texture for the surface of our mesh, rather than have it always be a solid white color. While we're at it, let's also replace our rim_color uniform with a second texture, to let us use a texture as the source of our rim light color—simply to make our rim light shader even more distinct from the engine provided RIM effect.

Adding textures to a shader in Godot is identical to how we did it in our openFrameworks projects. We simply declare two uniform sampler2D variables to store our texture (and have the editor build the UI necessary to let us set these variables), and then sample them in our fragment shader using the texture() function, like you can see in Listing 18-4.

Listing 18-4. Adding Texture Support to Our Rim Light Shader

```
uniform float rim_tightness;
uniform sampler2D albedo_color;
uniform sampler2D rim_color;
```

```
void fragment()
{
        vec3 toCam = normalize(world_camera - world_position);
        float rim = 1.0-dot(normalize(world_normal), toCam);

        EMISSION = texture(rim_color, UV).rgb * pow(rim, rim_tightness);  ❶
        ALBEDO = texture(albedo_color, UV).rgb;
}
```

You'll notice that we didn't have to explicitly pass any texture coordinates to our fragment shader. Instead, we used the Godot provided variable "UV," which passes mesh UV coordinates from the vertex to the fragment shader. As we'll see later in this chapter, you can modify this value in the vertex shader if you want to modify your UV coordinates, but since our vertex shader didn't write to this variable, Godot has written our mesh's UV coordinates to that variable for us.

With these changes, we can specify a texture both for the surface of our mesh as well as the source of color for our rim light effect. Figure 18-5 shows what this looks like if we set up a material to use a marble texture for our mesh and a wood grain texture for our rim light color.

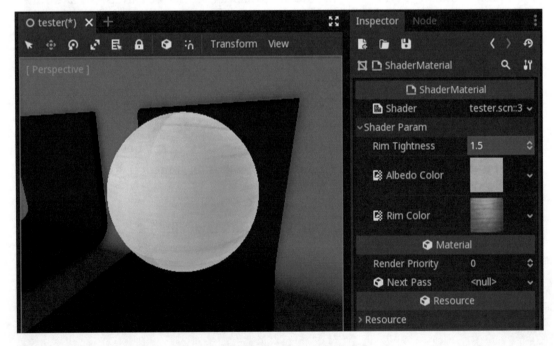

Figure 18-5. *The final output of our rim light shader*

Custom Vertex Shaders

So far, we've been perfectly happy to let the engine handle the work of getting our vertex positions and UV coordinates sent to the right parts of the pipeline, but there are lots of cases where you may want to take a more hands-on approach. For example, let's say we wanted our rim light shader to also add some time-based vertex animations, like we saw in Chapter 15. To do that, we tell the engine that we want to handle transforming our vertex position ourselves, and then add in the required math.

To specify that we're going to be handling the math ourselves, we need to add a new flag to the render_mode statement at the beginning of our shader. The flag we need to add is "skip_vertex_transform," and it can be chained with other render_mode flags as needed. Listing 18-5 shows a few examples of what this could look like.

Listing 18-5. Examples of render_mode Flags

```
render_mode skip_vertex_transform;
render_mode diffuse_lambert, skip_vertex_transform;
render_mode diffuse_burley,specular_blinn,skip_vertex_transform;
```

Shaders with skip_vertex_transform specified need to handle transforming both vertex positions and normals. Unlike our earlier projects, even with skip_vertex_transform enabled, Godot will still handle the projection matrix for us, so we only need to multiply things by a matrix that combines the model and view matrices, which Godot provides as the variable MODELVIEW_MATRIX. You can see an example of this, with our vertex animation from Chapter 15, in Listing 18-6.

Listing 18-6. Custom Vertex Animation in a Godot Shader

```
shader_type spatial;
render_mode skip_vertex_transform;

void vertex(){
    vec3 finalPos = VERTEX + vec3(0,sin(TIME),0);

    VERTEX = (MODELVIEW_MATRIX * vec4(finalPos, 1.0)).xyz;
    NORMAL = (MODELVIEW_MATRIX * vec4(NORMAL, 0.0)).xyz;
}
```

UV Animation

Applying animation to UV coordinates is even easier than animating vertex positions, since we don't have to handle the vertex transformations ourselves if all we want to modify are UVs. Listing 18-7 shows off a quick shader that scrolls a texture in the X direction of a mesh's UV space.

Listing 18-7. Simple UV Animation in a Godot Shader

```
shader_type spatial;
uniform sampler2D albedo;

void vertex()
{
     UV += vec2(TIME * 0.1, 0.0);
}

void fragment()
{
     ALBEDO = texture(albedo, UV).rgb;
}
```

Translucent Shaders and Blend Modes

Making translucent materials in Godot isn't much different from the shaders we've already written. By default, any fragment shader can write to the ALPHA output variable and become an alpha blended shader. To use a different blend mode, all it takes is another flag added to a shader's render_mode. Godot provides four possible blend modes to work with, which are summarized as follows:

- **Blend_Mix**: The default value used if you don't specify one. This is standard alpha blending, which we've seen before. The blend equation for Blend_Mix is:

  ```
  vec4 finalColor = src * src.a + (1.0 - src.a) * dst;
  ```

- **Blend_Add**: This is the blend mode you'll use for additive blending, which we've seen a few times already in this book. This corresponds to the blend equation:

```
vec4 finalColor = src + dst;
```

- **Blend_Sub**: We haven't seen this type of blending before, but it's called "subtractive blending." This corresponds to the blend equation:

```
vec4 finalColor = dst - src;
```

- **Blend_Mul**: Another blend mode we haven't seen before. This one is called "multiplicative blending," and its blend equation is:

```
vec4 finalColor = dst * src;
```

Using any of these is as simple as specifying which type of blending to use in the render_mode line, and then writing to alpha. For example, Listing 18-8 shows a multiplicative blending shader. Note that for blend modes other than blend_mix, you don't need to write to alpha in order to get that type of blending, since Godot will automatically set ALPHA to 1.0 if you don't write to it.

Listing 18-8. A Multiplicative Blending Godot Shader

```
shader_type spatial;
render_mode blend_mul, unshaded;

void fragment()
{
    ALBEDO = vec3(5,0,1);
}
```

If you put this shader onto an object, you're going to end up with a translucent object that boosts how much red you can see in everything behind it and remove any green. Since it's using multiplicative blending, the red increase will be proportional to how much red is already in the fragments that are rendered behind the mesh. Green will be completely removed, because we're going to be multiplying that channel by 0. Figure 18-6 shows an example of what this might look like.

Figure 18-6. *Using our multiplicative blending shader*

Passing Data from Code to Shaders

In addition to setting uniform values via the Godot editor, you can also set and change these values in code at runtime. Like most engines that have a material asset type, to pass uniform data to a material you can write code to set that property on the material object itself. To accomplish this, you need to call set_shader_param() on the material that you want to pass data to. This function takes two arguments: the first is the string name of the uniform that you want to write to, and the second is the data you want to write. Listing 18-9 shows a few examples of how to do this in GDScript (Godot's proprietary scripting language).

Listing 18-9. Setting a Uniform Value in GDScript

```
extends MeshInstance

func _ready():
    var mat = get_surface_material(0);
    mat.set_shader_param("albedo_color", Vector3(5,0,1));

    pass
```

You can use many different languages to write code for a Godot project, so the specific syntax that you'll use will, of course, change slightly depending on whether you choose to use GDScript or one of the other languages that Godot supports. However, the core concept of setting the parameter on a material object will remain the same no matter what.

The Future: Visual Shader Editing?

The last thing I want to mention in this chapter is that if you'd prefer to not write shader code, or want to be able to empower team members that don't know shader code to be able to create their own materials, the creator of the Godot engine is developing a visual shader editor that looks very similar to the one found in UE4. It was not available in the version of the engine I used when writing this chapter, but it seems poised to make an appearance in a future version of the engine, so perhaps by the time you're reading this, it will be another tool in your tool box.

For now, we're stuck writing shader code the fun way—by hand—and that means that we've wrapped up our chapter about working with the Godot engine. Of the three engines we've looked at, Godot's shading language is the closest to what we were writing in our openFrameworks projects, which means that if you're looking for a place to go next, Godot might be an attractive place to start putting everything we've learned in this book to use.

Summary

You've made it to the end of the book! Congratulations! Here's a quick summary of what we covered in this chapter:

- Godot shaders are written using a custom shading language, which is based on a subset of GLSL.

- The engine provides several built-in lighting model implementations, which can be selected using arguments passed to the "render_mode" declaration.

- Fragment shaders can control the appearance of the objects they render by writing to a number of engine provided "out" variables. A list of some of these values was provided in this chapter, and we saw an example of using some of these outputs to build a custom rim light shader.

- Vertex shaders also have several "out" variables that they can optionally write to. We saw an example that used these variables to implement custom vertex animation.

- The "render_mode" statement can also be used to specify what blend equation to use when rendering translucent geometry. We walked through an example of using the multiplicative blend mode.

- Data can be passed from code to shaders by using the set_shader_ param() function. We saw an example of how to do this in GDScript.

APPENDIX A

Important Code Snippets

There are two code snippets referenced in the text that are essential to being able to follow along with the examples on your own. In case you're reading this book without access to the online code examples, I've included these two snippets here.

Calculating a Mesh's Tangents

Listing A-1 contains the code necessary to calculate the tangent vectors for a mesh and store these vectors in the mesh's vertex color.

Listing A-1. The CalcTangents() Function

```
void calcTangents(ofMesh& mesh){
    using namespace glm;
    std::vector<vec4> tangents;
    tangents.resize(mesh.getNumVertices());

    uint indexCount = mesh.getNumIndices();

    const vec3* vertices = mesh.getVerticesPointer();
    const vec2* uvs = mesh.getTexCoordsPointer();
    const uint* indices = mesh.getIndexPointer();

    for (uint i = 0; i < indexCount-2; i += 3){
        const vec3& v0 = vertices[indices[i]];
        const vec3& v1 = vertices[indices[i+1]];
        const vec3& v2 = vertices[indices[i+2]];
        const vec2& uv0 = uvs[indices[i]];
```

K. Halladay, *Practical Shader Development*, https://doi.org/10.1007/978-1-4842-4457-9_19

```
        const vec2& uv1 = uvs[indices[i+1]];
        const vec2& uv2 = uvs[indices[i+2]];

        vec3 edge1 = v1 - v0;
        vec3 edge2 = v2 - v0;
        vec2 dUV1 = uv1 - uv0;
        vec2 dUV2 = uv2 - uv0;

        float f = 1.0f / (dUV1.x * dUV2.y - dUV2.x * dUV1.y);

        vec4 tan;
        tan.x = f * (dUV2.y * edge1.x - dUV1.y * edge2.x);
        tan.y = f * (dUV2.y * edge1.y - dUV1.y * edge2.y);
        tan.z = f * (dUV2.y * edge1.z - dUV1.y * edge2.z);
        tan.w = 0;
        tan = normalize(tan);

        tangents[indices[i]] += (tan);
        tangents[indices[i+1]] += (tan);
        tangents[indices[i+2]] += (tan);
    }

    for (int i = 0; i < tangents.size(); ++i){
        vec3 t = normalize(tangents[i]);
        mesh.setColor(i, ofFloatColor(t.x, t.y, t.z, 0.0));
    }
}
```

The ofxEasyCubemap Class

Listings A-2 and A-3 contain the source code for the ofxEasyCubemap class, which was written to allow you to create your own cubemap objects during the examples without having to write and OpenGL code yourself.

Listing A-2. ofxEasyCubemap.h

```
#pragma once

#include "ofURLFileLoader.h"
#include "uriparser/Uri.h"
#include "ofTexture.h"
#include "ofImage.h"

class ofxEasyCubemap
{
public:
      ofxEasyCubemap();
      ~ofxEasyCubemap();
      ofxEasyCubemap(const ofxEasyCubemap& other) = delete;
      ofxEasyCubemap& operator=(const ofxEasyCubemap& other) = delete;

      bool load(const std::filesystem::path& front,
                const std::filesystem::path& back,
                const std::filesystem::path& left,
                const std::filesystem::path& right,
                const std::filesystem::path& top,
                const std::filesystem::path& bottom);

      ofTexture& getTexture();
      const ofTexture& getTexture() const;

private:
      ofTexture textureData;
      unsigned int glTexId;
      ofImage images[6];

};
```

Listing A-3. ofxEasyCubemap.cpp

```cpp
#include "ofxCubemap.h"
#include "ofGLUtils.h"

ofxEasyCubemap::ofxEasyCubemap()
{
      glEnable(GL_TEXTURE_CUBE_MAP);

      textureData.texData.bAllocated = false;
      textureData.texData.glInternalFormat = GL_RGB;
      textureData.texData.textureID = 0;
      textureData.texData.textureTarget = GL_TEXTURE_CUBE_MAP;

}

ofxEasyCubemap::~ofxEasyCubemap()
{
      glDeleteTextures(1, &glTexId);
}

bool ofxEasyCubemap::load(const std::filesystem::path& front,
                          const std::filesystem::path& back,
                          const std::filesystem::path& right,
                          const std::filesystem::path& left,
                          const std::filesystem::path& top,
                          const std::filesystem::path& bottom)
{

      bool success = images[0].load(right);
      success |= images[1].load(left);
      success |= images[2].load(top);
      success |= images[3].load(bottom);
      success |= images[4].load(front);
      success |= images[5].load(back);
```

```
if (!success)
{
     fprintf(stderr, "ERROR: EasyCubemap failed to load an image");
     return false;
}

unsigned int faceWidth = images[0].getWidth();
unsigned int faceHeight = images[0].getHeight();

glGenTextures(1, &glTexId);
glBindTexture(GL_TEXTURE_CUBE_MAP, glTexId);

glTexParameteri(GL_TEXTURE_CUBE_MAP,
               GL_TEXTURE_WRAP_S,
               GL_CLAMP_TO_EDGE);

glTexParameteri(GL_TEXTURE_CUBE_MAP,
               GL_TEXTURE_WRAP_T,
               GL_CLAMP_TO_EDGE);

glTexParameteri(GL_TEXTURE_CUBE_MAP,
               GL_TEXTURE_WRAP_R,
               GL_CLAMP_TO_EDGE);

glTexParameteri(GL_TEXTURE_CUBE_MAP,
               GL_TEXTURE_MAG_FILTER,
               GL_LINEAR);

glTexParameteri(GL_TEXTURE_CUBE_MAP,
               GL_TEXTURE_MIN_FILTER,
               GL_LINEAR);

unsigned char* faceData[6];

for (int i = 0; i < 6; ++i){
     if (images[i].getWidth() != faceWidth ||
         images[i].getHeight() != faceHeight){

          fprintf(stderr, "ERROR: Not all textures are the same
          size\n");
```

373

```
                return false;
            }

            faceData[i] = images[i].getPixels().getData();

            glTexImage2D(GL_TEXTURE_CUBE_MAP_POSITIVE_X+i,
                        0,
                        images[i].getTexture().texData.glInternalFormat,
                        faceWidth,
                        faceHeight,
                        0,
                        ofGetGLFormat(images[i].getPixels()),
                        GL_UNSIGNED_BYTE, faceData[i]);
    }

    textureData.texData.textureID = glTexId;
    textureData.texData.bAllocated = true;

    return true;
}

const ofTexture& ofxEasyCubemap::getTexture() const
{
    return textureData;
}

ofTexture& ofxEasyCubemap::getTexture()
{
    return textureData;
}
```

Index

Printed in the United States
By Bookmasters